REFORMING UK PUBLIC POLICY THROUGH ELECTED REGIONAL GOVERNMENT

This book takes an in-depth look at the enormous challenges facing UK public services and considers what might be done to resolve them. The authors are confident that more of the same over-centralised approaches to public policy and so-called "levelling-up" policies will just not work. Instead, they argue for an application of radical measures, involving the creation of elected regional governments in England similar to the devolved arrangements in Wales, Scotland and Northern Ireland.

The book comprises four distinct parts: introduction and context; the need for major reform; policies for individual public services and cross-cutting themes. Following an introduction and discussion of the meaning of the terms public policy and public services, the first part goes on to discuss at length the substantial challenges to public policy and public services. The second part sets out the need for over-arching reforms, designed to address the issues discussed above, namely the development of elected regional governments. Each chapter in part three explores key themes concerning individual public policy areas and public services, while part four discusses a number of themes, which cut across all the public services already considered.

Although the book is focused on and is of great relevance within the UK, it also has international appeal, as many of the themes discussed will have resonance in other countries and the analysis of public policy in regional administrations will also be of interest in other jurisdictions. It will appeal to students and academics in the fields of government and politics, economics, finance and accounting, public administration, public service management and social policy, as well as policymakers, practicing civil servants, public service managers and elected representatives.

Malcolm J. Prowle has extensive experience of policy, strategy and finance in many public services, gained through holding senior financial posts in several public service organisations, senior positions with two major international consulting firms (KPMG and PWC) and professorial posts in various UK universities.

REFORMING UK PUBLIC POLICY THROUGH ELECTED REGIONAL GOVERNMENT

Edited by Malcolm J. Prowle

LONDON AND NEW YORK

Cover image: johnwoodcock/Getty Images

First published 2023
by Routledge
4 Park Square, Milton Park, Abingdon, Oxon OX14 4RN

and by Routledge
605 Third Avenue, New York, NY 10158

Routledge is an imprint of the Taylor & Francis Group, an informa business

British Library Cataloguing-in-Publication Data
A catalogue record for this book is available from the British Library

Library of Congress Cataloging-in-Publication Data
Names: Prowle, Malcolm, editor.
Title: Reforming UK public policy through elected regional government /edited by Malcolm J. Prowle.
Description: Milton Park, Abingdon, Oxon ; New York, NY : Routledge, 2023. | Includes bibliographical references and index.
Identifiers: LCCN 2022005788 (print) | LCCN 2022005789 (ebook) | ISBN 9781032063577 (hardback) | ISBN 9781032063560 (paperback) | ISBN 9781003201892 (ebook)
Subjects: LCSH: Municipal services—Great Britain | County services—Great Britain | Local government—Great Britain. | Great Britain—Politics and government.
Classification: LCC HD4645.A5 R44 2023 (print) | LCC HD4645.A5 (ebook) | DDC 351.4/1—dc23/eng/20220504
LC record available at https://lccn.loc.gov/2022005788
LC ebook record available at https://lccn.loc.gov/2022005789

ISBN: 978-1-032-06357-7 (hbk)
ISBN: 978-1-032-06356-0 (pbk)
ISBN: 978-1-003-20189-2 (ebk)

DOI: 10.4324/9781003201892

Typeset in Bembo
by codeMantra

CONTENTS

FIGURES

TABLES

CONTRIBUTORS

EDITOR

Malcolm J. Prowle has extensive experience of policy, strategy and finance in many public services. This was gained through holding senior financial posts in several public service organisations, senior positions with two major international consulting firms (KPMG and PWC) and professorial posts in various UK universities. Malcolm is an acknowledged expert on the economics, finance and management of public services. He has had extensive experience in the health, education, local government and central government sectors and has worked at the highest levels of government advising Ministers, Ambassadors, senior civil servants, public service managers and service professionals. He has been an adviser to two House of Commons Select Committees, an adviser to three shadow government ministers and a consultant to the World Health Organization. He has spoken and presented papers at a wide range of events and conferences, has authored many books and research reports, and has published papers on public service issues.

CONTRIBUTORS

Anna Birley brings extensive and varied experience in housing policy from several standpoints. She is policy officer for UNISON, one of the UK's largest trade unions. Her role involves publishing policy papers and briefings, and providing support to MPs on issues ranging from housing, the cost-of-living crisis to English devolution. Previously at the Co-operative Party, she led policy development in many areas including co-operative and community-led housing. As an elected member of the Lambeth Borough Council for 8 years, Anna was the Deputy Cabinet Member for Housing and Policy Lead on private renting which is a major issue in the borough.

Tony Garthwaite has over 30 years' experience in local government, culminating in being Director of Social Care and Housing Services in Bridgend County Council. He is a former policy adviser to the Welsh Local Government Association on Social Services issues. He was a Board Member of the UK Alliance (Sector Skills Council for Care and Development) and authored "Social Work in Wales: A Profession to Value", a major research project on the recruitment and retention of social workers. Tony has undertaken extensive research and publication on issues concerning social care provision and into the theory and practice of collaboration. He completed his PhD on inter-agency collaboration and is currently a visiting professor in the Welsh Institute of Health and Social Care (WIHSC) at the University of South Wales.

Nick Howe is currently Director of Institute of Policing at Staffordshire University. Prior to entering academic life, Nick served as police officer, for many years, rising to the rank of Chief Superintendent. He was also employed by Her Majesty's Inspectorate of Constabulary responsible for supporting the inspection of police forces throughout the UK. Nick holds a Master's degree in criminology and a PhD for doctoral research into partnership working between police and other public services.

Roger Latham's initial training was in economics and statistics and he subsequently held various economic posts in the private sector and in regional economic development. He then trained as an accountant and rose to be chief financial officer and then chief executive of a large county council where he was heavily involved in regional economic development. Roger has been involved in various government task forces and led the Local Government Association task group preparing the local government response to the Simms sustainability agenda. He is a former President of the Chartered Institute of Public Finance and Accountancy (CIPFA) and has been a visiting fellow at a number of UK universities.

Graham Lister initially worked in local government but subsequently joined the public sector consulting group of Coopers & Lybrand (now Price Waterhouse Coopers). He rose to be the partner in charge of the health sector consulting practice in the firm. In this role, he advised many hundreds of different clients on aspects of public sector and health systems reform and economics at national, regional and local levels in England, Scotland, Wales and Northern Ireland and 45 other countries. He has been a visiting professor at London South Bank University and Senior Fellow of the Graduate Institute of Geneva. He served as Chair of the College of Health, Fellow of Judge Business School, Cambridge and also served on national and regional committees including the NICE Partners Council, Buckinghamshire Health Authority and the Health Protection Agency, Global Health Technical Sub Committee. Graham has published over 20 research reports and papers on various aspects of health systems and has spoken at a wide range of events.

Terry Mackie A career educationalist for over 30 years, his experience covers Wales, England and international education contexts. He has extensive experience of both classroom teaching and education management and leadership at a senior level in several local authorities including a period as Chief Education Officer of an LEA. He has had extensive senior experience concerning school improvement, schools' resourcing, SEN/inclusion and governor support. On leaving local government he founded a specialist education consultancy service and worked for clients in Wales, England and overseas. He has written many discussion papers on education topics and is author of a controversial book on education policy.

Peter Murphy is Director of the Public Policy and Management Research Group at Nottingham Business School. Prior to academic life he had a long career as a senior civil servant in four Whitehall departments and prior to that he spent 23 years in local government rising to Chief Executive. While at Nottingham Business School, Peter has focused on emergency public services and has conducted a range of consultancy and research projects for fire and rescue authorities and for the National Fire Chiefs Council. He has been the Joint Editor of the *International Journal of Emergency Services* and has edited special editions of various public management journals.

ABBREVIATIONS

3SOs	Third Sector Organisations
AI	Artificial Intelligence
ALMO	Arms-Length Management Organisation
BBC	British Broadcasting Corporation
CCC	Climate Change Committee
CCG	Clinical Commissioning Group
CSD	Circulatory System Disease
DCLG	Department for Communities and Local Government
DfE	Department for Education
ERA	Education Reform Act
EU	European Union
FE	Further Education
FRS	Fire and Rescue Service
GCSE	General Certificate of Secondary Education
GDP	Gross Domestic Product
GNI	Gross National Income
GVA	Gross Value Added
HE	Higher Education
HEI	Higher Education Institution
HMICFRS	Her Majesty's Inspectorate of Constabulary and Fire & Rescue Services
HR	Human Resource
HSC	Health and Social Care
ICP	Integrated Care Partnership
ICS	Integrated Care System
ICS	Integrated Children's Service
IGE	Inter-generational Equity

ILEA	Inner London Education Authority
IMD	Index of Multiple Deprivation
IT	Information Technology
LEA	Local Education Authority
MAT	Multi-Academy Trusts
MP	Member of Parliament
NAO	National Audit Office
NATO	North Atlantic Treaty Organisation
NCD	Non-communicable Diseases
NCVO	National Council for Voluntary Organisations
NHS	National Health Service
NI	Northern Ireland
NICE	National Institute for Clinical Excellence
NCS	New Community Schools
NPF	National Performance Framework
OECD	Organisation for Economic Co-operation and Development
ONS	Office for National Statistics
PAC	Public Accounts Committee
PCC	Police and Crime Commissioner
PCT	Primary Care Trust (of the NHS)
PFI	Private Finance Initiative
PISA	Programme for International Student Assessment
PPP	Public/Private Partnerships
PWLB	Public Works Loan Board
QUANGO	Quasi-autonomous Non-governmental Organisation
RDA	Regional Development Agency
REF	Research Excellence Framework
TEF	Teaching Excellence Framework
TMC	Tenant Management Cooperative
TMO	Tenant Management Organisation
UK	United Kingdom
UN	United Nations
UNEP	United Nations Environment Programme
UNHCR	United Nations High Commission for Refugees
VAT	Value Added Tax
VFM	Value for Money
WHO	World Health Organization

PREFACE

The title of this book suggests that public services in the UK face a catastrophic future which has already commenced. While this may sound dramatic and alarmist, we sincerely believe this to be accurate. The reasons for this are discussed in the early chapters of the book but in summary these might be seen as:

- the current alarming situation in health and social care consequent on inadequate finances, an inability to recruit staff and the impact of Covid-19;
- the ongoing pressures of reconciling growing demands for many public services with, at best, stagnant financial and human resources;
- the ongoing and longer-term implications for public services of the Covid-19 pandemic and any future pandemics, which are increasingly likely;
- the ongoing fall-out from the UK's decision to exit the European Union (whether that is seen as right or wrong) which again impacts on public services particularly with regard to human resources; and
- the immense global challenges posed by climate change which has almost unimaginable implications for public services.

We believe that, fundamentally, the UK's very centralised system of government is just not up to the task of dealing with all of these issues simultaneously. In Chapter 2, we comment that the UK used to rule a global empire from offices in London but today it tries to rule the rest of the UK, from offices in London. The problems of both these approaches are similar – being out of touch. At the time of writing, after the early problems relating to the pandemic, we have seen a picture of the UK government thrashing around trying to deal with a stream of largely predictable problems, without any clear vision or purpose when many of these issues were best dealt with locally. However, this criticism is not new and does not apply just to the current government. As we discuss in Chapter

2, the history of public policy in the UK, over the last few decades, has largely been one of ongoing public policy failure by governments of all political parties. Add to this the issue of sleaze and corruption, which historically is often associated with power as demonstrated by the following quotations:

> *Those who seek power are not worthy of that power* (Plato)
> *Power corrupts, absolute power corrupts absolutely* (Lord Acton)

While the UK is not a corrupt state by global standards, looking at modern UK political history, over the last 50 years or so, it does seem that UK governments of all parties get tainted with corruption and sleaze to a lesser or greater extent. One has to ask whether the existence of the centralised UK state, with the vast bulk of power centralised in a small number of hands in London, breeds such corruption and sleaze.

This book is about the government and governance of the UK, the complete mess of the current system and the urgent need for radical reform. The main thrust of the book is the case for dismantling the over-centralised and London-centric approach to government policy making leading to endless policy failures and disenchantment of the electorate, particularly in those areas of the UK outside of the South East which represent 80% of the UK population.

In its place, we describe, in considerable detail, an alternative approach, namely the development of federal state with a system of elected regional government for the whole of the UK with a corresponding reduction in the scope, power and size of national UK government. An elected regional government would include English regions as well as existing governments in Scotland, Wales and Northern Ireland. Such an approach has often been mentioned in discussions by many people, but what this book does is flesh out in detail how such a system of regional government might be formed and how it might operate. Furthermore, we consider how public policy, in specific policy areas such as health and social care education, might be formulated and implemented by regional governments. We do not claim to have "dotted every i" or "crossed every t" in these areas, but we have provided a framework for further work to be done to flesh out the proposals.

Why are these changes necessary? There are probably two main reasons. First, the union of the UK seems in serious trouble. Scotland seems to be moving inexorably towards a referendum on full independence which may well succeed eventually due to the numbers of younger voters who will be eligible to vote. In Wales, a similar trend may be seen. Polls show that Welsh voters (and indeed many English voters) have been more approving of the Welsh Government's response to the coronavirus crisis than that of the UK government at Westminster. This increased confidence in self-government in Wales has been linked to significant rise in support for Welsh independence particularly among younger people. In Northern Ireland, support for a referendum on the province leaving the UK seems to be growing. A recent poll undertaken on behalf of the BBC found that some 43% of the region's voters would vote to leave the UK, while 49% of the region's voters would vote to remain and 8% were undecided. However, 51% said they believed Northern Ireland would no longer be part of the UK in 25 years, with 37% saying they believed it would still be.

All of the authors who have contributed to this book are firm supporters of the UK union, but we look with alarm at the above figures and wonder why this is the case. We do not think the devolved administrations of the UK are perfect examples of government, without blemish, but they are trying to plan, deliver and tailor public policy and public services based on local knowledge of the needs of their population as opposed to having these things determined from offices in the centre of London. It is a mistake to see this move towards the break-up of the UK as, merely, some form of nationalist resentment by the Celtic nations towards England and the English. It is more to do with a picture of a London-based UK government which is both out of touch with what is happening outside of London (including English regions) and which shows deep incompetence with regard to public policy and public services in these areas.

Second, in the book we examine the UK closely and we highlight the massive inequality (on almost every measure) that exists between the South of the country (mainly London and the South East) and Scotland, Wales, Northern Ireland and the majority of English regions. Such inequalities seem likely to worsen as a consequence of the pandemic. It would be wrong to link these regional inequalities purely to the policies of the Conservative and coalition governments of the past 11 years, even though they have presided over a period of financial austerity. These inequalities have persisted for many decades and governments of all parties have, seriously, failed to address social, but especially economic inequalities, between North and South when in power. I would go as far as to suggest that Labour governments (which also tend to have very centralising tendencies when in government) are more culpable since they have ignored the needs of what were once regarded as their heartland constituencies in the North, Midlands, Wales and Scotland. Such voters have subsequently been attracted by the "levelling-up" rhetoric of the present government which, of course, will come to nothing because they are attempting to deliver improvements using the failed centralised approach which just does not work.

There is no doubt that achieving the sorts of changes in government and policy referred to in this book will be an extremely difficult (if not impossible) task given the large-scale resistance that will be generated by powerful vested interests of many kinds. Such changes as described will be greeted with reflex cries of "fantasies", "madness" and "ludicrous" by many, but the reality is that they are common in many, if not most, developed countries. Such resistance will derive from an inherent superiority complex of the London elite coupled with fears about the changes being proposed impacting on vested interests about factors such as income, wealth, property, influence and honours.

We are not naïve and, to be frank, we see little chance of any of the changes described above ever taking place, in the foreseeable future, whatever the views of the electorate and whatever government was in power. This is not because what we outline is incorrect, illogical or impractical, and such systems of regional government operate perfectly well in many other developed countries. It is because the vested interests involved are just too great. The absolute power of London and these vested interests involved make such changes virtually inconceivable. Our overall conclusion is that this inability to change shows the limits of UK democracy. Hence, our primary purpose in writing this book is to describe the mess we are in regarding public policy and public services and to outline some possible alternative approaches to see if they have any longer-term resonance.

However, as already noted, in the absence of such changes, we foresee a nightmare scenario involving the break-up of the UK as a nation state and the creation of a nationalistic and insular English state beset with major social problems caused by ongoing and growing inequalities.

Thanks are due to a number of people – first and foremost, the contributors to this book. In an era where the word "expert" is often used loosely I have been extremely fortunate to be able to call on a group of real experts in a diverse number of fields. Taken together they bring expertise and extensive experience covering the local, regional, national and international aspects of government and policy making in the main areas of social and economic policy. A majority of the contributors have also worked extensively in public services in a London environment including Whitehall and Westminster. They also combine academic experience with extensive practical experience in their field of specialism. What they also bring is a broad consensus view about the extreme challenges facing public policy and public services in the UK and the difficulty of finding responses to these challenges. Thanks are also due to Kristina Abbots of Routledge Publishing who had faith in the concept of this book from an early stage.

Finally, I must emphasise that this preface reflects my personal views only but I believe there is broad consensus about the content of the book among the contributors.

Malcolm J. Prowle
December 2021

PART A

Introduction and context

1

INTRODUCTION AND CONTEXT

Malcolm J. Prowle

Introduction

> Just about every aspect of our current national impasse proves that the old centralised game is up, and that England needs a new constitutional settlement. Power needs to be taken from the centre and dispersed. If we do not begin this revolution soon, we will carry on bumbling from one crisis to the next, as Whitehall and Westminster fall into more scandal and disgrace and the commands barked from on high continue to fade into white noise
>
> *(Harris, 2020)*

At the time this book was being written, the UK (and most other countries in the world) was in the midst of the Covid-19 pandemic. Now many will argue that much could have been done over the years to reduce the chances of a new viral disease occurring and to minimise the extent of disease transmission within and between countries. However, this did not happen and governments around the world had to deal with the immense and unprecedented problems of coping with the pandemic and protecting lives, while minimising the collateral economic damage.

This was the case in the UK during the period of the pandemic but it is easy to forget that the UK already faced a number of other significant challenges which, at the time, seemed to have taken a back seat. One of these is, clearly, coming to terms and adapting to the changed situation caused by the UK's departure from the European Union (EU). Another is the ongoing debate about immigration to the UK – whether that be immigration from the EU or other countries outside the EU. A third is the resolution of the dilemma as to how to provide public services in an environment of growing demand and, at

DOI: 10.4324/9781003201892-2

best, stagnant resources. Fourth and perhaps the biggest challenge is that posed by climate change. All of these, and other, matters concern public policy in the UK and this is the topic of this book.

All the authors of this book see huge weaknesses and concerns with the London-centric approaches to government and public policy formulation in the UK and are convinced that these weaknesses are unresolvable under the current arrangements and major reforms are required. This statement should not be seen, solely, as a criticism of the current Conservative Government although they have played their part over the last couple of years, or even longer. These criticisms can be made at all political parties and, indeed, it could be argued that the Labour Party has more guilt to bear as it is their traditional heartlands in the North, Midlands, Wales and Scotland that have borne the burden of the huge UK inequalities and the unbalanced UK economy (as well as the Covid-19 pandemic) which we discuss later. Many will argue that these matters are the prime cause of the loss of Labour "heartland seats" in these areas.

What we outline in this book is a programme for change involving the development of devolved regional government across the UK as a whole (including England) and along the lines of the existing UK devolved governments, but with significant enhancements.

In this chapter we discuss:

- The nature of public policy
- Public services in the UK
- The nature of the problems
- Structure of the book

The nature of public policy

What is public policy?

Getting agreement on a single, all-inclusive definition of public policy is very difficult if not impossible. Initially, we might say that a public policy is simply what government (and perhaps any public official who influences or determines public policy) does or does not do about a problem that comes before them for consideration and possible action. Public policy can be seen as having a number of key attributes (Project citizen):

- Policy is made in response to some sort of issue or problem that requires attention.
- Policy is what the government chooses to do (actual) or not do (implied) about a particular issue or problem.
- Policy is made on behalf of the "public" but that "public" should also encompass future generations as well as the current generations

- Policy is oriented toward a goal or desired state, such as the solution of a problem.
- Policy is ultimately made by governments, even if the ideas come from outside government or through the interaction of government and the public.
- Policy making is part of an ongoing process that does not always have a clear beginning or end, since decisions about who will benefit from policies and who will bear any burden resulting from the policies are continually reassessed, revisited and revised.

Without doubt, there are many problems in our communities that need to be solved. Some problems may readily be dealt with by actions taken in the private sphere (individuals and families) or by our civil society (social, economic or political associations or organisations). Public policy problems are those that must be addressed by government.

Public policy and social policy

At the outset we need to distinguish between public policy and the management of public services. Policy defines the problem faced by public services and the expectation rights and duties of citizens with regard to public services. Management of public services defines how services are provided in a fair and effective manner. We return to this later under the heading of implementation.

The term "social policy" sits alongside public policy. However, the difference between them does not seem to be clear. To some, the terms mean the same thing and often are expressed as social and public policy. However, to others, social policy is a part of public policy but is distinctive in that it is that part of public policy which is concerned with public welfare and how societies across the world meet human needs for education, work, health and well-being. However, we see this as something of a moving feast since it could be argued that issues such as policing, the environment and economic development also contribute towards social policy. In this book we will use the term "public policy".

The public policy process

In one way or another the public policy process is normally conceptualised as sequential parts or stages (Jordan and Adelle, 2012). These are:

1 Problem emergence
2 Agenda setting
3 Consideration of policy options
4 Decision-making
5 Implementation
6 Evaluation

However, it must be recognised that the political perspective of the government in power, its manifesto commitments and its values will also have a strong influence on the public policy agenda.

According to this "textbook" view of policy, individuals and groups must first get a particular problem on the agenda for discussion and, if possible, consideration by policy makers. This could be achieved via representations from political groups, professional organisations, lobbyists, local communities, etc. However, the reality is that some groups and individuals are less effective at articulating and expressing their views than other groups. Disparities of knowledge and articulation can lead to policy makers receiving very biased sets of views, on a particular issue, not all representative of the community at large. This is exacerbated when the policy is developed in London and the bulk of views impacting on the policy makers are also London based. Views of people and individuals living far from London cannot expect to get the same degree of attention as those based in the metropolis. What is needed here is the development of advocacy skills among those lacking the skills and confidence to express their views (see for example Lister).

Policy makers then select the best course of action based on evidence and specialist advice, make the policy, then hand it to administrators and managers for implementation. This stage-based view emphasises that policy is a process involving many different parts of government. But in practice, policy issues are interconnected; policy makers look around for solutions in the context of great uncertainty and many internal and external constraints. Past practice often has a determining effect on how new issues are processed. To counter such uncertainty, increasing use should be made of scientific evidence to guide policy development. Multiple policy "tools" such as expert reports, consultation, focus groups, polls, cost-benefit analysis and impact analysis are employed by governments to provide such decision support (Jordan and Turnpenny, 2015). However, in practice, policy making may sometimes (or even often) fail to reflect the above process. Policy decisions may be made which are influenced by over-strong lobby groups (usually London based), political correctness (usually London derived), corruption, political time pressures or many other factors. Sometimes policy is made not on evidence (because none exists) or may be a function of negotiation within the decision-making body sometimes referred to as "negotiated order" (Cox, 2019).

A multitude of different models and theories have been developed to explain policy making (see Dryzek and Dunleavy, 2009; Hill, 2009). *Pluralists* believe that political power is widely, although unevenly, spread throughout society. Although powerful groups exist in particular policy sectors, no single group is continuously capable of shaping the entire policy process. In policy terms, pluralists assume that agenda setting is open and competitive, with the government acting as an honest broker. Once adopted, though, policies must still be steered through the implementation process. Because of the competitiveness of the policy process, outcomes are unpredictable. Another group the *neo-pluralists* argue that business occupies a privileged position compared to other groups. Instruments like the mass media help to structure environmental politics by removing "grand majority" issues, concerning the fundamentals of the political order, from the agenda, leaving citizens to debate residual secondary concerns (Lindblom, 1977). Whereas pluralists assume that grievances are openly debated, neo-pluralists argue that they are organised out of politics by institutional rules and routines. Policy making occurs within small and stable groups of actors (or networks) clustered around particular government departments. Policy outcomes then generally reflect business preferences rather than those of environmentalists, who find it difficult to access decision-makers or are deterred from even trying. Finally, *structuralists* believe that the state is under powerful structural pressure to nurture economic growth regardless of the environmental implications (Benton, 1984). On this view, most environmental controls are nothing more than a sham, introduced to pacify critics and keep the conflict between economic classes to manageable levels. For Marxist scholars, environmental problems are rooted in the unequal distribution of resources within society. There can be no lasting solution to such problems until the social system is structured more equally.

Levers of public policy

One outcome of the public policy process, particularly in democracies, is that political leaders will have to decide what levers they intend to use to achieve the policy they wish to implement and the objectives they have set themselves. There are a finite number of levers, and it is suggested that the main ones are as shown below:

- **Legislation** – the passing of laws and associated regulations by the legislature of a country or state.
- **Regulation** – various bodies exist to regulate the activities of certain private or public bodies. An example here might be the Care Quality Commission, in England, which regulates the activities of both public and private providers of health and social care.
- **Taxation** – new taxes can always be introduced or existing taxes varied by government. Although one aspect of taxation is to raise revenues, taxes can be used by governments to try and change the behaviours or citizens or organisations in order to affect a particular policy. Examples here would be increases in taxes on cigarettes or fizzy drinks to reduce consumption of these items.
- **Subsidy** – government subsidies can be used to sustain or promote activity in a particular area in order to affect a particular policy. For example, subsidies can be paid to private providers of child care in order to increase the capacity of this sector as a means of enhancing the labour force.
- **Nudge approaches"** – this is a concept in behavioural economics, political theory and behavioural sciences which proposes positive reinforcement and

indirect suggestions as ways to influence the behaviour and decision-making of groups or individuals in society. Nudging contrasts with other ways to achieve compliance discussed here such as legislation and enforcement.

- **Direct provision** – as is well known, governments are a major direct provider of public services in many areas including health services, schools and social care. However, in addition to direct provision, governments may use other levers to enhance private capacity in the same fields.
- **Leadership and exhortation** – government Ministers and their expert advisers may provide leadership and exhortation to try and influence public behaviour in support of a particular policy. Much has been seen of this lever during the Covid-19 pandemic.

Locus of public policy

Most people would expect that in a nation state, the main locus for public policy would be that of central government. This would involve various actors such as ministers, legislators, civil servants and lobbyists. Undoubtedly this is the case but it must be recognised that public policy can also be developed at other levels including:

- **Supra-national bodies** – for example, the EU develops a variety of public policies that are applicable in member countries of the union. The UN and the World Trade Organization are other examples of supra-national organisations whose activities will impact on domestic public policy such as refugee policies.
- **Sub-national government** – these will also have some involvement in public policy formulation and implementation, as it affects their own region or state. The extent of involvement in public policy depends on the type of sub-national government that exists in a country.

We might also think of more local bodies like local government having an involvement in public policy albeit within a national or regional framework. To a large extent this will probably be concerned with refining national policy to fit local circumstances but this is often constrained by the actions of central government. Also, we must recognise that a local government may not be able to utilise all the levers of public policy referred to above.

Implementation of public policy

As noted above, one of the stages of the policy process is that of implementation. In some cases, the implementation stage may be an integral part of the policy process but in other cases implementation may be a separate component with the tasks of implementation being undertaken by persons different from those who formulated the policy. This separation of policy formulation and policy implementation is a well-established weakness of UK public policy, particularly where policy is developed by a London-centric centralised government but implemented by local authorities in disparate parts of the country. At the evaluation stage it is not unknown for a particular policy to be deemed a failure only for it to remain unclear whether the problem was in the conception and/or implementation of that policy.

Now this weakness of the policy formulation/implementation phase might seem an argument for the implementation and management of public services to be undertaken by central government – it is not. First, it retains the problem of policy formulation being undertaken by groups divorced from the communities being served and second, we do not think civil servants would have the aptitude or the wish to undertake the operational management of public services such as refuse collection and road maintenance. What needs to be done is for the task of policy making to be devolved to a level where it naturally integrates with the process of implementation

Public services in the UK

What are public services?

At first thought, one might think that public services are those services provided by the public sector for the benefit of the general public, usually free at the point of receipt. This differs from private transactions involving payment to a private sector organisation for some goods or services. However, things are more complicated than this and we have to consider two aspects of public services:

- Who provides those public services – a public-, private- or third-sector organisation?
- Who ultimately pays for those services – a public or private source?

If we combine these two aspects together we can see four possible combinations as shown in Figure 1.1.

Now this sort of analysis can be undertaken for any public service, in any country, but the size of the segments will differ from case to case. Perspectives on the UK situation are as follows:

	Public Provision	Private Provision
Public Funding	A	B
Private Funding	C	D

FIGURE 1.1 Public service finance and provision

- **Segment A (public/public)** – this is clearly a public service since it is publicly provided and publicly financed. Examples here would be state schools, most NHS services, etc.
- **Segment D (private/private) –** this is clearly NOT a public service but a private transaction between a private organisation and a customer for the provision of a service in return for payment. Private healthcare in a private hospital or private security guards are examples.
- **Segment B (public/private) –** this is a situation where a service is provided by a private sector organisation but paid from public funds. An example of this is an NHS patient treated in a privately owned hospital but with payment being made to the private hospital by the NHS. Arguably, this arrangement does constitute a public service since the service has been financed from public funds.
- **Segment C (private/public) –** this involves someone receiving service from a public service provider but making full payment for that service themselves. An example might be a patient having a surgical operation in the private wing of an NHS hospital. Arguably, this does not constitute a public service but involves a commercial transaction between a public provider and an individual consumer.

Types of public services

Clearly public services are numerous and varied and many of them probably do not impinge on our consciousness to the same extent as others which are more visible. However, we can attempt a broad classification of public services of which the main groups would be as follows:

- **Defence and foreign relations** – this involves relations with other countries (diplomatic service) and defence of the country (armed forces).
- **Economic management –** this involves a wide range of economic issues including the promotion of economic growth, the management of public finances, public debt management, regional economic development and trade relations.
- **Law and order** – a key role of the state is to maintain law and order in society. Thus, in this group would be included such services as police, prisons, courts of law and probation services.
- **Population welfare** – these are concerned with the basic well-being of the individuals and the society at large. Thus, they could include such services as education, health, social care, and social protection. In many developing countries, such services may not be provided, formally, by governmental organisations but, informally, by family members, voluntary groups, etc.
- **Physical infrastructure –** the maintenance and development of the physical infrastructure of the country including roads, housing, airports,

communications, and power. This may be done by direct provision by government or the use of private companies regulated by government.

- **Environmental protection and management** – this has always been an important area of public policy in all countries but in recent decades the increasing importance placed on the problems of global warming and climate change has significantly increased the emphasis placed on various aspects of the environment. This trend can be expected to continue in the future. A wide variety of issues fall under this heading concerning waste disposal, energy, water supply, land management, pollution control, etc.
- **Health protection** – health protection is a term used to encompass a set of activities within the Public Health function. It involves such matters as the safety and quality of food, prevention of communicable diseases, managing outbreaks and other incidents that threaten the public health. Health protection has both a domestic and an international dimension and its importance has been greatly magnified in recent months because of the Covid-19 pandemic.

Organisation of public services

There can be a number of different public service organisations that provide a range of different services. The relationship between the organisation and the services provided is complex and will vary considerably from country to country.

First, as discussed above, many, if not most, public services will usually be provided by a public sector organisation but some services will may be provided by a private or third-sector organisation.

Second, public services will be provided by a wide range of organisations including the following:

- **Supra-national organisations** – the EU provides certain services for member countries of the Union. Examples are vaccine procurement and external border security.
- **National governments** – in most countries national governments may provide a wide range of services such as defence, policing and health services.
- **Sub-national governments** – as will be discussed at length, in most large countries in the world it is more usual to find some form of sub-national government. In the UK the only examples of sub-national government are the devolved governments of Wales, Scotland and Northern Ireland. In England, up until 2010, there were "Government Offices" in each of the English regions but these were abolished by the incoming Cameron government. There is now no form of regional government in England but while there are various approaches to taking account of regional views these seem flawed and have been constantly amended over time.

- **Government agencies** – in many countries there are a variety of agencies concerned with delivering public services but which are not a part of central government or local government. However, they might be regarded as operating at arm's length from central government. In the UK, government agencies might be created by the UK government or the devolved governments.
- **Local government** – in most countries in the world, including the UK, there is a structure of local government involving hundreds of elected local authorities charged with the delivery of public services.

The linkage between types of public services and providers of public services is complex and a particular public service can involve many state and non-state organisations. Some UK examples are given in Figure 1.2.

Mention must also be made of public service partnerships. These are not separate public service organisations but a series of organisations working

SERVICE SECTOR	ORGANISATIONS INVOLVED IN SERVICE DELIVERY
Defence	• Ministry of Defence • Government agencies • Armed forces (army, navy, air force) • Private contractors
Education	• Department for Education • Devolved government departments of education • Government agencies • Local Government • Schools • Universities and colleges
Health	• Department of Health and Social care • Devolved government departments of health • Government agencies • NHS Commissioners • NHS Providers (e.g. hospitals) • Local Authorities (Public Health) • Private companies • Third sector organisations
Social Care	• Department of Health and Social care • Devolved government departments for social care • Government agencies • Local authorities • Private companies • Third sector organisations
Economic Development	• HM Treasury • Other government departments • Bank of England • Devolved governments • Government agencies • Universities/Colleges • Local Authorities (Economic Development Units)

FIGURE 1.2 Public service delivery

together in a partnership arrangement to meet local service needs. At this point, we should distinguish between two types of partnerships:

- **Public-public partnerships** – such partnerships often exist largely because the organisational boundaries between different public service organisations do not reflect the continuity of some services across those boundaries. Others exist because of the potential for obtaining economies of scale in public service provision. Partnerships can show great variety. Examples of organisations working in partnership arrangements could include local government, health services, police and third sector.
- **Public-private partnerships (PPP)** – it should also be noted that there are a wide range of partnerships in existence that involve public service organisations working in partnership with the private sector. There are a variety of different forms of public private partnerships already in existence.

Finally, the problems of collaborative working need to be mentioned. There are often difficulties with different organisations in the same sector collaborating with one another. An example here might be difficulties in collaboration between the primary healthcare sector and the hospital sector. However, another problem appears to be collaboration between organisations in different sectors where there seems a clear need to do so. The challenges to public services outlined in Chapter 2 point to a greater, not lesser, need for multi-agency collaboration in service provision. However, this issue has been ongoing for many decades and while some improvements have undoubtedly been made, there still seems much to do and the problems seems almost intractable. The whole issue of improved coordination, collaboration and integration in public services will be discussed later in Chapter 13.

The nature of the problem

This book is focused on the myriad of problems that are seen to be consequent on unsatisfactory and inappropriate governmental structures and policy-making processes in the UK. The key aspects of this are listed below and discussed more fully in later chapters.

- The huge scale of challenges facing public services in the next few decades coupled with the likelihood of limited economic growth and limited growth in public service funding.
- The enormous inequalities between London and the South East, and the rest of the UK. There are other sorts of inequality in the UK but these seem secondary in scale to the geographic issue.
- The large imbalances in the UK economy in terms of both economic sectors and geography.

- The degree of political fracture in the UK with the possibility of Scotland, Wales and Northern Ireland leaving the Union coupled with a political and social schism between the North and South of England.
- The over-centralisation of government at all levels in the UK which is inhibiting successful public policies in the UK. I once described this as being a situation in UK public services where "*every tier believes the tier below it is incompetent*". This means that every tier in the hierarchy wishes greater power devolved to them but they are reluctant to devolve any power to lower levels.
- The inadequacies of current processes of public policy formulation and implementation leading to a significant track record of public policy failure by governments of all parties.

We do not see the solutions to the above as being "*more of the same*", namely an improved approach to centralised London-centric policy making applied to the whole of England and, to a lesser degree, Wales, Scotland and Northern Ireland. Watchers of the famous TV series "Yes minister" will recall the episode where the Permanent Secretary (Sir Humphrey) exhorts his Minister to "*centralise, Minister, centralise*".

Instead we believe solutions to the problems mentioned above as being along the following lines:

- The creation of a federal system of government involving elected regional governments in England comparable to the elected governments in Wales, Scotland and Northern Ireland. However, for English regions and Wales, Scotland and Northern Ireland, there is also a need for much greater powers regarding a range of public policy issues but especially that of regional economic development. Coupled with this would be a reduction in the number of MPs sitting in a federal parliament and a very large reduction in the number of London-based civil servants no longer needed in London since many policy responsibilities had been devolved to regions.
- A need for competence in government and policy formulation. First, it is desirable that governments come to power with adequate and thought-out policies rather than just trying to attract votes through sound-bites. In this way, they will avoid wasting a first term in office learning how to use the levers of power (IfG, 2010). Second, that policy-making processes and personnel are competent, innovative, recognise regional differences and outlooks, and understand the complexities of implementation. Third, that policy making has a strong degree of transparency such that voters and other interested parties can understand the reasons why particular policies were accepted and alternatives rejected.

These are the issues which this book is concerned with. However, at the outset we must strongly emphasise that the authors of this book (three who are Welsh and five who are English) are all strong supporters of the union of the UK. We are not promoting nationalism or independence in the devolved nations and we want to see a strong UK that is based on strength throughout its four corners. In all parts of the UK, we want to see local diversity respected through local problems being capable of being addressed by local action, not dependent on an ever-distant government in London. Our aim is to help to keep the UK together not weaken it or see it weakened. However, as we discuss later in the book, we fear that if something is not done to alleviate the problems of remote government, social and economic inequality, and failed public policy, then the UK as a nation state will dis-integrate.

A word of clarification is needed concerning the terminology we use in writing this book. We refer to the UK as a "nation state" with a seat at the UN, the G7, etc. Within the UK, there are four countries or nations, namely England, Scotland, Wales and Northern Ireland, although the situation of Northern Ireland is anomalous because of the Good Friday agreement, the Brexit Trade Deal, etc. Throughout the book we refer to the regions of England, of which there are currently nine. We use the term "UK regional governments" to mean nine English regional governments plus the existing three devolved governments. In terms of powers and responsibilities, we see no reason why the English regional governments should have any greater or lesser powers/responsibilities compared to the existing devolved governments but we propose an increase in powers/responsibilities of all the UK regional governments.

Structure of book

The book is structured in four parts.

- **Part A**: Following this introductory chapter, which has discussed the concepts of public policy and public services, Chapter 2 considers the huge range of challenges facing public policy and public services in the years ahead.
- **Part B**: This section comprises three chapters. Chapter 3 discusses the concept of regionalism and regional government and describes the way in which regional governments exist and operate, successfully, in many other countries. Chapter 4 considers, in some detail, the key issues which would need to be addressed to implement regional government in the UK. Chapter 5 outlines the need for a complete overhaul of the way in which public services are financed in the UK to provide for greater sustainability.
- **Part C**: This section concerns the development and application of public policy in a number of key policy areas. However, policy development and implementation is addressed in the context of a devolved regional government in the UK where regional governments have considerable discretion over the policy approaches developed and applied in their particular region. The key policy areas we have considered are economic planning and development, health, social care, schools and post-16 (non-university)

education, housing and other public services. While not an exhaustive list the section does include the main policy areas which effect the everyday lives of citizens.

- **Part D**: This section considers three key issues which are not specific to any one area of public policy but have relevance to several or even most policy areas. These issues concern: resource trends and resource planning, collaboration and integration of public services and the role of community development and the third sector. Each of these issues is considered in the context of a framework of devolved regional government throughout the UK.

References

Benton, T. (1984), *The Rise and Fall of Structural Marxism: Althusser and His Influence*, Macmillan.

Cox, S. (2019), An Examination of the Negotiated Order of NHS Commissioning: Decisions in the Absence of Objectivity, PhD thesis, Nottingham Trent University.

Dryzek, J. and Dunleavy, P. (2009), *Theories of the Democratic State*, Palgrave Macmillan.

Harris, J. (2020), https://www.theguardian.com/commentisfree/2020/may/25/pandemic-failings-centralised-state-councils-coronavirus

Hill, M. (2009), *The Public Policy Process*, Routledge.

IfG (2010), An Evening with Tony Blair, Institute for Government, https://www.institutefor government.org.uk/blog/evening-tony-blair

Jordan, A.J. and Adelle, C. (2012), *Environmental policy in the EU*, Routledge.

Jordan, A.J. and Turnpenny, J.T. (2015), *The Tools of Policy Formulation: Actors, Capacities, Venues and Effects*, New Horizons in Public Policy Series, Edward Elgar Publishing.

Lindblom, C. (1977), *Politics and Markets: The World's Political Economic Systems*, Basic Books.

Lister, E.G., Building Leadership for Health, https://www.building-leadership-for-health.org.uk/sfgh-training-toolkits/

Project citizen, What Is Public Policy, https://www.civiced.org/project-citizen/what-is-public-policy

2

ONGOING AND FUTURE CHALLENGES TO UK PUBLIC POLICY AND PUBLIC SERVICES

Malcolm J. Prowle

Introduction

This chapter aims to outline the enormous range of challenges that face public policy and public services in the UK and, to a large extent, other countries across the globe. Some of these challenges have been with us for decades, others are fairly recent and yet others are just appearing over the horizon. These factors will have implications for the demand, supply, organisation and financing of public services. Any consideration of the future of public policy development and the delivery of public services would be pointless without some consideration of these factors.

Various challenges have been considered under the following headings:

- The legacy of austerity
- Ongoing and increasing demands for public services
- Social and economic inequalities in UK regions: a nation divided
- An unbalanced UK economy
- UK public policy failure
- Climate change and environmental degradation
- Limited economic growth
- Legacy of public debt
- Political alienation and voter apathy
- The legacy of the Covid-19 pandemic

Legacy of austerity

The term "economic growth" is well known which means the annual growth in the Gross Domestic Product (GDP) of a country's economy. Also, the term

DOI: 10.4324/9781003201892-3

"recession" is widely understood which means a contraction in the size of a country's economy. Technically, an economic recession is defined as a contraction in a country's GDP in two successive quarters. Recessions are not new and the biblical story of Joseph describes a country where seven years of a bountiful harvest (growth) was followed by seven years of famine (recession). In modern times, we are used to scenarios less serious than in Joseph's time whereby we would expect four to five years of economic growth in a country to be followed by, perhaps, up to a year of recession.

The economic recession of 2008/2009 (now referred to as the Great Recession) was a landmark event in economic history and was different from other recessions for four main reasons:

- **Breadth** – historically, many recessions might have occurred in one or a small number of countries. The Great Recession impacted on a large number of countries across the globe and even those countries that did not have a technical recession (e.g. China) suffered a sharp economic slowdown.
- **Length** – after two quarters of economic contraction (a recession), quite often economies come out of recession and into growth fairly quickly but this was not the case with the Great Recession. In the USA, the Great Recession was deemed to have lasted eighteen months while in the UK, France and Australia it lasted for five quarters. Other countries were even longer in recession.
- **Depth** – at the time, the Great Recession was the deepest UK recession since the Second World War. Manufacturing output declined by 7% by the end of 2008 and the recession affected many sectors including banks and investment firms, with many well-known and established businesses having to fold. The unemployment rate rose to 8.3% (2.68 million people) in August 2011, the highest level since 1994.
- **Recovery Time** – this concerns the length of time it took for an economy to recover to pre-recession levels of economic growth. An economy typically recovers to its previous peak output in less than a year. However, in the case of the Great Recession the recovery time was much longer. Having shrunk by more than 6% between the first quarter of 2008 and the second quarter of 2009, the UK economy took five years to get back to the size it was before the recession.

An economic recession has two main impacts on public services and public finances:

- A reduction in tax revenues because of lower company profits and lower levels of earnings
- An increase in demands for social benefits and some public services (e.g. health services)

In terms of public finances, the traditional model in the UK was for governments to suffer public budget deficits in times of recession because of the two factors mentioned above. During this time public services would be financed through some form of borrowing which added to public debt. In times of economic growth, governments usually generated public budget surpluses and these could be used to repay public debt. In the UK, somewhere along the way, this went wrong as illustrated in Table 2.1.

Between 1999 and 2001, the UK government applied the conventional model of running a public budget surplus at a time of economic growth. However, from 2002 to 2008, the then government was suffering public budget deficits during a period of economic growth, which was sometimes quite substantial growth. In 2009, the Great Recession hit with a huge impact on government revenues and spending and the public budget deficit went "through the roof". In 2009/2010, the UK borrowed a record £155 billion.

Government borrowing at this level could not go on indefinitely since the UK may have seen a decline in its credit rating. Hence, in 2010 the newly elected coalition government had to decide what action to take. Many advocated having an increased level of borrowing for a limited period of time in order to invest in the UK economy and promote higher levels of economic growth which might, in turn, generate additional tax revenues that could be used to repay the debt. However, the new government introduced a policy which became known as "austerity" and which comprised two main elements:

- Some higher levels of taxation notably VAT
- Significant cuts in funding for many (but not all) government expenditure programmes

TABLE 2.1 UK public finances

Year	*Growth/contraction in GDP*	*Government surplus-deficit as % of GDP*
	%	%
2009	−5.25	−12.8
2008	0.55	−5.5
2007	2.53	−2.7
2006	2.85	−2.7
2005	2.15	−3.3
2004	2.98	−3.7
2003	2.80	−3.7
2002	2.13	−2.0
2001	2.45	0.6
2000	3.90	3.7
1999	3.70	0.9

Source: Various.

The initial objective was to have reduced government borrowing to zero by the end of the Parliament but this was subsequently changed to 2018. However, while annual government borrowing was reduced substantially over this period, in 2019/2020 (the last full year before the Covid-19 pandemic) the UK government was still borrowing £56 billion, equivalent to 2.5% of GDP (House of Commons 2021).

This is not the place to discuss the merits of the austerity policy or whether other approaches to the borrowing crisis might have been more appropriate. What is certain, however, is that this level of financial austerity had not been seen in the UK for almost a century and its impacts on UK public services and society were profound and substantial. Much has been written about the impact of austerity on UK public services and this will be discussed further in Chapter 5 but for the moment it must be noted that this legacy of ten years of austerity had major implications for UK public policy and public services.

Ongoing and increasing demands for public services

In the UK and many other countries, we see an ongoing and increasing demand for certain public services. There are probably four main issues that drive increasing demands for services.

- **Population growth** – the global population keeps expanding. In 1960, the global population was 3 billion while today it is 7 billion. By 2050, it is expected to be 10 billion. Nor is this just a phenomenon of the developing world. Projections suggest that the population of the UK will rise from 63 million in 2010 to 67 million by 2020 and 72 million by 2035 (Macrotrends). Clearly, population growth of any kind will have implications for the demand of a range of public services such as health, education and housing. However, the other side of the coin is that such an increase in population *may* result in higher levels of economic growth and tax revenues to government but this is very uncertain.
- **Ageing population** – this is the well-known phenomenon, in both developed and developing countries, of the ageing population brought about by continuing declines in all-age all-cause mortality rates, meaning that more and more people are living into their 80s, 90s and beyond. In addition, there is the phenomenon of declining fertility rates (and new births) which means that populations are becoming skewed to the older end of the spectrum. There are two effects of this. First, it is well established that a growing proportion of elderly in the population has resource consequences for a range of public services, most notably health and social care. Second, the ratio of those who are economically active (and thus contribute to tax revenues) compared to the economically inactive (being the sum of those who are children or have retired) will rise significantly. This is referred to as an increasing age dependency ratio.

- **Scientific and Technological developments** – these have implications for the demand for public services and two aspects of this should be noted. The first concerns medical science and technology. New developments create demand for services where none previously existed. Consider the following: artificial joint replacements, organ transplants, drug therapies, imaging techniques. Before such developments took place, the demand for such services was zero. However, the existence and supply of such treatments, in turn, creates and fuels the demand that previously was non-existent. This is expected to continue.

  In addition, the IT and digital revolution is well known and understood. In the last 30 years, we have seen a wide range of technological developments such as personal computing, networks, e-mail, Internet, video communications and now artificial intelligence. Such developments have truly changed the world and have revolutionised many aspects of human life including the delivery of public services. One example concerns education, whether that be school or post-16 education. The Covid-19 pandemic has forced education providers to deliver learning via the Internet (using Teams, Zoom, etc.) and at the end of the pandemic it is likely that, to some extent, these technologies will be here to stay. Such developments have resource implications for public authorities and are likely to do so in the future.
- **Societal trends** – this concerns broad societal trends such as family breakdown, loss of the extended family and the numbers of persons living in one-person households. Such trends have, over the last few decades, had major implications for many public services and seem likely to do so in the future. Also, to be noted are increased public expectations of what public services will deliver and an enhanced sense of "entitlement" which probably has its origins in the "choice" agenda of the 2000s.

Social and economic inequalities in UK regions: a nation divided

The scale of inequalities between different parts of the UK is enormous but let us first start by looking at the global picture.

Global inequalities

The work of Thomas Piketty in his two books *Capital in the 21st Century* and *Capital and Ideology* (Piketty 2014, 2020) demonstrated that, globally, in the post-war period, inequality in both income and wealth first declined in the period 1945–1980, and has subsequently increased in the period 1980 to present. Income inequality in the UK is such that the top decile has 40%–50% of income, and 50%–55% of wealth. The income of the top decile is as much earned from the possession of wealth as it is from employment or self-employment, so that the inequalities become self-reinforcing, and at the current time begin to approach the extreme of inequality of the late 19th and early 20th centuries.

In recent decades, we have seen the growth of economic globalisation. Proponents of globalisation argue that the economic boom that results from globalisation has increased trade in goods and services, between countries, thereby increasing average income within countries, and reducing inequality. However, Nobel Laureate Eric Maskin (World Bank 2014) arrives at a different conclusion. He theorises that while average income has been rising as a result of more trade and global production, so has inequality risen within countries. Overall, the balance of evidence would seem to support Maskin that while globalisation leads to increased incomes for all groups in societies it also substantially increases inequalities between groups in a country and between countries.

Such inequality breeds political instability. Picket and Wilkinson in their books *The Spirit Level* and *The Inner Level* (Pickett and Wilkinson 2009, 2018) argue that the rising level of inequalities has had several consequences for public policy including:

- A negative relationship between mental and physical health and inequalities. The higher the inequality in a particular country, the lower the health and well-being of the population.
- Increasing levels of social dissatisfaction as the "have-nots" aspire to the culture and status of the "haves" but are unable to attain them.
- Increasing pressures on internal state security – with increasing levels of criminality.
- Increasing levels of GDP have not brought increasing levels of perceived well-being in most developed economies.

Inequality in the UK

Lipset and Rokkan (1967) suggest that modern societies had experienced two revolutions – the national revolution and the emergence of the nation state, and the industrial revolution and the emergence of a full market economy with its change from a patronage culture to contractual social arrangements. From these two revolutions came four major political cleavages:

- A cleavage between centre and periphery (central regions being those close to the political or economic capital, and those regions remote from these capitals)
- A cleavage between central government and the churches
- A cleavage between industrial and agricultural sectors
- A cleavage between ownership of the means of production between employers and workers

A particular concern in the UK is the first of the cleavages between centre and periphery, because increasingly in the late 19th and 20th centuries the political and economic capitals in the UK coalesced around London and the southeast, leaving the old economic powerhouses of the North behind. In more modern times the development of the neoliberal economic model has exacerbated this cleavage since the older traditional industries of the North have become those most likely to be affected by the globalisation of the world economy. The migration of the most mobile and highly educated populations from the regional periphery towards the centre increased the decline of the peripheral regions.

The impact this has had on the extent of regional inequality can now be set out. In summary, the situation is that London and the South taken together dominate the UK, demographically, politically, economically and in other ways, to an extent not seen anywhere else in the developed world. Some aspects of this are discussed below.

First is demographic. In demographic terms, in 2018 London and South East had 27% of the UK population based on just 8% of the land area of the country.

London is not only the largest city in the UK by far; it is also the centre of political power. The Monarchy, the Executive, the Legislature, the Supreme Court, the Media, numerous other influential state agencies together with the City of London, many leading universities and the headquarters of large businesses are all located in London. Aside from the relatively recent and small devolution changes in Wales, Scotland and Northern Ireland, political power in the UK is focused almost entirely in London. At one time, the other regions had economic development agencies and government offices of their own but even this is no longer the case. With political power goes influence on decision making about public and economic policy and the distribution of public resources. As already noted, it may also breed corruption and sleaze.

On the economic front a range of indicators show a wide disparity between London/South East and the rest of the UK. These include:

- Gross value added
- Income
- Wealth

Gross Value Added (GVA) is a measure of the productive economy of a region or country. The situation for the UK is shown in Table 2.2 using data derived from the Office for National statistics.

On these measures, the domination of London and the South East can be clearly seen.

In terms of income, the UK has the seventh most unequal incomes of 30 countries in the developed world. While the top fifth of the population have nearly 50% of the country's income, the bottom fifth have only 4% of the income (Equality Trust). Looking at this from a regional standpoint, we see the following picture in Figure 2.1.

This map shows the gross inequalities between London/South East and the rest of the UK. The UK's regional inequality is worse than 28 other advanced OECD countries.

TABLE 2.2 UK regional gross value added

	GVA (2017)	*GVA per head of population (2017)*
	£m	£
North East	53,235	20,129
North West	173,607	23,918
Yorkshire and Humber	116,772	21,426
East Midlands	104,243	21,845
West Midlands	133,128	22,713
East of England	152,799	24,772
London	**431,161**	**48,857**
South East	**267,126**	**29,415**
South West	130,635	23,499
Wales	62,190	19,899
Scotland	138,231	25,485
Northern Ireland	39,613	21,172

Sources: ONS (2018).

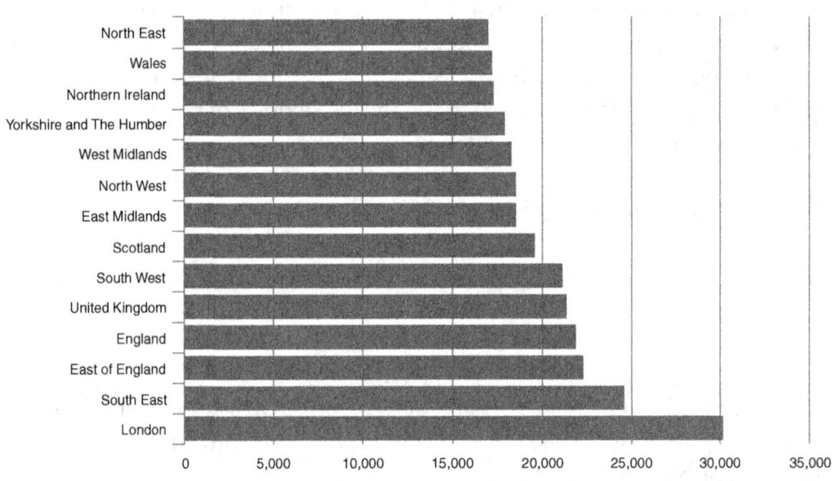

FIGURE 2.1 Regional gross disposable household income per head
Source: Office for National Statistics – Regional gross disposable household income (GDHI).

Wealth is also unevenly spread across the UK. As can be seen in Figure 2.2, levels of wealth in London and the South East are massively greater than any of the other ten regions.

This economic domination by London/South East has hugely detrimental effects on the rest of country and leads to the concept of the two nations – a prosperous South and a relatively (by UK standards) impoverished North. This is

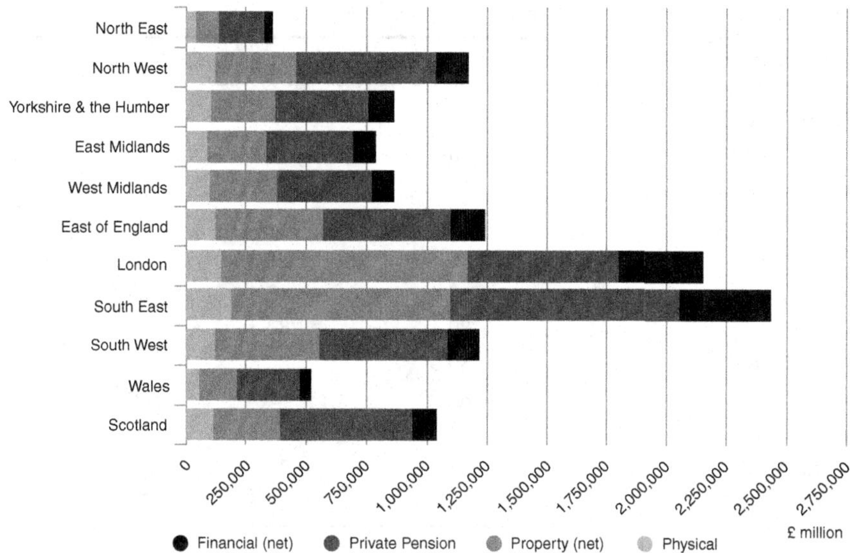

FIGURE 2.2 Aggregate household wealth by region for 2014–2016
Source: Wealth and Assets Survey. Office for National Statistics.

also exacerbated by the dominance of the London-based financial services sector on the rest of the UK economy and the focus of economic policy on protecting the financial sector of the economy to the detriment of other sectors.

If we look beyond the economic and consider other matters such as health status in different parts of the UK, we again see a north-south divide. The highest life expectancy is found in the southern regions and the lowest in the north. This is illustrated in Table 2.3 for males. Similar data exist for females.

The causes of these variances in life expectancy are complex but must be influenced to some degree by the economic inequalities referred to earlier. Many other examples can also be found of significant inequalities in health status between the North and the South in England. These include:

- Infant mortality rates
- Mortality rates for CSD, cancers and respiratory disease
- Prevalence of life-limiting illness.

Inequalities in relation to other social factors (e.g. education, housing) can also be quoted and other data can be used to describe the picture of the North/South inequality in the UK.

What is shown above is just the tip of the iceberg. An immense amount of *recent* evidence illustrates the social and economic problems of the North and the levels of inequality in the UK. Examples are Bradshaw (2020), Liddle and Shutt (2020) and the House of Commons Library (2020). Furthermore, at the time of writing,

TABLE 2.3 UK regional life expectancy

REGION	*2014–2016*	*2015–2017*	*2016–2018*
North East	77.8	77.9	77.9
North West	78.2	78.2	78.3
Yorkshire and Humber	78.7	78.7	78.7
East Midlands	79.3	79.4	79.4
West Midlands	78.8	78.8	78.9
East of England	80.4	80.4	80.3
London	80.4	80.5	80.7
South East	80.6	80.6	80.7
South West	80.2	80.2	80.2
Wales	78.4	78.3	78.3
Scotland	77.1	77.0	77.1
Northern Ireland	78.5	78.5	78.7

Source: ONS Life expectancy at birth and at age 65 years by local areas, UK.

the UK (along with many other countries) has recently been in a state of "lock-down" because of the Covid-19 pandemic and various other measures are still in place. Consequently, large parts of the UK economy were effectively shut down with many thousands of people being either furloughed or made redundant. While at the time of writing no firm data are available, there are serious concerns about the impact of lockdown on inequalities in the UK (Tabner 2020) with increasing inequality taking place. Some commentators (BBC 2021) also suggest that the expansion of inequalities will impact between social classes and between UK regions with a growth in the North-South divide. Clearly, the strength and longevity of these impacts remains to be seen but may be permanent.

An unbalanced UK economy

The failure of the Keynesian-based post-war economic consensus, in the 1970s, resulted in a resurgence of free-market economic thinking reinvented under titles such as "monetarism". With the collapse of communism in the late 1980s and early 1990s it became the unchallenged basis of political economy. However, subsequently, China now has the second largest economy in the world which is state-controlled.

The combination of free-market economics, and the development of the Internet and communications technology, led to the evolution of globalisation. This is also often linked to the rising inequalities experienced in developed liberal economies like the UK because of its intense dependence on trade, the effects of technology and over exposure to volatile financial markets. This has led to a UK economy which is hopelessly unbalanced in terms of two dimensions – geographic and sectoral.

Geographic imbalances

There exist huge imbalances between the regional economies of London and the South East compared to other UK regions. This is illustrated earlier in Table 2.2, which shows the gross value added per head of population for the UK regions, where London and the South East dominate. Such a situation existed for many years prior to the large growth in the financial services sector but the situation has worsened over the last 20 years. If we look at regional unemployment (ONS 2015), while we find relatively high rates of unemployment *in parts* of London, unemployment rates in the South of the UK are significantly lower than in northern English regions, Scotland, Wales and Northern Ireland. In other words, not only does London dominate the UK demographically and politically but it is also much richer.

Sectoral imbalances

If we look at a variety of countries, we see differences in composition of their economies. Table 2.4 shows the composition of the economies of a sample of countries broken down over three mains sectors of agriculture, industry and services.

At one level we can see significant differences between low-, medium- and high-income countries. Low-income countries tend to have larger agricultural sectors and correspondingly smaller industry and service sectors. Compared to low-income countries, middle-income countries show shifts from agriculture into the industrial and service sectors. High-income countries have tiny agricultural sectors and much larger service sectors.

However, if we look more closely at high-income countries which are more comparable to the UK we see that most of them have larger industrial sectors and much smaller service sectors. This is an ongoing problem. Between 2000 and 2007 there was a large overall growth in the total GDP of the UK (44%) but a significant contraction in the proportion of that GDP from the manufacturing sector. In fact, the absolute contribution from manufacturing hardly increased at all and the bulk of the GDP growth came from the financial and real estate sectors, much of which is concentrated in London and the South East.

The UK financial services sector is a large part of the services sector with half of the sector's output being generated in London. In fact, of the 1.14 million jobs in the UK financial services sector, 46% of these jobs were in London or the South East.

Now the financial services sector is, clearly, an important part of the UK economy generating economic output and overseas earnings and jobs. However, the downside of this is that it leaves the UK with an imbalance between the different sectors of the economy which impacts negatively on the regions of the UK outside of London and the South East. Such imbalances in economies are very serious and are not restricted to the UK. *The Economist* (2010) once published a special report focusing on the need to rebalance the US economy following the

TABLE 2.4 Composition of economies

		Agriculture	*Industry*	*Service*
		%	%	%
High income	UK	0.7	20.1	79.2
	France	1.7	19.5	78.8
	Spain	2.6	23.2	74.2
	Italy	2.2	23.9	73.9
	Germany	0.7	30.7	68.6
	Sweden	1.6	33.0	65.4
	Norway	2.3	33.7	64.0
	Ireland	1.2	38.6	60.2
	Russia	4.8	32.4	62.8
Middle income	China	7.9	40.5	51.6
	India	15.4	23.1	61.5
	Central African Republic	43.2	16.0	40.8
Low income	Liberia	34.0	13.8	52.2
	Ethiopia	34.8	21.6	43.6

Source: Various.

financial crisis and the same applies to the UK. However, while the imbalances in the US are different to those in the UK they are, arguably, easier to resolve.

So, what are the implications of this double imbalance in the UK economy? First, this variability is an intrinsic weakness in itself because it impedes recovery when one part of the economy is overheating, while other parts are still suffering recession, and it creates vulnerability for public services if all the UK's "eggs are in one basket", so to speak. Looking beyond this:

- The wide inequalities in income, wealth, health status and housing standards create public sector community dependency, increasing the need for public sector financial support.
- The strength of London/South East leads to certain parts of the UK being over-reliant on public sector employment because of the lack of private sector jobs.
- The pressures on the housing market in the South East result in a situation where low-income workers, essential for the local economy, are unable to afford housing, and first-time buyers cannot get a foot on the housing ladder.
- The overheated housing market in the South East leads to inflationary pricing bubbles which eventually burst. This has contributed to the 2009 "credit crunch".
- The UK, outside of London and the South East, suffers dis-proportionately as a consequence of economic recession even though this recession had its genesis in the London-based financial sector. Insolvency rates,

unemployment levels and the state of household finances across the UK for the period 2008–2010 show the same skewing of recessionary pain and hardship towards regions of the UK other than the South East.

- The UK manufacturing sector now comprises just 11% of GDP but delivers 50% of UK exports. However, the UK still has a trade deficit in goods and a trade surplus in services. The lack of domestic confidence and demand means that export-led growth is critical to the recovery. An under-represented manufacturing sector means the UK economy may not be able to take full advantage of any significant recovery in global demand.

The consequences of these economic imbalances are huge and have needed urgent attention by policy makers. However, governments have usually been extremely half-hearted in addressing these imbalances preferring to focus on the overall headline growth of a deregulated economy rather than aiming for a suitable balance between regions and sectors. The social and financial problems involved have been mitigated by higher levels of public spending underpinned by the buoyancy of the financial services sector but any slowdown in this sector with the loss of tax revenues means we inevitably face large-scale cuts in public spending. Add to this concerns that have often been raised in the past about a "*one-size-fits-all*" monetary policy for the UK. Quite often it appeared that monetary policy was changed to deal with perceived issues affecting the London economy with little consideration of the impact of such changes on other regional economies. While being beneficial to the UK, as a whole, this approach is seen, by many, as delivering a privileged elite, largely based in London and the South East to the detriment of the bulk of the population throughout the rest of the UK.

UK public policy failure

Overview

For a long period of time, Great Britain ruled an empire that at its height was the largest in history. Consequently, the model of public administration and policy making which evolved during that period was strongly influenced by the need to rule an empire as well as ruling the home country. Hence, it was a very centralised model driven largely from London. Fast forward to modern times and in 2002, the late Robin Cook (a former UK Foreign Secretary) stated that "*Britain was the most centralized state in Europe*" (The Guardian 2002). Others also argued that the UK is one of the most centralised states in the world. Indeed, in 2010, *The Economist* magazine once suggested that the UK was "*the second most centralised country in the developed world after New Zealand*" which is, after all, a quite small country compared to the UK.

Such centralisation has clear limitations and examples of its implications abound. Just after the end of the Second World War, there was a failed attempt by the British government to cultivate tracts of Tanganyika (modern-day Tanzania) with peanuts

(Cavendish 2001). After many problems, the project was finally abandoned, in 1951, as unworkable and at considerable cost. While the causes of failure were many, the major weakness was the attempt to plan such a development from offices in London with only limited input from people on the ground in Africa. This case was a striking example of the arrogance of colonial rule leading to public policy failure.

However, the above example is now 60 or more years old, and better and more recent cases can be found in a postcolonial Britain. If we look for examples of public policy failure, we need to go no further than Crossrail, HS2, Smart Motorways, repeated reorganisations of the NHS, the development of independent schools' trusts, the 1992 GMS contract for primary health care. Track and Trace, Connecting for Health, etc. All of these were dominated by London-centric thinking and London-centric attitudes and problems. In many ways, this is very similar to the colonial thinking referred to above but with much shorter distances involved.

Most recently, in writing about the failures of the UK government in managing the Covid-19 pandemic *The Economist* (2020) stated that "*In a federal system, like America's, the central government's failings can be mitigated by state and local authorities. In a centralised system, they cannot*". This is exactly the case in the UK where the hugely centralised system means that local authorities did not have the powers or the resources to compensate for the failings of central government.

Available evidence suggests a significant degree of public policy failure in the UK, over many decades, which has possibly accelerated in recent years. A report from the Institute of Government (IfG 2010) asked political science academics to judge from a list of government policies, over the last three decades, what they thought were successes. The results showed little consensus about what were policy successes and all policy choices (apart from Northern Ireland and minimum wage) received low scores. Furthermore, a recent blog (2019) by Professor Bob Hudson on the LSE website concluded,

> it has always been the case that the likelihood of policy failure is at least as high as policy success. However, the currency of modern politics seems to be squarely that of failure – indeed major failure. The most prominent current British examples are Brexit, closely followed by Universal Credit, and now a new NHS Ten Year Plan that disavows the extensive reforms to the service introduced only six years previously.

Many more cases could be added to the list. In their popular exploration of "policy blunders", the distinguished political academics Anthony King and Ivor Crewe (2013) identified 12 government policies that were said to have failed in their objectives, wasted large amounts of public money, "wrecked the lives of ordinary people' and were foreseeable.

Even where policies were not seen as a total failure, they were often inadequate or inappropriate because they were based on a London-centric perception of what was needed. For example, the reality is that for most people such things as the question of competition between schools, or by hospital trusts may make sense in London but make little sense in smaller urban and rural areas where the issue is the quality of your local hospital rather than the possibility of going somewhere else – which generally is not a credible proposition.

Over-emphasis on structures

There are many aspects to UK public policy failure which could be mentioned here such as an absence of data, lack of options and inadequate (and too hasty) analysis. However, perhaps one key issue that should be highlighted is the obsession among politicians and civil servants with organisational structures and structural change as a solution to problems, with disregard of other aspects of change. The ancient words of the Roman Caius Petronius Arbiter writing in AD 60 resonate here:

> We tend to meet any new situation by reorganizing, and a wonderful method it can be for creating the illusion of progress while producing confusion inefficiency, and demoralization.

There are many examples of this which could be quoted from UK public services but a good example concerns the health service reforms during the period of the Blair/Brown governments. A key component of the NHS in England is that of the commissioner role which is responsible for deciding what health services are needed in a particular area and for commissioning those services from service providers such as NHS Trusts. During this period, the English NHS commissioning role went through a number of structural changes including the formation and subsequent elimination of the following organisations: district health authorities, primary care groups, primary care trusts, mergers of primary care trusts, GP practice commissioning, clinical commissioning groups and now integrated care systems (ICS). By and large, all of these structural changes were seen to have failed because of the simple reason that they were all altered after just a few years. Now it only needs a fairly elementary knowledge of the principles of organisational performance (Lee and Yu 2004, Shahzad et al. 2012) to understand that it is not structures that are the key driver of organisational performance but the twin factors of process (how things get done) and, most importantly, organisational culture (the attitudes towards doing these things). There is a famous quote attributed to management guru Peter Drucker that "*culture eats strategy for breakfast*". This implies that the culture of the organisation always determines success regardless of how effective strategy and other factors may be. Unfortunately, this simple fact does not seem to resonate in the UK governments. We will return to this issue several times in this book but one specific example discussed in Chapter 13 concerns collaboration in public services. This is usually seen, in government, as a structural issue involving the formation of partnerships sometimes through statute whereas any study of organisational performance suggests it is more to do with softer factors such as culture and trust.

Failure to reduce inequalities

We have already noted the failure of public policy in achieving any sort of balance between the North and South of England. Earlier we outlined a picture of the domination of London/South East in recent years in economic, social and other terms. This picture is not new – the reality is that this has virtually always been the case in modern times. Geary and Stark (2015) in their analysis of UK regional inequality in the 20th century indicate that regional inequality in the UK is not a new phenomenon but one that existed throughout the 20th century albeit with variations in the level of inequality at different points in time. Table 2.5 illustrates this.

It can be seen that a large-scale inequality existed in the UK throughout the 20th century but while the UK became a more equal nation during the post-war years, since 1979 this process of narrowing inequality reversed sharply.

Moreover, evidence suggests that the UK has a higher level of regional inequality than any other large wealthy country. Analysis by McCann (2018) has shown that the UK is more inter-regionally unequal than the USA, France, Germany, Spain, Sweden and South Korea. The only wealthy countries with higher levels of regional inequality are Slovakia and Ireland.

In the light of this and the previous comments about public policy failure, we believe it can be argued that this failure to reduce the gross inequalities between London/South East and the rest of the UK is a consequence of ongoing failure in public policy over many decades. It can, therefore, be argued that this can be seen as, perhaps, a key cause of Brexit which is discussed below.

In addition, it must be emphasised that these failures apply to all political parties, when in government, albeit to different degrees. The problem is with

TABLE 2.5 History of UK regional equality Standardised GDP per person (UK = 100)

	1901	*1931*	*1951*	*1961*	*1981*	*2001*
London	**134.2**	**144.2**	**138.6**	**145.3**	**129.3**	**132.6**
South East	**107.0**	**114.0**	**84.8**	**88.1**	**108.4**	**118.0**
East of England	**83.7**	**82.7**	**89.0**	**92.4**	**96.3**	**103.8**
South West	91.7	92.3	89.3	88.9	92.9	91.1
West Midlands	86.0	95.7	104.0	104	90.0	89.5
East Midlands	92.4	86.6	95.8	94.7	96.3	91.3
North West	103.7	88.6	104.0	95.9	93.5	89.7
North East	85.8	65.0	88.6	89.6	92.5	79.0
Yorkshire and Humberside	88.3	86.4	97.5	94.1	91.7	84.2
Wales	80.3	81.1	84.9	90.7	82.8	76.4
Scotland	90.5	94.2	89.3	89.0	95.6	92.9

Source: Geary and Stark (2015).

the bus itself not with the bus driver which means it is with the system of government and policy making in the UK not with who is in power. It is pointless opposition MPs imagining that they can solve the problems when they gain power because it is the system that is broken. Whatever political party they come from, aspirant ministers come into power expecting to solve problems using the London-centric model, only to fail and leave office chastened.

Climate change and environmental degradation

For almost two years, the UK and the rest of the world have been in the grip of the Covid-19 pandemic which is sometimes (perhaps wrongly) described as the greatest crisis since the Second World War. This has created situations which would have been seen as unimaginable a year ago. However, many commentators from a variety of backgrounds have suggested that a greater challenge than Covid-19 is that relating to climate change and environmental degradation. For example, the then Governor of the Bank of England, Mark Carney, when talking about the impact of climate change, said that "*The world is heading for mortality rates equivalent to the Covid crisis every year by mid-century unless action is taken*" (BBC 2020). Furthermore, many will argue that the climate and environmental changes that have already taken place may actually be a causal factor in the creation of the SARS-CoV-2 virus responsible for the pandemic. For example, Dr Andrew Bernstein, Director of the Harvard Chan School of Public Health, has stated that

> We don't have direct evidence that climate change is influencing the spread of COVID-19, but we do know that climate change alters how we relate to other species on Earth and that matters to our health and our risk for infections.
>
> *(Bernstein)*

Thus, we can see that climate and environmental matters pose a huge challenge for every country on earth. This will have serious implications for a wide range of public policies and for the organisation and delivery of public services. This will be further discussed in Chapter 4.

Limited economic growth

Prior to the start of the 20th century, and for many centuries previously, the involvement of government and the state, in the UK, and most other developed countries, was largely limited to three areas of activity, namely:

- **Defence of the realm** – expenditure on armed forces
- **Maintenance of law and order** – police, courts, prisons, etc.
- **Trade –** regulation and promotion of trade matters

However, the role of the state has expanded enormously and Figure 2.3 illustrates the growth in public expenditure in the UK in the 20th century and beyond.

It can be seen that over the last 100 years or so UK public expenditure as a percentage of GDP has grown substantially with strong peaks during the times of the two world wars. Several phases of development (excluding world wars) can be identified in most countries which contributed to the significant upward trend in public expenditure in the 20th century, leading to public services being much larger and complex and having a greater direct impact on the life of the average citizen. In the early part of the 20th century, the state became increasingly involved in improving the social welfare of its citizens. Major welfare reforms took place in the early part of the century, which resulted in an increase in the size and scope of government involvement in social welfare issues. The main aspects of this were two key pieces of legislation. These were the Old Age Pensions Act of 1908 which provided for a non-contributory but means tested pension and the National Insurance Act of 1911 which provided a contributory but non-means tested cover against sickness and employment for some classes of worker.

The years following the Second World War saw a major expanse in the scope of the welfare state. This was consequent on the publication of the Beveridge report and its five "Giant Evils" in society: squalor, ignorance, want, idleness and disease. Beveridge proposed significant changes to the delivery of public services. Following the end of the Second World War, the new Labour Government

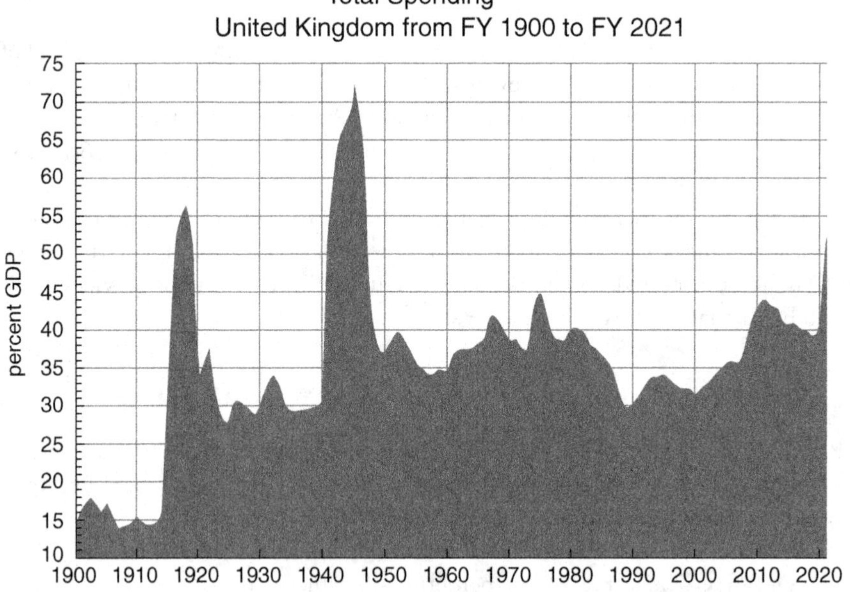

FIGURE 2.3 UK public spending as % of GDP

embarked on a huge programme of improvements in social welfare, which basically involved the implementation of the Beveridge recommendations. Beveridge made recommendations for the development of comprehensive systems of social security and the development of a national structure of health services. The social security developments were underpinned by the passing of the National Insurance Act of 1946 and the National Assistance Act of 1948. The National Assistance Act of 1948 replaced the Poor Law. However, perhaps the flagship policy of this period was the creation of the National Health Service (NHS) in 1948, which brought into public ownership large numbers of what were previously private or voluntary hospitals. The 1944 Education Act brought together, in a nationally set-up but locally administered system, the existing dispersed arrangements for education through church, charitable and local authority responsibilities. This provided for the provision of universal, free, state secondary education and provided the framework for the education services we have today.

There is now a general recognition that in a modern state, governments need to be actively involved in many aspects of social welfare (e.g. education, health, pensions). Politicians of the left and right may argue and debate the extent of that involvement but few politicians of the right would suggest that the welfare state be contracted back to pre-First World War levels. Indeed, the role of the state has arguably expanded even further in the early years of the 21st century and expanded, even further, during the Covid-19 pandemic.

The key point is that this growth in the UK welfare state and public services had to be financed and the two sources of that finance were:

- Ongoing annual growth in the GDP of the UK economy (economic growth)
- An increasing proportion of that GDP being committed to public services

During the years following the Second World War, although there were cycles of growth and recession, the UK economy managed to grow overall at a rate sufficient to sustain the growth in public services without placing an intolerable tax burden on the electorate.

This matter will be discussed further in Chapter 5 but the basic problem for the future is that it is not clear how the UK is going to generate the levels of economic growth needed to finance the growth required in public services and public expenditure. Politicians and some economists are optimistic about this but it is difficult to see what that optimism is based on. It seems that we now live in a culture where optimism is a prime requisite for respectability and being realistic is somehow seen as "letting the side down". Some are of the view that there is little chance of significant economic growth in terms of GDP/capita for decades ahead not least because of the impact of climate change. At the same time, there seems to be little public aptitude for higher levels of taxation. I suggest this is a time for realism not false optimism based on a dream that science and technology will provide all the solutions.

Legacy of public debt

In Chapter 5, we discuss in detail how, in recent years, UK public debt has risen to over 2 trillion pounds and is set to continue rising. It should also be noted that a business debt is at a record high level as consequent on the pandemic. UK businesses took on debt at more than twice the normal average growth rate since the crisis began and are on course to have borrowed £61 billion in total by the end of 2021 (Partington 2021). Such a level of debt seems likely to be a drag on economic performance. Household debt is also high but reduced during the pandemic but this includes student loans which are less likely to be repaid now.

Two things can be said about debt of any kind, namely, that interest will be charged on that debt and the debt will have to be repaid sometime in the future. The problem is that this legacy of debt will be left to our children and our grandchildren to deal with. This introduces the concept of intergenerational equity which has economic, psychological and sociological contexts. It is the concept or idea of fairness or justice between generations and can be considered in relation to fairness between children, youth, adults and seniors. It can also be applied to fairness between generations currently living and generations yet to be born. Increasing public debt is a major issue of intergenerational inequity, as future generations will shoulder the consequences. This is discussed further in Chapter 5.

Political alienation and voter apathy

In recent years we have seen turbulent political times. Just think about the following:

- Far-right political parties gaining power in European countries (e.g. Austria, Italy, Slovenia) something which would have been unimaginable in the years after the end of the Second World War.
- The substantial growth in electoral support for far-right and nationalistic parties in many European countries, but not the UK. For example, the recent presidential election in France resulted in the far-right party of Marine Le Pen taking second place to President Emile Macron and polling well-above the more established parties.
- The election of a right-wing nationalist candidate (Donald Trump) to the presidency of the USA. Although President Trump lost the 2020 presidential election, he won an additional 10 million votes (compared to the 2016 election) from a number of unexpected sources including black and Latino voters.
- At the 2019 UK general election, the Conservative Party had a net gain of 48 seats in England while the Labour Party had a net loss of 47 seats. Many of these seats lost by Labour were in what were traditionally strong Labour areas which had never previously elected a Conservative MP. This is often referred to as the breaching of Labour's "Red Wall" in the north. An internal party report suggested that Labour may never win back some of these

seats. At the same time as Labour was losing seats in its traditional heartlands it was gaining support in what is termed "Middle England" which traditionally voted Conservative.

What on earth is going on? Political scientists draw a distinction between voter apathy and political alienation. Voter apathy describes a person's indifference to voting and/or the voting process. One aspect of this concerns trust in politicians which is low in the UK. Just before the 2019 general election a poll suggested that trust in politicians had fallen by five percentage points and they had displaced advertising executives as the least trusted profession in the survey. At the start of this general election campaign, just 14% of the public said they trusted politicians in general to tell the truth – a five percentage point fall since 2018. Trust in politicians has always been in short supply, but this figure matches previous lows recorded in 2016 (15%), 2011 (14%) and 2009 (13%)

However, politically alienated people may feel compelled to vote, but are restricted by their sense of insignificance in the system. They feel that they are under-represented or not represented at all by those running for office; their best interest or concerns are not regarded. One aspect of this concerns the EU referendum of 2016. Many believe that, in essence, the vote in favour of Brexit came as a consequence of deep-seated economic and societal issues which had remained unresolved, by all political parties, for many decades. Older working-class communities in the North took their anger out at being "left behind" by the political elite of all parties. They did this notwithstanding the fact that all the economic evidence pointed to the fact that their individual communities, with a high dependence on public sector funding and more vulnerable in terms of manufacturing base, would be adversely affected by the decision to leave the EU. Arguments against leaving the EU on an economic basis simply cut no ice against the cultural and visceral underpinnings. Thus, Brexit became a conduit for bringing to the surface major economic and societal concerns which previously existed but which were not fully recognised by politicians of all parties. These concerns still exist and have huge implications for UK political parties.

The legacy of the Covid-19 pandemic

At the time of writing, it is almost two years since the onset of the Covid-19 pandemic. The pandemic has impacted on every country in the world, to some degree, and in the UK, it has had major implications in many areas of life including working practices, retail behaviours, travel arrangements, leisure activities, social interactions and purchasing patterns.

Although the existence of effective vaccines now provides hope for the future, it is unclear what the longer-term impact of the pandemic might be. While one does not want to be overly pessimistic, it is important to be realistic and recognise that getting back to "normal" or "near normal" might take much longer than we anticipate and may be different from the current "normal". Early assessments, particularly by politicians, about a return to normality have been shown to be wildly inaccurate. To take just one example, on 24 March 2020, UK Prime Minister Boris Johnson was reported as saying that he believed the country could "turn the tide" within 12 weeks (Meredith 2020), while in the USA, President Donald Trump had suggested the US could open up again "fairly soon". Both predictions were spectacularly wrong but there have been many subsequent predictions from various quarters which have also proved wayward.

The longer-term impacts of Covid-19 are impossible to predict at this point in time but there are considerable uncertainties about a number of factors which will have serious implications for a number of public services. These include:

- The impact on children of having missed many months in the classroom
- The impact on patients needing hospital care which was delayed because of the pandemic
- The impact on the mental health status of many people in society as a consequence of lockdown
- The potentially large number of latent cases of domestic abuse that will emerge post lockdown
- The future employment prospects of many people made redundant during the pandemic
- Future working practices – will many people continue to work at home?
- The impact on participation in sports and leisure activities
- Possible "burn-out" of front-line staff who have been at the forefront of the pandemic for many months. For example, this could result in a big increase of medical and nursing staff wishing to take early retirement
- The need to protect the country from new strains of Covid or other new diseases which derive from environments similar to the source of Covid
- The need to continue social distancing for an indefinite period

This is a daunting list of uncertainties but not necessarily exhaustive. Later in the book we discuss in more detail the impact of Covid-19 on the economics and financing of public services but it must be recognised that the challenges to public services of Covid-19 go beyond just finances but permeate virtually every aspect of public policy and public service provision and will do so for many years into the future.

Conclusion

It is no exaggeration to say that the above list of challenges to UK public policy and public services is daunting and even frightening. In particular, we see huge uncertainties regarding the legacy of this pandemic, and possibly future pandemics, plus the challenges and implications of dealing with climate change. It seems clear that we cannot address, successfully, challenges of this magnitude by "more of the same" in terms of existing government structures and public policy. In the next chapter, we start to consider what really needs to happen.

References

BBC (2020), Mark Carney: climate crisis deaths 'will be worse than Covid', 5 February 2020, https://www.bbc.co.uk/news/business-55944570

BBC (2021), UK 'cannot duck' post-Covid inequalities, report warns, https://www.bbc.co.uk/news/business-55536722

Bernstein, A. Coronavirus and climate change, https://www.hsph.harvard.edu/c-change/subtopics/coronavirus-and-climate-change/

Bradshaw, J. (2020), Child poverty in the North East Region, CPAG, https://cpag.org.uk/sites/default/files/files/policypost/Child%20poverty%20in%20the%20NE.pdf

Cavendish, R. (2001), Britain abandons the groundnuts scheme, *History Today* 51, 1, p. 52.

Equality Trust, The Scale of Economic Inequality in the UK.

Geary, F. and Stark, T. (June 2015), What happened to regional inequality in Britain in the twentieth century? *The economic history review* 69, 1, pp. 215–228.

House of Commons (2021), The budget deficit: a short guide, House of Commons Library, https://commonslibrary.parliament.uk/research-briefings/sn06167/

House of Commons Library (2020), Income inequality in the UK, https://commonslibrary.parliament.uk/research-briefings/cbp-7484/

Hudson, R. (2019), Why policy failure is so common in the UK, https://blogs.lse.ac.uk/businessreview/2019/01/26/why-policy-failure-is-so-common-in-the-uk/

IfG (2010), What makes a 'successful' policy? https://www.instituteforgovernment.org.uk/sites/default/files/PSA_survey_results.pdf

King, A. and Crewe, I. (2013), *The Blunders of or Governments*, One World Publications.

Lee, S. J. K. and Yu, K. (2004), Corporate culture and organizational performance. *Journal of Managerial Psychology*, 19, 4, pp. 340–359.

Liddle, J. and Shutt, J. (2020), *The North East after Brexit: Impact and Policy*, Emerald Publishing.

Lipset, S. M. and Rokkan, S. (1967), "Cleavage structures, party systems, and voter alignments. An introduction." In *Party Systems and Voter Alignments: Cross-National Perspectives*, eds. S. Rokkan, S. M. Lipset. New York Free Press, 2019.

MacroTrends, UK population trends, https://www.macrotrends.net/countries/GBR/united-kingdom/population

McCann, P. 2018, Perceptions of regional inequality and the geography of discontent: insights from the UK. *Regional Studies* 54, 2, pp. 256–267.

Meredith, S. (2020), When will life return to normal? Health experts on a possible exit strategy to the pandemic. *Health and Science*, https://www.cnbc.com/2020/03/24/coronavirus-health-experts-look-at-when-will-life-return-to-normal.html

ONS (2015), Regional Labour Market: October 2015, https://www.ons.gov.uk/employmentandlabourmarket/peopleinwork/employmentandemployeetypes/bulletins/regionallabourmarket/2015-10-14

Partington, R. J. (2021), Debt levels soar for business as UK economy struggles to recover from Covid, https://www.theguardian.com/business/2021/feb/08/debt-levels-soar-for-business-as-uk-economy-struggles-to-recover-from-covid

Pickett, K. and Wilkinson, R. G. (2018), *The Inner Level*, Penguin Books.

Pickett, K. and Wilkinson, R. G. (2009), *The Spirit Level: Why More Equal Societies Almost Always Do Better*, Bloomsbury Press.

Piketty, T. (2014), *Capital in the Twenty-First Century*, Belknap Press.

Piketty, T. (2020), *Capital and Ideology*, Harvard University Press.

Shahzad, F., Luqman, R. A., Khan, A. R. and Shabbir, L. (2012), Impact of organizational culture on organizational performance: an overview. *Interdisciplinary Journal of Contemporary Research in Business*, 3, 9, pp. 975–985.

Tabner, I. T. (2020), Five ways coronavirus lockdowns increase inequality. *The Conversation*, 8 April 2020.

The Economist (2010), Time to rebalance, April 2010.

The Economist (2020), Why governments get covid-19 wrong, 26 September.

The Guardian (2002), Cook: Britain is most centralised state in Europe, 3 November 2002.

World Bank (2014), Theorist Eric Maskin: globalization is increasing inequality, https://www.worldbank.org/en/news/feature/2014/06/23/theorist-eric-maskin-globalization-is-increasing-inequality

PART B
The need for major UK reform

3

TOWARDS STRONGER UK REGIONALISM

Roger Latham

Introduction

So far, in this book, we have set out the principal challenges to the future of public policy and public services in the United Kingdom. In Part C of this book we will look at the specific issues that face individual public services, but in this part (Part B) we will give the context of the overall constitutional, organisational, and financial reforms which will be necessary to meet the challenges facing public services and the increasing levels of crisis. The first big challenge was the financial crisis of 2008/2010, while we are now in the midst of the second, the Covid-19 pandemic. The third, which we are now just beginning to face up to, is the existential crisis of climate change and the environment of the planet under human influences.

In this chapter we look at some of the over-arching changes that will be necessary to provide the resilience and flexibility to deal with these future crises. In the next chapter, we will consider what needs to be done to implement these changes.

Public policy is not going to be effective in the United Kingdom under the current over-centralised and inadequate arrangements. Reforms must involve changes to government structures, economic policy formulation, and public policy formulation and implementation. We will argue that this demands the development of regional governments in England to complement the existing arrangements in Wales, Scotland, and Northern Ireland. We will argue that the United Kingdom has occupied a halfway house for many years with a quasi-federal arrangement of three devolved administrations (which administer only 16% of the UK population) coupled with an English-dominated and centralised UK government. Resolving this unsatisfactory situation will be key in facing future crises effectively.

DOI: 10.4324/9781003201892-5

This chapter is structured as follows:

- The (dis)United Kingdom
- Regionalism and regional government elsewhere
- Towards a new regionalism for the United Kingdom

The (dis)United Kingdom

The United Kingdom of Great Britain and Northern Ireland, Great Britain, Britain, the British Isles, England and Wales – take your pick. Unlike some countries we have a plethora of names to describe the various semi-federal structures that have grown up over time. This is to say nothing of the devolved administrations of Scotland, Wales, and (for some of the time) Northern Ireland. To add to this there is the peculiar arrangement with the Irish Republic whereby citizens of England, Wales, and Scotland can travel to the Irish public freely, and vice versa. The complication of the lack of a physical border between the Irish Republic and Northern Ireland, which was a key part of the Good Friday agreement, which established a cessation of hostilities between the warring communities of Northern Ireland, proved to be the unforeseen (or ignored) stumbling block of the Brexit arrangements which could trigger a return to hostilities.

The complexity is patterned in history. The United Kingdom was established when the kingdom of Scotland and the kingdom of England (and Wales) were joined together in 1603 on the death of Queen Elizabeth I, who having no successor caused James VI of Scotland to become James I of England and established the Stuart dynasty which lasted most of the 17th century. In 1707 it became Great Britain when the Scottish parliament was prorogued, and its government moved to Westminster when the Bank of England (there is no Bank of Britain) bailed out the Scottish nation from impending bankruptcy after the disastrous failure of the Darien project.

When devolution came in 1999, the Scottish parliament was re-established, though as a devolved administration of the Westminster government. At the same time the Welsh Assembly was created with somewhat lesser powers which have subsequently been enhanced. The Northern Ireland assembly was an outcome of the Good Friday agreement.

So, given this historical background what on earth has kept this disparate group of countries together in a union for several centuries? Linda Colley and other contemporary historians suggest it was three elements:

- Protestantism
- Empire
- Successful wars

It was Protestantism that led to James succeeding Elizabeth, it was Protestantism that underpinned the English Civil War (or as historians now properly call it The

Wars of Three Kingdoms – recognising the separateness of Scotland Ireland and England), it was Protestantism that led to the successful invasion of William of Orange in opposition to the Catholicism of James II, and it was Protestantism that led to the introduction of the Hanoverian dynasty as the Stuart dynasty and its inherent Catholicism faded away. Interestingly, this assertion of Protestantism resulted in Britain being ruled by foreign monarchs for almost 200 years!

Chapter 5, the economic development chapter, will make clear that the peculiar establishment of England as a trading empire in the 17th–19th centuries created a major economic dependence on England and its industrial revolution to become a major world power with the result that the English pound became the uniting national currency (even though, peculiarly, Scottish and Northern Irish banknotes still circulate as legal tender).

The successful wars of empire also pulled together, militarily speaking, Scots, Irish, Welsh, and English regiments to maintain imperial ambitions. As politicians throughout the centuries have discovered successful wars are a great form of community cohesion. As the chapter on economic development will point out these three sources of unity were dealt a near fatal blow by the First World War. Protestantism, Empire, and war no longer bind together the disparate countries, and they begin to pull apart.

The Irish situation is of course quite unique. Invaded in Norman times it had repeated plantations of English Protestant settlers in a largely hostile Catholic country. In 1801 Ireland joined the union of England and Wales, and Scotland. The political driver for this was again Protestantism. Great Britain, at war with France, feared that the Catholics of Ireland would provide an ally in a potential French invasion. Fearing it to be a security risk, William Pitt then Prime Minister secured his military flank by the act of Union. It immediately created the beginning of a long-term problem in that Ireland was simultaneously thought of as part of the home countries but treated as an imperial possession. And while Protestantism as a source of unity has virtually died away in England Wales and Scotland, it remains a potent force in Northern Ireland. Throughout the 19th century the principle of a united Ireland having "Home Rule" was one of the most contentious issues debated in the Westminster Parliament. As war loomed in 1914 it was not the developing danger in Europe that exercised politicians of the day, it was Home Rule for Ireland. The thought of the English (and Scottish)-planted Protestant settlers of Northern Ireland being absorbed through some form of devolved imperial arrangement into a majority Catholic community was unacceptable and remained unacceptable even after the passage of the Home Rule Act in 1914. War suspended the implementation of the Act, but the 1916 Easter Rebellion showed that there were still Republicans for whom Home Rule was insufficient. The Irish Civil War that erupted in 1922 resulted in a division of Ireland into northern and southern Ireland on a religious split, which remains a strategic division. However, the rapid reduction of the influence of the Catholic Church in the Irish Republic, and its increasing prosperity in the EU, together with the complications created by Brexit may yet provide a pressure for

Northern Ireland to integrate with the Irish Republic in due course following the referendum procedure set out in the Good Friday agreement.

Throughout the nationalist movements of the 19th century, language was also a key symbol of the demand for independence. In Ireland, a resurgence in Gaelic was associated, and remains associated, with Republican nationalism, as do national sports. Similarly, in Wales the Welsh language (spoken by 17% of the population) is associated with nationalism. While this driver was and remains important in Ireland and Wales, it is much less the case for Scotland. In Scotland Gaelic remains a minority language, mostly found in the Western Isles and has never been a cause of community cohesion for Scotland.

Today, the glue that held together the quasi-federal arrangement that existed of four independent countries coming together under a common Westminster Parliament is coming unstuck. The problem that exists is England and the dominance of England, within the United Kingdom, being the elephant in the room. In 1801 the census (which excluded Ireland at that point) indicated that 54% of the population lived in England. By 1871 that proportion had risen to 70%, and by 2011 the English population represented 84%, as against Scotland's 8.4%, Wales' 4.2%, and Northern Ireland's 2.9%. This predominance of population in England is mirrored in Parliamentary seats and power. England can simply dominate all the other countries in the union. What England wants England gets and politicians frequently speak of Britain when they mean England. For example, if an individual wants to become a naturalised British citizen, they must pass a test in the history of Britain. This test (which has been much criticised by historians for its simplicity, inaccuracy, and promulgation of tropes and myths) is much more about the history of England than it is of Britain. The dominance is considerable. The difficulties this could create have been bought off by giving the devolved administrations a greater share in public resources. In 2018/2019 public spending per person in the United Kingdom was £9,584. In England it was £9,296 (3% below the UK average). In Scotland it was £11,247 (17% above average); in Wales £10,656 (11% above UK average); and in Northern Ireland £11,590 (21% above average). These figures come about through the application of the Barnett formula agreed back in the 1970s to prevent constant haggling over the resources that should be distributed to the now devolved nations because of decisions taken by an English-dominated UK Parliament (often only with England in mind).

But there is also a mini-elephant in the room – if that makes sense! Greater London represents almost a nation within a nation in England. In 2011 there were 8.8 million people living in Greater London – 13% of the UK population, which is almost as much as Scotland, Wales, and Northern Ireland put together. We have earlier drawn attention to the dominance of London which includes the dominance of London not only in physical terms but also in economic terms. That is also mirrored in public expenditure per head, which stands at £10,425 (9% above the UK average). The dominance of London goes beyond public expenditure. Many policies of the English Westminster government are based on circumstances which apply predominantly in London. Choice in hospitals and choice in education make sense in the urban density of London but made little sense in more rural communities where choice does not bring effective competition into education or health leading to improved outcomes, because there is truly little choice available. Instead the populations in these places simply hope that the local hospital or school is of a reasonable quality. Of course, the preponderance of London and the expenditure that it attracts mean that the rest of England gets substantially less. In the South East region and East Midlands, the figure is 8% below the UK average – the lowest of any of the regions. And these discrepancies were borne out in the Brexit referendum which exposed these long-term issues. The devolved administrations of Scotland and Northern Ireland voted to Remain, Wales voted to Leave, but only by a small margin. London, with its diverse metropolitan base, voted to Remain. England outside Greater London voted to Leave, and significantly so – enough to make the decision into a marginal Leave majority. So, the pressure that is now being felt to break up the existing union with its centralised English government covering Scotland, and to a lesser extent in Northern Ireland and Wales is also driven by the feeling in English regions outside of London that they were being "left behind" and ignored by a largely political metropolitan elite based in London and responding to London issues and London values. It was the capture of these disgruntled voters outside London that gave the Conservative government under Boris Johnson such a significant majority in the 2019 election. While Brexit may have been a symptom rather than a cause of the disunity of the union, the issues that it has created will act as a catalyst to future change. We turn now to what must be done if the United Kingdom is to remain united.

Regionalism and regional government elsewhere

Regional arrangements are already commonplace in a great many countries, and indeed the EU (of which the United Kingdom was most recently a part) was pressed to ensure that European regional, social, and cultural funds could be distributed to match the obvious inequalities that existed both across the EU, and within the component parts of each individual EU member state. In some countries, notably England and the Republic of Ireland, such regional bodies as were created had little or no political or economic clout. They were simply there as administrative requirements. Such policies were administered in these regions under EU funding that had to be authorised by national governments, and when the EU negotiated individually with regional bodies on individual development proposals this was greatly resented by UK central government. It is notable that in the United Kingdom the decision to replace the older EU funding with UK government funding directly is not being delegated to UK regions and devolved governments but will be managed and directed centrally.

A report by the European Commission (2017) identifies four countries that operate as federal or quasi-federal administrations – Austria, Belgium, Germany, and Spain. The remaining 23 countries are all noted as having unitary governments, yet these 23 countries all have different patterns of regional organisation, and there is no common agreement as to the significance of the sub-national governments in these countries. They occupy a spectrum. Some countries have few truly autonomous regions, such as Portugal where places like the Cape Verde islands and Madeira are, historically, out of reach of central administration. Italy has a regional structure which is widely subvented by national and other sub-national bodies with only a few exceptions, like Sicily. Other countries operate regional administrations but strictly under national policies, while others, like the Irish Republic and the United Kingdom, have no regional administrations or function (except in devolved administrations in the case of United Kingdom).

Table 3.1 taken from a review of Regional Government in European Countries commissioned by the Constitution Unit of University College London (Hopkins) gives some flavour of the range of functions carried out regionally in several European countries. They classified regional activities under four headings:

- Region only – where the region was the only policy-making body and the public service area.
- Regional policy – where regions introduce policies in the particular service area but there was also a national level of policy.

TABLE 3.1 Functions of regional governments in Europe

	Region only	*Regional policy*	*National framework*	*Regional administration*
Belgium (Federal)	• Education • Planning • Environment • Health	• Transport • Economic Development		
France (Unitary)		• Transport • Planning • Environment	• Economic Development	• Education
Germany (Federal)	• Police • Education	• Transport • Economic Development • Environment		• Health
Italy (Unitary)			• Transport • Planning • Environment	• Health

Source: Hopkins.

- National framework – where regions made policy within guidelines established at national level.
- Regional administration – where regions simply administered national policy.

When we come to look at the United Kingdom, we find that the information from the European Union is unable to classify it in simple structures; in fact it needs four pages of documentation to explain the differences that exist between England, Scotland, Wales, and Northern Ireland. This peculiarity draws attention to the fact that the United Kingdom has a curiously unacknowledged and historic federal structure that labours under a centralised government. When we come to look at the history of the economic development function in the public services, some part of the economic history of the British Isles will provide some of the rationale for this history of unacknowledged federalism.

Towards a new regionalism for the United Kingdom

Faced with the current problems of the United Kingdom with the imbalance between the devolved nations and England, and the massive imbalance between London and the rest of England, one solution appears to be plain – an increased level of regionalism within England to accompany the existing devolved governments. In this section we will examine the possible pattern for regionalism, the scope for regional autonomy, and the constitutional issues that would be involved in moving towards a more federal system. A number of approaches have been proposed.

English parliament

One suggestion has been the creation of an English parliament which would sit alongside the existing devolved governments in Wales, Scotland, and Northern Ireland and sit under a federal UK government. At the outset this would resolve the so-called "West Lothian" question whereby under current arrangements Scottish and Welsh MPs can vote on issues of relevance only to England (e.g. the NHS in England). However, we cannot see that this would resolve the many problems described in this book:

- The four parliaments/assemblies within the United Kingdom would still be creatures of UK Parliament and would still be subject to interference and control by the UK government. There would be no constitutional protections. Already, we see the Johnson government attempting to undermine the existing devolution arrangements.
- The powers given to the English parliament would probably be similar to those in the existing devolved areas and, therefore, very restrictive in scope.

- The English Parliament would be responsible for the welfare of 84% of the population of the United Kingdom with the other three parliaments/assembly being responsible for the remaining 16%. This looks a very unbalanced position.
- We suspect there would be huge pressure to base the English Parliament in London in the same city as the UK Parliament. We suspect this would not provide for much devolution of power to the North and Midlands of England. In fact, it would reinforce the existing domination of London.
- Even if the English parliament were based outside London (e.g. Birmingham) it would still be geographically remote from places like Newcastle and Cornwall and would suffer the same problem as the current UK government of failing to recognise regional differences in policy matters.

Overall we do not see this approach as a desirable option.

Regional government across England

To repeat what was said in Chapter 1, the terminology we use in writing this book the term United Kingdom is used to describe a "nation state" and within the United Kingdom, there are four countries or nations, namely England, Scotland, Wales, and Northern Ireland. We use the term UK regional governments to mean nine English regional governments plus the existing three devolved governments. English regional governments should not have greater or lesser powers/responsibilities compared to the devolved governments.

Our proposals involve the creation of a series of directly elected and constitutionally protected regional governments across England operating in a similar manner to Wales, Scotland, and Northern Ireland. However, some will argue that while devolved governments for Wales, Scotland, and Northern Ireland make sense, as they are distinctive countries in their own right, with their own history and culture, England is also a distinctive country in its own right and should not be regionalised. We do not see the idea of a united England as a persuasive argument in historical terms or in today's terms. First look consider history. While England can be regarded as being in *political* unity ever since the crowing of Æthelstan as king of the English in 927AD, England was not necessarily unified. Parts of England have never really been happy under the rule of one central authority and there have been many rebellions against an overbearing and despotic king in London. While many of these occurred in Scotland, Wales, or Ireland, there have also been a number of revolts in outlying regions of England including the Peasants Revolt of 1381, the 1497 Cornish rebellion, the 1489 Yorkshire rebellion, and the rising of the North in 1569. Today, for example, Cornwall is a distinctive entity within England with its own history, culture, economic structure, and even language. Similarly, the North East is a part of the United Kingdom which is distinctive in social and cultural terms from many other parts of England, especially London and the South East. The EU referendum highlighted this situation where Remainers (concentrated in London) had very different views on social and cultural issues like immigration, race, sexual orientation, globalisation, and the English language compared to Leavers based in the North (YouGov 2019).

So, the question needs to be asked – on what basis should the English regions be established? A simplistic answer is to look at the regions that are already formally established based on economic factors but which still reflect cultural differences in the United Kingdom. But we need to recognise that within these regions there are other cultural and societal groupings that might make a claim to being a regional entity. So, within the West Midlands anyone who has worked in Birmingham will be acutely aware of the differences between Birmingham and the Black Country, which despite their economic similarity have substantial cultural and historical differences. So, marked is the distinction that you can virtually draw a boundary line between them. Similarly, within the North East there are substantial differences between Teesside, Tyneside, and Northumberland. The North West will show big differences between Merseyside, Greater Manchester, the northern mill towns, and the countryside and Fylde coast. You could multiply the examples.

However, this concern about sub-regions should not undermine the basic principle of economic regions. Within the existing devolved administrations there are similar sub-regional elements. Wales has a north-south split and arguably West Wales and South East Wales are different again but it still makes a cohesive unit. Scotland has long been divided between Highland and Lowland regions, and within the Highland area is split between East and West, particularly regarding the Western Isles. The Northern Isles of Orkney and Shetland have long been considered vastly different, partly because of their Norse heritage of which they are so proud. Geography plays a part as well. A Shetlander will happily point out to you that Lerwick is closer to Oslo than it is to Edinburgh. Nevertheless, there is a clear element of Scottish unity. In the case of both Wales and Scotland this is based around an idea of civic nationality and inhabitants of both areas are encouraged to play the democratic role irrespective of their country of origin or their race. Northern Ireland is slightly more peculiar in this regard given the legacy of the Protestant glue but even there this is beginning to diminish as the communities in Northern Ireland feel that their welfare is neglected by a nationalistic England where Brexit matters more than constitutional unity. These elements of civic nationality contrast markedly with English nationalism which appears to have been expropriated by extreme right-wing groups and has a significant undertow of racism where the true English patriot is seen as white, and individuals who have been born in England but are of different racial or cultural heritages are somehow considered to be un-English and subject to further tests of their loyalty as in the notorious Tebbit cricket test.

So, the proposals that we make here are based upon the principles of the existing 12 regions of the United Kingdom. This represents a balance between an English government and a plethora of extremely small regions, and it provides units which are large enough to be semi-autonomous and balanced against the devolved administrations. If we look at the population of the different regions of the United Kingdom we see the following picture in Table 3.2.

Thus, we can see that while there is a wide range of populations, the nine English regions and the three devolved countries are all of the same order of magnitude. However, it should also be noted that the current devolved areas are at the smaller end of the population spectrum when compared to most of the English regions. If the current devolved areas are big enough for devolved government then surely the same must apply to the larger English regions.

The proposals that we are making need to balance up the economic, political, and social imbalances that exist in the United Kingdom. It needs to recognise that within the devolved administrations there is already that element of micro-nationalism. To match that regionalism based upon economic development alone, or a move towards decentralisation, is not going to cut it. The English regionalism that we are now proposing must move towards democratic enhancement and become a parallel to the already existing devolved administrations. The essence of this will be federalism. We envisage this is applying to both the devolved administrations and the new English regions. The new regional bodies would have sweeping authority consisting of:

- The ability to legislate within their own area to meet locally determined objectives.

TABLE 3.2 UK regional populations

	Population (2020) million
South East	9.2
London	9.0
North West	7.3
East of England	6.2
West Midlands	5.9
South West	5.6
Yorkshire and Humber	5.5
Scotland	5.5
East Midlands	4.8
Wales	3.2
North East	2.7
Northern Ireland	1.8

Source: ONS.

- Control of the key services of education, health, police, housing, economic development, social care and welfare, transport and environment, and physical planning.
- The ability to raise taxes in their own right from a variety of sources, and the ability to issue debt in their own name.
- The power of general competence to undertake such activities as they felt necessary for their region, to include the ability to cooperate with other regions in the achievement of their objectives.

These UK regions would easily be large enough to manage, effectively, the vast bulk of public services that would fall under their jurisdiction under a federal arrangement. Indeed, most of these regions are larger than many existing European countries such as Denmark Finland, Ireland, and Slovakia to name just a few.

However, there will still be a need for a UK federal tier of government with responsibility for certain government activities which need to be undertaken at a UK level:

- Foreign affairs involving relationships with other nation states
- Defence
- Strategic networks (including transport, digital, and public utility networks)
- National security and safety functions (such as national security, Coast Guard)
- Trade agreements
- Major disaster responses
- Monetary policy

The federal government could also undertake common service administration and provision as agreed by the regions such as unified systems for the national collection of direct and indirect taxes. Also, there could be clear roles for a federal government in coordinating (but not controlling) certain aspects of public policy across all regions. Environmental policy would be seen as a key issue here.

The proposal here is to re-strike the balance between regional and federal functions much in the line of the balance between the Lande and Federal governments in Germany, where the Lande has the capacity to do what is necessary to provide for public welfare, unless it is agreed that the federal level takes over priority. In Germany this can be at the behest of the federal level alone which therefore cuts out the Lande from activities by incremental stages. They proposed here that this automatic takeover function would not apply, and that such arrangements would be subject to approval by the regions.

In the next chapter, we consider how such a model of regional government could be implemented in the United Kingdom.

References

Colley, L. (1992), *Britons: Forging of a Nation 1707–1837*, Yale University Press.

European Commission (2017), A comparative overview of public administration characteristics and performance in EU28, https://op.europa.eu/en/publication-detail/-/publication/3e89d981-48fc-11e8-be1d-01aa75ed71a1/language-en

Hopkins, J. Regional government in European countries, The Constitution Unit University College London, https://www.ucl.ac.uk/constitution-unit/sites/constitution-unit/files/5.pdf

YouGov (2019), Leavers v remainers: how Britain's tribes compare, *The Guardian*, 2 May 2019, https://www.theguardian.com/world/ng-interactive/2019/may/02/leavers-v-remainers-how-britains-tribes-compare

4

IMPLEMENTING ELECTED REGIONAL GOVERNMENT IN THE UK

Roger Latham

Introduction

The previous chapter discussed the idea of regional government in a federalised government structure and contrasted the over-centralised UK to comparable countries elsewhere.

This chapter is concerned with the details of implementation of UK regional government and covers the following themes:

- Constitutional and organisational issues
- Regional economic policy and development
- Regional public policy making and implementation
- Prospects for change

Constitutional and organisational issues

A move towards a federal/regional arrangement for the UK would have major implications in a number of areas. Primarily these would be:

- Constitutional changes
- Structural changes
- New electoral systems
- Management and administrative changes

Constitutional changes

Almost no modern Western nation, other than the UK, functions without a written constitution. Although we pride ourselves on having an unwritten

DOI: 10.4324/9781003201892-6

constitution, in truth the constitution of the UK does have significant elements which are written down, but it is un-codified, and is based historically on a mishmash of documents, precedents, and legal judgements. The idea of not having a codified written constitution is treated as a further example of British (or rather English) exceptionalism. England has always been so good in its governance arrangements that it has led the world. We were the first to establish the principle of rule by consent through Magna Carta; we were the first nation to have a representative Parliament; we were the first nation to establish an industrial revolution; we were the first nation to establish a trading empire that was the envy of the world; we were the first nation to establish the principles of a constitutional monarchy and the sovereignty of Parliament; and so on. Inevitably this English exceptionalism proves to be less solidly based in history than some of its proponents would care to think. It leads to what Gavin Esler (2021) describes as nostalgic pessimism – a feeling that things were better in the past when we were "top dog" (variously place it somewhere in the 18th and 19th centuries) and that things have gone downhill since. "Since what" is variously described as numerous cultural changes, the failure of politicians' nerve, or the fault of some group or other. It is the basis of populism throughout the ages where politicians curry favour with the electorate by playing on national myths, and falsehoods about the events of history, identifying villains or groups to be blamed, and promising simplistic solutions that they are generally incapable of delivering.

One part of this exceptionalism was the myth that the unwritten constitution showed that the British were better at governing themselves than any of the other nations who had to rely on a written document, even though British constitutional experts wrote a great many of those documents in the past. The unwritten constitution allowed us to revel in the "magic" as Bagehot described in "the British Constitution"; it permitted flexibility to meet new changes and challenges without being tied to written documents that went out of date, and gave the government the ability to take decisive action when required to. It also allowed governments the freedom to do whatever they chose without checks on civil liberties, or constitutional safeguards. It allowed the development of what Lord Hailsham famously called an "elective dictatorship". Two things (as described by Esler 2021) permitted this unwritten constitution to function effectively:

- A process of "*muddle through*", which was more pithily described by Churchill as KBO – "*Keep Buggering On*"
- Self-restraint by politicians in power based on "*faith in chaps*"

"Muddling through" sounds as if it is a reflection of the fact that democracies are a contention of ideas within a framework for the assessment of policy failures and successes, backed by processes for the transfer of power without violence. Perhaps it is no bad thing. However, muddling through does not take into account the proper assessment of long-term consequences of short-term decisions, often taken with a limited perspective. This might be illustrated by a story told by Rabbi Jonathan Sacks (Sacks 2021) in *Morality* which was his last book before he died:

> An old man and a young man are together on a train that is speeding towards its final destination, the hometown of the old man. The young man, seeing that they are approaching their destination, asks the older man if he can tell him the time. The old man does not reply. Thinking that possibly he is a little deaf the young man repeats his question but speaks a little louder and a little more slowly. The old man continues to ignore him. The young man is sure that the older man has heard him so he asks "Excuse me sir, but I've asked you twice if you could tell me the time and I'm sure that you've heard me, but you have ignored me. Why is that?

The old man looks at the young man and replies:

> Young man, if I answer your question I will establish a relationship with you. The train is nearly at the final destination and you are a stranger. Under the tradition of our faith I will feel obliged to offer you hospitality. You are a handsome young man, and I have a beautiful daughter. You will meet, you will be attracted to each other, you will fall in love, and you will want to marry. So, I must ask myself, do I want as a son-in-law a man who can't afford a watch!

Rabbi Sacks uses this story to illustrate two points: the difference of perspective from the old man and the young man – the young man is looking to the immediate situation, the old man is looking long term; and the fact that the old man knows that small decisions taken in the short term can have long-term consequences.

But if muddling through was a successful strategy in the past, it will not be a successful strategy for the future. We are already facing a series of crises that will require more than the marginal variations and "adjustments" to existing arrangements if they are to be successfully addressed. In the financial crisis of 2008/2010, the collapse of private money (i.e. the credit created by financial institutions in the form of loans, overdrafts, and financial instruments traded as money) meant that the public sector had to step in and effectively "nationalise" substantial elements of private money in order to stabilise the public trust in money, and prevent a disastrous collapse of world economies and trading. The problems began in the financial sector but like a corrosive acid a lack of trust seeped through to the real economy. The public sector threw unheard-of amounts of money at the problem, but the debt overhang that was created in the public sector, commercial sector, and household sector resulted in a long period of austerity which, over ten years, still failed to achieve its overall objectives, but at a cost of a fall in real household income, and the progressive erosion of public services. Muddling through simply would not do – even though complacent bankers thought that it might.

The second crisis that we are currently experiencing, the pandemic, is another example where muddling through will not do. Initially preparations for the crisis were limited to unimaginative assumptions that any major virus outbreak would be similar to the annual influenza infection, but a bit worse. That clearly has not been the case. As the virus became endemic, it was clear that significant changes needed to be made in people's behaviour, expectations, and significant resources in the future will had to be deployed to prevent long-term damage to world economies. Yet, in the early days, inadequate preparation meant that the history of the pandemic has been one of attempting to "muddle through" by half-hearted attempts to procure equipment, run effective test and trace facilities, and implement substantial community testing. Fortunately, after a year or more into the crisis, science has ensured that effective vaccines became available and a vaccine policy been developed, but even that is fraught with difficulties such as virus mutants. The attempt to continue with the muddle through thinking is evident in the short-term financing decisions, however significant those have been, and the failure to plan effectively to provide health and social care functions that will be robust in the face of an inevitable further pandemic.

The third crisis, that of climate change and the human environmental impact on the planet, is beyond the possibilities of "muddling through", even though that still seems to be the approach. To meet targets aimed at stabilising the effect on the planet will require, it has been estimated, 20% of current employment in economic activities to be replaced by "green alternatives". This is an economic revolution that goes well beyond the technological changes that have been experienced in past decades, and if one takes the assumptions of Schumpeter's "creative destruction" (Schumpeter 1942) then leaving it to market forces to "muddle through" will not be possible. Nor is it permissible to meet this crisis in a partial and ineffective way. Getting this wrong is truly existential – it becomes an extinction event.

But more serious still is the reliance in British public life on "*faith in chaps*". This phrase conveys several assumptions about the class of politicians and civil servants:

- The assumption of a hierarchy of rulers and ruled, with the rulers feeling that they have a sense of entitlement to rule – because they know best and will always serve the public interest.
- The assumption that there is a "code of honour" between those in power so they all know how best to behave that they will not break precedent or act in a way that favours themselves or their friends.
- A feeling that to be questioned on their actions, or to be called to account is offensive to their personal dignity.

- The assumption that if a "chap" goes astray or does something that offends against the code of honour then other "chaps" will have a quiet word and that the offending "chap" will always accept their judgement and, if necessary, step down quietly from their position of power.

So, it is commonly felt that in such circumstances a written constitution is unnecessary because you can always rely on "chaps" (and historically it usually is chaps) to do the right thing. Unfortunately, this idea that the British constitution is safe has taken something of a hammering. In the past there have been patrician politicians who have taken an honourable way out in line with the code of honour. But such examples are few and far between. In 1947, Hugh Dalton, then Chancellor of the Exchequer, famously resigned because he had accidentally leaked a budget announcement to the press before he had briefed Parliament. In 1954, the Crichel Down affair saw the resignation of the Minister responsible. And more recently the invasion of the Falkland Islands by Argentina in 1982 saw Lord Carrington, then Foreign Secretary, resign – not because he had done something wrong but because it had happened "on his watch". But such examples of "decent chaps" are rare in recent political life. Recently, Health Secretary, Matt Hancock, did not immediately resign following the release of images which showed he was guilty of breaching his own pandemic social distancing regulations – a very serious action. However, when this was coupled with evidence that he was having an extra-marital affair with a member of his staff, the resignation was forthcoming.

One of the changes from the historical model has been the rise of the professional politician. In the 19th and 20th centuries many politicians had an active career outside politics or came to politics only after retiring from such a career. Currently the career of politicians is increasingly one of individuals leaving university, joining think tanks, or acting as a political researcher for a political party, before standing for Parliament, without ever touching the "real world".

The rise of populism as a political force, common in many countries, is a potential threat to civil liberties and good governance. Politicians who adopt this approach generally have a scant connection with the truth. Lies and misstatements are made without shame, and even when exposed, they are not corrected. Any contrary evidence to the impact of policies is dismissed as "fake news". Such politicians retain and expand on historical tropes and myths which are at best simplistic and in some cases totally false. The inherent nature of populism, to find someone or something to blame, is divisive and is likely to lead at a minimum to a lack of community cohesion, and at worst to intercommunity violence. In places where there is a written constitution there is the possibility (but not a guarantee) of some degree of check on the policies and activities of such politicians.

The US Constitution was drawn up to affect the separation of powers between the legislature, judiciary, and executive functions based, almost perversely, on a misreading on the pattern of British governance by Montesquieu. The US Constitution, as written, builds in its checks and balances to the point where it can result in almost political deadlock. That is a weakness. There is also a view that the US constitution, written two centuries ago, is seen as so sacred, to many people, that it inhibits societal progress in the modern world. The battle between those who are originalists and those who believe in a living Constitution is an ongoing issue in the USA. To avoid this in the UK, suggests there should be some mechanism to review the constitution and make amendments as needed. However, such a constitution does add as a check on a populist president like President Trump by limiting what he can do. The UK with its unwritten constitution provides no such check to the rise of the populist politician.

In summary, the issues described above suggest, to us, there is a strong argument for a written constitution in the UK irrespective of the changes we discuss in this book. A written constitution becomes essential to meet the kind of changes that we are now proposing to meet the huge range of challenges facing the UK which were outlined in Chapter 2. Furthermore, it is important that the principal of elected regional government is enshrined in the UK constitution to avoid interference in, and undermining of, regional government by the federal government in the same way that the present UK government tries to undermine the devolution settlements in Wales and Scotland.

Structural changes

The introduction of a written constitution is undoubtedly the most significant change that we are proposing, based on a federal structure of governance. Inevitably, a new constitution will involve a statement of broad democratic objectives; have safeguards for individuals' rights and liberties; place limits on the arbitrary powers of government; and provide for arrangements for constitutional changes subject to democratic processes and a minimum level of public support. Such a constitution will need to decide between the traditional Anglo-American model where the rights of individuals are safeguarded by a Bill of Rights against the possibility of tyrannical government, and the French or continental model where these rights are expressed as legitimate demands on government to provide for individuals and to meet their needs. The first sees government as essentially antagonistic to the liberties of individuals, the second sees government as a collective expression of "the will of the people" and their objectives. This is no small matter to decide and most of the modern constitutions are an expression of the latter rather than the former, even though the contradictory demands of individuals and groups to have their rights "respected" often involve the making of value judgements about their contradictory demands. Such is democracy.

What we are discussing here, however, are the arrangements that lie below the constitutional level within a proposed federal/regional arrangement for the UK. In looking at these, we will use the usual description of the three branches of government shown in Figure 4.1.

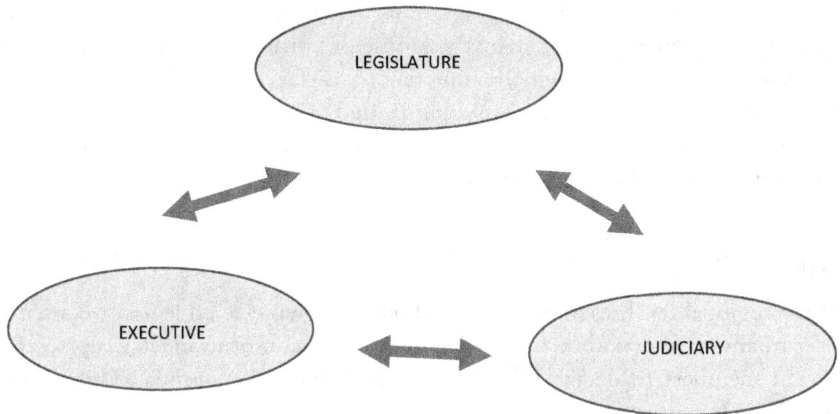

FIGURE 4.1 Branches of government

Legislative branch

This is discussed twofold.

Federal tier

At present the UK has a bicameral legislative system, as is the case in many other countries, that is unique in that the second chamber, the House of Lords, is unelected. We work on the assumption that a federal UK government would continue to function with two chambers.

The proposals that we are making suggest that the House of Commons could not function as a purely English assembly, since most of the service provision and decisions are now being made at a regional government level. Along the lines of the USA it might better be named the House of Representatives and would be the body accountable for federal government activities. We suggest that it would comprise around 100–150 members drawn from all parts of the UK.

We would also suggest that the House of Lords, in its present form, should be abolished. In its place, there could be a "Senate" which would not be directly elected but which would be appointed. What is important is that the Senate should have strong representation from UK regions (as is the case in Germany) as a counter-balance to the elected chamber. Perhaps 50% of the Senate would come from the regional assemblies in proportion to their populations, while 50% would be nominated from businesses, trade unions, faith communities, community and environmental groups, etc. In this way, the regional voice will be heard, directly, at the federal level. It would therefore provide a forum in which the federal functions could properly be discussed and would have legislative capacity in respect of those functions, but only after the proposals had also been passed by the Senate which would exercise a federal and regional oversight to ensure that the federal level in the Commons was not exceeding its functions or impinging on the authority of individual regions. This would more accurately balance out the current arrangements whereby the House of Lords may have a delaying and refining function but is essentially impotent in the face of a Commons majority. The arrangements might get more sophisticated over time involving, for example, the need to achieve a certain percentage majority for bills that had a significant regional impact from the regional delegates

Regional tier

At the regional level, each region would have its own elected legislative assembly/parliament and within the constraints of the constitution, it is up to the elected members to decide how the region should be organised. This would include such matters as:

- The organisation of the regional tier itself
- The structure and functions of local government within the region including numbers and types of local authorities and existence of mayors
- The organisation of other services such as police, and fire and rescue in the region

In doing this, we would hope that the elected regional government would consult widely, within the region, about these structural issues and would not just look at the matter simplistically or in, purely, political terms. The key point is that it is for the elected regional government to decide these matters as they are closest to the communities they serve. They do not require standardised guidance, instructions, etc. from Whitehall/Westminster which is what happens today.

A key question now arises about the position and functions of a democratically elected local government in a region with an elected regional assembly. As originally envisaged, in the 19th century, local government was a democratically elected local body, which did not have legislative capacity or a power of general competence, but which was instead limited by national statute to those functions and decisions decided on by central government. Nevertheless, historically for many decades, local government exercised considerable initiative in the Victorian and Edwardian periods, introducing public utilities, transport, and undertaking health and education responsibilities. However, in the post-war period many of these functions were stripped to be taken into national bodies like the National Health Service, government agencies, and nationalised industries. Successive reforms of local government sought to make it more effective through amalgamations into bigger units, audit, inspection, etc. However, at the same time central government often became irritated when local government (often in the hands of opposition parties rather than the party of government) resisted government policies using the legitimate argument that they, too, were elected to power. Successive measures were taken to strip local government of its functions and take them into centralised bodies.

Example of this is its control of education, and increasingly over social care. Those who have read Yes Minister (still the best guide to the operation of Whitehall) will remember Sir Humphrey browbeating the Minister with "centralise Minister, centralise".

Local government continues to be highly dependent on central or devolved government funding, and increasingly the limited power of local council taxation was constrained and reduced to the point where local government is now largely a local administration and has few powers of independent action. The period of austerity substantially diminished the resources given to support local government and the Covid pandemic created further pressures on local authorities such that local government is now significantly financially stressed, and there is the possibility of major authorities effectively going bankrupt.

Under our proposed regional government arrangements, local authorities would fall under the purview of regional government. Under this arrangement there will always be the temptation for a regional government to try to interfere with the workings of local authorities and to strip them of powers in the same way as Westminster/Whitehall has done. Indeed, there have been criticisms of both Welsh and Scottish governments that having had power devolved to them, they did not devolve power further down the chain but took power away from local government. This is a difficult issue and one which would need to be addressed within each region.

Executive branch

At the federal tier, the Prime Minister of the UK would appoint his or her Cabinet (and other ministers) from the House of Representatives and/or the Senate, which will comprise the federal executive branch. However, this Cabinet and the associated government departments will be much smaller in number and size than the current situation. This is for the simple reason that many of the traditional UK departments of state will no longer be needed (or will be vastly diminished in size) since their powers and responsibilities will have been transferred to regional governments. So, for example, we see no need for a large UK Department of Health or a large Department of Education, at the federal level. Regional governments are quite capable of dealing with most of these functions themselves without guidance or prescription from Whitehall. We recognise the federal tier may well have coordinating roles, across regions, in many areas of activity but the term is "coordinating" not control and the size of such functions should be small and might be accommodated in a single department for the regions.

The devolved governments of Scotland, Wales, and Northern Ireland already have executive branches consisting of a First Minister and Cabinet members and this might be the model for regional governments in England. However, once more, we must emphasise that this is an issue to be decided by elected regional governments not laid down by Whitehall.

Judicial branch

Finally, we cannot leave the section on constitutional change without commenting on the role of the judiciary. Within the federal proposals we suggest that the role of the judiciary will be largely unchanged. While recognising that Scotland has a separate judicial system, the arrangement for the English regions, Wales, and Northern Ireland would be the present arrangements of High Court, Court of Appeal, and Supreme Court. The one variation would be that since the regions have independent legislative ability under the federal arrangements we are proposing that if an issue arose with the exercise of executive authority within a region, it would be decided initially at the relevant Crown Court for that region. It could be, however, that the issue raised was of greater than regional significance, going beyond, for example, a judicial review, and if it raised an issue that related to a general point of law affecting all regions, or it related to legislative functions between federal authority and region. In that case, the issue would be transferred by the relevant Crown Court to the High Court for decision. Clearly, a lot more work would be needed to flesh out these arrangements.

Beyond this we would further recommend that in recognition of the federal arrangement, the activities of the High Court and Supreme Court could be more peripatetic, transferring the location, but not the function, to different regional centres from time to time.

However, we cannot leave untouched the issue of the lack of diversity in the UK judiciary. A recent article in the Law Society Gazette stated that "*Senior judges 'most socially exclusive' of all professionals*" (Fouzder 2019). The article states that 65% of senior judges were educated at an independent school while 75% attended Oxford or Cambridge. This seems very much like a manifestation of the phenomenon of "faith in chaps" which was discussed earlier. Having freed regional governments from an over-bearing central government through constitutional protections, it makes no sense to leave it at the mercy of a judiciary which lacks diversity and interprets legislation from a London-centric and elitist concept of UK society. We believe that a constitution should provide for some form of consultative mechanism involving federal and regional tiers to ensure diversity in the judiciary. Improving diversity does not mean reducing competence – it is arrogance of the highest level to suggest otherwise.

One final observation would be that the political role of Lord Chancellor should revert to being a position only held by an individual with a legal qualification, instead of a politician as a present.

New electoral systems

At present the system of "first past the post" is commended by supporters of centralised government on the grounds that it provides a strong and stable government by giving political parties a majority in the House of Commons by which to enact their legislative programme. While undoubtedly this is correct, it also means that political choice is highly restricted to a few political parties (which being internal coalitions often driven by factions and groups) which may, if they gain power, enact more extreme measures on the entire population. It also means that since the Second World War only a very few administrations have commanded a majority of the popular vote, and most are able to control Parliament and set up a government with only 40% of those of the electorate who actually voted casting their vote for them for them. The objection to alternative forms of voting in the form of proportional representation does not seem to be one of principle since the devolved administrations all have different forms of proportional representation. There can be therefore no objection in principle to moving towards a system of proportional representation (the simplest is the single transferable vote system) for all elections to public bodies in the UK. This would lead to a greater variety of political parties that more accurately represented diverse opinion, and the likelihood that coalitions of political parties will be necessary to form a government which would act as a brake on the danger of small minority groups within larger political parties becoming dominant and able to govern on an exceedingly small minority of the popular vote.

Management and administrative changes

The last point that we raise in this section concerns the management and administrative functions that support governments at federal and regional levels. There are many concerns, already expressed, about the capability of the UK civil service in relation to policy formulation and implementation. Over many years, there has been much criticism from various sources about the efficacy of the UK civil service. Former UK Prime Minister, Tony Blair, once strongly, criticised the UK civil service, saying there is a "*genuine problem with the bureaucracy*" of the country (The Guardian 2017). He said that he found civil servants "*frankly just unresponsive*" when it came to major changes, such as healthcare or education reform. Former Tory Cabinet Office Minister, Angus Maude, once said that he became disillusioned with the Civil Service, not with civil servants but that the Civil Service as an institution is deeply flawed, and in urgent need of radical reform. Much of the criticisms of the Civil Service concern its generalist approach and lack of technical expertise at senior levels, its concern with protecting Ministers rather than developing policy, its resistance to radical reform, etc. Recently, the former Chief of Staff in 10 Downing Street, Dominic Cummings, entered the fray stating, among other things, that the civil service lacked people with "*deep expertise in specific fields*". While there has been much criticism of Cummings's comments, given his antagonistic approach, there has also been support for his views. He maintains his opinions even though now out of office and has invited Commons Select Committees to seek those opinions which he is most willing to give. It seems clear to us that the civil service, in terms of culture and approach, has, in reality, changed little since the Fulton Report over five decades ago and hence needs reform. The major changes resulting from the creation of a federal tier would provide a suitable impetus for doing that.

Thus, when it comes to the staffing of a regional government (be that called the "civil service" or some other title) there must be a focus on high-quality policy development, advice, and analysis to regional government ministers. This implies a different model to the UK civil service with a stronger focus on technical expertise, the provision of advice and less emphasis on protecting Ministers from the folly of their actions. Indeed, there seems a case for strengthening, in regions, the system of Ministerial directives now found in Whitehall. Under this process, civil servants must seek Ministerial cover for a decision to spend money if it does not meet all of the four tests of regularity, propriety, value for money, and feasibility. In such a circumstance, the Accounting Officer must in these circumstances ask for a written direction to continue from Ministers. The Accounting Officer then implements the decision – but it is the Minister who bears responsibility for that use of public money.

During our interviews with individuals well experienced in functioning within devolved administrations and federal organisations it became apparent that advice, efficiency, and functioning of administrative officers were deeply influenced by their career prospects working within a unitary state. Civil servants and others who were assigned to work with devolved administrations often found that their career prospects could be severely damaged if they took a regional view as opposed to reflecting national policies of the central government. There were therefore instances of legitimate policy decisions at a devolved level being delayed or deliberately thwarted when it was believed that these were contrary to the wishes of national politicians. The proposals that we are making here would clearly focus on providing an administrative framework in which such national dominance was substantially weakened, and careers could be established by working at federal or at regional level independently, with career changes being subject to competitive appointments rather than career assignments.

One issue often mentioned is the costs of establishing regional government in the UK. In 2004, a referendum took place in North-East England as to whether or not to establish an elected assembly for the region. Almost 80% of those voting were against such a development. Subsequently, this result has often been used as the argument against any form of regional devolution in the UK. The campaign against the proposed assembly was successfully led by a local businessman who argued that the institution would have no real powers, would be expensive and a "white elephant" and too centric to Newcastle upon Tyne. These are strong and valid arguments and voters correctly realised that the additional cost of setting up the assembly would not be defrayed by cost savings in the London-based civil service. However, the model we propose in these pages is different. The regional assembly would have real powers and the costs of creating must be offset by enormous reductions in the London civil service (since many government departments would be abolished) coupled with the lower costs associated with being based outside of London. This might actually reduce the overall costs of government.

Regional economic policy and development

Earlier in this book we compared the way in which today's London-based UK governments relate to UK regions as being analogous to the way London-based UK governments of the 19th and 20th centuries related to overseas UK colonies. One commentator on the "*ground nut scandal*" referred to earlier stated that it was "*primarily a political project pursued in haste for primarily political ends, ignoring locals and experts, which will so often end not just in tears but in a massive cost to the taxpayer and a political price for the government*" (Westcott 2020). A case of policy making being made by people who had little knowledge and understanding of the environment and cultures of the places affected by the policy and who were unlikely ever to visit such places. The same is true, to some degree, of UK public policy making today.

However, another analogy is that of overseas aid. The UK (and other world) governments provide aid to low-income countries which can't support public services from the proceeds of limited economic growth. Ironically, this is often the case in the UK where government neglect over many decades has meant that most UK regions have economies so under-developed that they could not support an adequate level of public services from their own economies and so need to receive "*overseas aid*" from London. For regional government to be effective and sustainable, this situation must be reversed. The current arrangement is inequitable and demeaning.

Thus, UK regions need to develop sustainable economies, which will increase economic growth, improve the living standards of their populations, and generate funds to pay for public services. At the moment, the economic inequalities in the UK mean that northern regions, in particular, are reliant on handouts from the UK government in the form of regional aid, government grants, etc. In many ways, this approach looks familiar to the process of overseas aid given to poor countries around the world. This situation is often commented on acerbically by some people in the South East in the same way that overseas aid is mentioned.

To develop sustainable economies, regions need to have access to funds to develop transport infrastructure, communications technology, education and training, etc. This means regional governments having tax-raising powers (which is already the case in Wales and Scotland) and borrowing powers but also the means having a *transparent and equitable mechanism* for sharing existing public resources and investment across the UK which is NOT the case at the moment. Current approaches are unfairly and outrageously biased towards London and the South East. A recent report from the IPPR North (Raikes 2019) illustrated the inequity in distributing transport infrastructure funds between UK regions. Over the next decade, investment per head of population in London will be three times that in the North. For regional economies to develop, a fairer distribution of infrastructure investment is needed. To some extent, this investment could be found by abandoning vanity projects planned for the South East such as HS2 and Third Heathrow runway. Even a fraction of the funds spent on these projects would have an enormous economic impact if spent in regions outside the South East. For those who think large-scale economic development outside the South East is impossible, Raikes (2017) showed that if the North had the same per capita spending as London over the last ten years then £66 billion more would have been spent in the region. One can only imagine the economic impact on the North of that level of investment.

There must also be a recognition that regions do not equate to cities. Having tried to re-balance the position of Northern Regions compared to London, we don't want to end up in a position where there are major inequalities between towns and cities within a region. Thus, public and economic policy within a region must also effect changes in towns and rural areas. Linked to this will be the development of communitarian approaches in local communities by empowering local authorities to focus on their assessment of community needs rather than have to implement targets set from "on high".

One critical area in this arrangement is the control of monetary policy. It has long been recognised that a common currency is an implicit requirement for a federal nation. Alexander Hamilton, Secretary to the Treasury in the newly born USA, knew that his establishment of a single currency separate from that of Great Britain was an essential step in nationhood. A single currency is essential within the UK. As already noted, under a federal structure, monetary policy (and trade policy) must be the responsibility of the federal tier of government. Earlier in this chapter, we noted concerns about the "one size fits all" approach to monetary policy resulting in decisions being made by the monetary authorities to resolve issues that have had variable impacts on different sectors of the economy. Writing in the context of the Indian economy, Singh and Rao (2015) cite empirical evidence of this fact that they express as follows:

> We find that the impact of a monetary policy shock at the sectoral level is heterogeneous. Sectors such as, mining and quarrying, manufacturing, construction and trade, hotel, transport and communications seems to decline more sharply than aggregate output in response to a monetary tightening.

In the UK, there have, in the past, been decisions made by the monetary authorities that have had significant detrimental effects on the non-financial services parts of the UK economy. Inevitably, because of the structure of the UK economy it means that these detrimental effects fall predominantly in regions outside London. Furthermore, looking at the current membership of the UK Monetary Policy Committee it appears that all of its members are London based and are predominantly involved in the financial sector. Hence, we get this London-centric thinking about monetary policy. In future, we suggest that the MPC must have a more balanced membership in terms of sector and location and that decisions made should consider the impacts on all sectors of the economy and achieve an appropriate balance.

But there are always tensions in establishing monetary policy. The control of liquidity and interest rates which is the essential core of that policy must balance the pressures of external trade imbalances with the requirements to smooth out fluctuations in the domestic economy. Given the predominance of London as an international monetary centre there has always been a pressure to maintain the value of sterling by monetary policy despite the damaging effects this could have on the domestic economy of many of the regions and devolved nations. Given the instability in finance and monetary matters since the resurgence of free-market liberalism from the 1980s, culminating in the disastrous financial collapse of 2008/2010, most countries have adopted the principle of an independent Central Bank to limit the political manipulation of monetary policy. Despite this, the economic predominance of London still dominates. Mark Carney (2021) in his recent book *Values* relates a story about his concern that he would not be accepted as a Canadian as Governor of the Bank of England. He says that he was reassured that "once you go north of Birmingham, the Governor of the Bank of England is an alien creature. No one will know the difference". The hint of metropolitan arrogance is hardly reassuring! Retaining that element of independence will be essential in any new constitutional arrangements, although as we will see in Chapter 5, which deals with the current situation in public finances, the independence of the Bank of England may be threatened by the level of current public debt. So, a further safeguard against the regional implications of monetary policy retained by central government would be to adopt the German federal arrangement whereby representatives of each of the regions are appointed to the Board of the Central Bank to make sure that their interests are heard, notwithstanding the fact that the Bank of England already has a regional arrangement for data collection and assessment of the regional economic situation.

Similar arguments apply to trade policy and there is a need for regional voices in UK trade negotiations as is the case with regions in other developed countries.

Chapter 6 will further develop the ideas around regional economic development under a model of elected regional government.

Regional public policy making and implementation

Public policy making needs to be far more systematic than the "muddle through" approach which currently seems to exist. Effective policy requires effective process. Various models exist to describe the policy process and these may be stage 3, stage 4, etc. One such policy model is summarised below:

- **Stage 1: Agenda setting** – as the first stage in the cycle, agenda setting helps policy makers decide which problems to address. Topics for discussion go through several types of agendas before these individuals may move them forward.
- **Stage 2: Policy formation** – in policy formation, solutions to problems are shaped and argued. This stage is characterised by intense negotiation between

parties. Leaders, bureaus, and other factions must fight for their own needs and desires, often in opposition to one another. Public policies are therefore formed far more by the act of bargaining than by any other means.

- **Stage 3: Policy legitimation** – "legitimacy" means that the public considers the government's actions to be legal and authoritative. To gain legitimacy, a policy must be moved through the legislative process. Once this happens, it is considered the law of the land and can be implemented as such.
- **Stage 4: Policy implementation** – this stage puts policies into action. Responsibility passes from policy makers to policy implementers, and the policies themselves may again develop further while this happens. Whether a policy succeeds can often be traced back to this stage; a well-written policy with a poor implementation can end in failure.
- **Stage 5: Policy evaluation** policy makers conduct evaluations to determine if the policies they create are effective in achieving their goals. When determining this, they must consider how to evaluate outcomes effectively, how to measure the outcomes, and how to navigate between the efficiency of a policy and its effectiveness (the former is often easier to measure than the latter). Evaluation may occur either during implementation or after the policy in question is finished.
- **Stage 6: Policy maintenance, succession, or termination** – once implemented, policies are periodically gauged for their relevancy and use. This may result in their continuation, amendment, or termination. These incidents often occur due to policy makers' shifting goals, values, beliefs, or priorities.

However, it is important to stress that the above model requires a cyclical approach to be fully successful, in that the evaluation/review ought to lead back to adjustments in the formulation of the policy or its implementation and so on.

Now we may look at the above stages and question to what extent these stages are, currently, undertaken and how well they are undertaken. For example, earlier we mentioned Universal Credit and it is not clear as to what extent the failures are due to poor policy evaluation and/or poor implementation. The problem is that while policy issues are shrouded in secrecy in Whitehall, it is difficult to get a clear picture as to how good the policy process really is. Furthermore, in stage 2 on policy formulation, it was stated that "*Public policies are therefore formed far more by the act of bargaining than by any other means*". There is much evidence (e.g. Cox 2019) to suggest that this is indeed the case but it will probably surprise most people who think that policy is developed based on data and evidence. However, we repeat the words of Professor Hudson quoted earlier "*the currency of modern politics seems to be squarely that of failure – indeed major failure*".

In future, governments, at both federal and regional levels, need to introduce more robust policy processes to improve the extent of policy success and be able to reduce regional inequalities. Improvements could include:

- **Data and data analysis** – as far as possible, policy should be based on evidential data that have been collected for policy development purposes.

Furthermore, much greater use should be made of modern data analysis techniques such as big data analytics and dynamic modelling. The recent comments by Dominic Cummings the Prime Minister's former chief adviser on the need for government to recruit far more data scientists are pertinent (ResearchLive 2020).

- **Restrictions on lobbying** – while it is important to take a wide range of opinions on matters of policy, the influence of professional lobbyists (who by definition are paid to promote their clients' interests) should be minimised. Examples can be quoted of where external influences have completely distorted policy decisions contrary to the opinions of those public servants responsible for its implementation. This is a form of corruption. Improvements in the availability of evidential data should also reduce the influence of inappropriate lobbying bordering on the corrupt.
- **Diversity of policy makers** – the term "diversity" is often used as a statement of "political correctness" used to mean differences in gender, age, race, sexuality, etc. Diversity is much more than this and needs to incorporate differences in backgrounds, experiences, geography, etc. However, diversity of people is seen as a key driver of innovation (Hewlett et al. 2013) and effective policy making requires a strong element of innovation. UK government policy making does not seem to involve much diversity. There is a commonly held view that power and influence in the UK is the province of white men who have been educated at independent schools and studied liberal arts at Oxbridge and thus dominate policy making in government. While this may be dismissed as a caricature, available evidence suggests a strong degree of truth. The social background of politicians and civil servants is increasingly restricted. A recent report by the Sutton Trust and the Social Mobility Commission (2019) threw a lot of light on this issue. In a study entitled "Elitist Britain" it showed how power and influence on public policy in the UK is dominated by those who attended independent schools followed by Oxbridge universities. In saying this let us remember that only 7% of school age children attend independent schools (ISC) but over 40% of places at Oxbridge are taken up by students from independent schools. This report contains much information and we give below just a few examples:
    - Fifty-nine percent of Permanent Secretaries of government departments attended independent schools and 56% attended Oxbridge
    - Forty-five percent of Chairs of public bodies attended independent schools and 40% attended Oxbridge
    - Thirty-nine percent of members of Cabinet/Shadow Cabinet attended independent schools and 57% attended Oxbridge

  No wonder UK public policy fails. There is a need for far more diversity among the policy-forming classes.
- **Transparency** – aside from policy areas where issues of national security are concerned, the policy process should be far more transparent. The options put to Ministers and the advice given on these options should be open to public examination, as should the results of any subsequent evaluation.

Conclusions

Changes of this magnitude may strike the reader as being impossible to achieve. Less ambitious attempts have been made in the past but have failed. However, doing all these things together makes for a coherent change in UK governance. In the past the "muddle through" attitude of small incremental changes has not proved effective. As noted earlier, proposals to establish a regional level of governance in the UK were promoted by John Prescott when Deputy Prime Minister in the Blair administration but failed, largely because it was presented by its opponents as being a further level of bureaucracy in an otherwise unchanged national system – which it was. Similarly, an attempt by the Liberal Democrats when in coalition with the Conservatives to introduce proportional representation also failed because it was not linked at all to changes in governance and was strongly opposed by principal political parties who saw it as a limit to the exercise of power (despite being in coalition at the time).

Yet despite this apparent support for strong central government the fact remains that the devolved administrations represent an already halfway house towards a federal system. Scotland, Wales, and Northern Ireland have their own arrangements regarding the health function (it may be a National Health Service in name, but in practice it is different across the four administrations). Similarly, education is handled differently in each of the devolved administrations, as is social care. No one seems to balk at all but the fact that there is not one Chief Medical Officer for the UK, but four – one in each of the devolved administrations. Too often these represent the overhang of historical arrangements rather than a thoroughgoing reform of the whole system to make it more effective to meet the future crises.

If changes on the scale of those described above are not implemented, we see there being little or no progress made in reducing inequalities between the devolved administrations and England and London/South East and the rest of the English regions. Merely sticking to the existing approaches to government and policy and giving a few billion pounds, more to the regions in the form of regional aid will just not suffice. UK economic history shows this to be the case.

London is almost the absolute centre of power and influence in the UK as it contains a concentration of elitist groups with immense power and influence. This includes strong degrees of overlap along with the aristocracy, politicians, civil servants, the media, public schools, the City, business leaders and Oxbridge and London universities. Given this concentration, it should not be surprising that decision making on economic policy and public policy is developed, almost entirely through the eyes of the London elite, and lacks virtually no degree of diversity across other societal groups or other parts of the country (outside of Wales, Scotland, and NI). The minor efforts to demonstrate awareness of other parts of the UK such as moving some governmental departments are tokenism as, in reality, nothing really changes.

We also need to recognise where federal arrangements have been established in European countries; in recent years these have often been in response to a national crisis. The federal arrangements in Germany and in Italy were established in the wake of the fascist dictatorships that had dominated those countries in the 1930s and which had been responsible for leading them into a disastrous war in which they had been defeated by an alliance of democratic countries. Both recognised the need to establish a regional level of government which balanced the regions so that the predominance that had existed of one region over another was counteracted. There was a similar experience in Austria, which had experienced a fascist takeover in the Anschluss, and the post-war division of the country between the Allied powers. The same could be said for Spain, where the federal arrangements followed years of the fascist dictatorship of Franco and an extreme unitary national state with increasing corruption and economic failure. The reversion to a more regional system under a restored monarchy was given a severe shock in 1981 with a failed military coup, which resulted in a much more federal system being established to recognise legitimate claims of regions such as Catalonia and the Basque country, a federal system which was significantly advanced by the inclusion of Andalusia to the greater level of autonomy envisaged in the federal structure. In Belgium, the federal arrangements with all their language, culture, and geographical complexities came about following significant civil disturbances in the 1970s when the Flemish regions felt that they were being oppressed by a French-speaking Brussels-dominated government.

There is perhaps a lesson here for the UK. The rise to power of populist right-wing governments with an authoritarian streak and a heavy nationalistic flavour led to disaster in many European countries which was "solved" by adopting federal arrangements which dispersed power and limited the ability of minorities to take over the functioning of the state. Rebellions in semiautonomous regions, particularly in Spain, remain an issue to the present day. It does not take much to see that if the Brexit experiment turns out to be an economic and political disaster, then it may create a crisis which results in either the collapse of the UK as an entity, or a more radical reform of government. Similarly, if the effect of the Covid pandemic becoming an endemic part of the future of the country, with repeated restrictions of liberty, being run and overseen by an overly dominant metropolitan capital elite there may be a backlash in terms of public consent which may only be assuaged with significant changes to the over-centralisation of power, reflecting a greater awareness of the fact that in the pandemic the devolved administrations each implemented different responses from that of England.

References

Carney, M. (2021), *Values: Building a Better World for All*, William Collins.

Cox, S. (2019), An examination of the negotiated order of NHS commissioning: decisions in the absence of objectivity, PhD thesis, Nottingham Trent University.

Esler, G. (2021), *How Britain Ends, English Nationalism and the Rebirth of Four Nations*, Blackwell.

Fouzder, M. (2019), Senior judges 'most socially exclusive' of all professionals, *Law Society Gazette*, June 2019.

Hewlett, S.A., Marshall, M. and Sherbin, L. (2013), How diversity can drive innovation, *Harvard Business Review*, December 2013.

Raikes, L. (2017). State of the North 2017: The Millenum Powerhousre, IPPR

Raikes, L. (2019), Transport investment in the northern powerhouse, IPPR.

ResearchLive (2020), Cummings calls on data scientists to join No 10, 6 January 2020.

Sacks, J. (2021), *Morality: Restoring the Common Good in Divided Times*, Hodder and Stoughton.

Schumpeter, J. (1942) *Capitalism, Socialism, and Democracy*, Harper & Bros.

Social Mobility Commission (2019), Elitist Britain, 24 June 2019.

The Guardian (2017), Tony Blair: UK civil service has genuine problem with change, 24 August 2017.

Westcott, L., https://boydellandbrewer.com/blog/african-studies/nuts-why-the-groundnut-scheme-still-matters/

5

FUTURE FINANCING OF PUBLIC SERVICES

Roger Latham and Malcolm J. Prowle

Introduction

Since the start of 2020, the UK, along with many other countries, has been in several states of lockdown in response to the Covid-19 pandemic, although the details of the lockdown varied between the various nations of the UK. Over and above lockdown, it seems likely that there will be a continuation of other policies such as social distancing for a considerable period of time, while the longer-term situation regarding the pandemic remains unclear.

Public services and especially the health and social care systems in the UK have been extremely important during the pandemic and most people would agree that these services have performed extremely well, in difficult circumstances, during the crisis. In addition, recognition should be given to other groups of workers in public and private sectors including emergency services, armed forces, refuse collection staff, and couriers. All of these staff have helped many to deal with a difficult situation.

In spite of this huge degree of uncertainty, it is, now, worth giving some thought to the future of public services post-pandemic and the funding implications of those services.

In this chapter, we will consider the following:

- Approaches to funding public services
- The public expenditure situation pre-Covid
- The impact of Covid-19 on public expenditure
- Other longer-term expenditure pressures
- Public finance futures
- The importance of inter-generational equity
- Conclusions

We will also consider the financing of public services from an over-arching point of view. In later chapters, aspects of financing specific public services will be discussed.

DOI: 10.4324/9781003201892-7

Approaches to funding public services

Clearly, someone has to pay for public services and there are only a limited number of sources of funding available. Before looking at ways of dealing with the current situation, we would first like to summarise the options available for funding public services.

Taxation

The 18th-century English writer Dr Samuel Johnson once commented that "*the only certain things in life are death and taxation*". This may well be true and indeed taxation is an integral part of everyday life in most countries today. At its simplest, it can be said that the two main purposes of taxation in a country are:

- **To raise funds for the government to finance public spending**. This has been the case since medieval times where kings levied taxation on their subjects to finance foreign wars. It is of critical importance today.
- **To promote the social and economic objectives of the government**. These days, governments may have a range of social and economic objectives including the following:
    - Stimulate investment
    - Promote/curtain consumption
    - Reduce income inequalities
    - Promote economic growth
    - Reduce regional inequalities in a country
    - Promote price stability

Various taxes can be utilised to achieve these social and economic objectives but it will also be important to be aware of the impact on government revenues of changes in tax policy.

The most important source of revenue for a government is taxation. A tax is basically a compulsory charge or fees imposed by a government on individuals and corporations. The key point about a tax is that the amount paid is not linked to the level of consumption, by an individual or corporation, of any particular public services. The persons who are taxed have to pay the taxes irrespective of any corresponding return from the goods or services by the government.

Taxes may be imposed on the income, consumption, or wealth of persons or corporations but the rates of taxes being applied will vary between countries and over time. Indeed, it almost seems to be the mark of a good finance ministry that they can conjure up new and innovative types of taxation. However, taxes should not just be conjured up out of thin air but should have criteria by which they should be judged. The 18th-century economist, Adam Smith (1776), set down four principles (or canons) of taxation which are:

- **Canon of fairness** – in canon of fairness, taxation should be compatible with taxpayers' conditions, including their ability to pay in line with personal and family needs.
- **Canon of certainty** – it should mean that taxpayers are clearly informed about why and how taxes are levied.
- **Canon of convenience** – it relates to the ease of compliance for the taxpayers: how simple is the process for collecting or paying taxes?
- **Canon of efficiency** – it touches on the collection of taxes: basically that the administration of tax collection should not negatively affect the allocation and use of resources in the economy, and certainly shouldn't cost more than the taxes themselves.

However, modern economists have added the following canons to that list being:

- **Canon of productivity** – this canon states that only those taxes should be imposed that do not hamper productive effort of the community. Thus, a tax is said to be a productive one only when it acts as an incentive to production.
- **Canon of elasticity** – this canon implies that a tax should be flexible or elastic in yield. It should be levied in such a way that the rate of taxes can be changed according to exigencies of the situation. Whenever the government needs money, it must be able to extract as much income as possible without generating any harmful consequences through raising tax rates. Income tax satisfies this canon.
- **Canon of simplicity** – this canon suggests that tax rates and tax systems ought to be simple and comprehensible and not to be complex and beyond the understanding of the layman. It seems unlikely that the UK tax system would comply with this canon.
- **Canon of diversity** – this canon suggests that there should be a multiplicity of tax systems and sources of a diverse nature rather than having a single tax system and source of revenue.

When we turn to public services, the reality is that, across the globe, the bulk of public services are paid for by the proceeds of taxation. This is especially true in the UK. Taxation is a complicated subject but taxes can be considered in three dimensions as illustrated in Figure 5.1.

- **Direct/indirect** – a direct tax is a tax, such as income tax, which is levied on the income or profits of the person or company who pays it, rather than on goods or services they purchase. An indirect tax is a tax, such as VAT, which is levied on the purchase of goods and services. The mix of taxes in the UK is illustrated in Figure 5.2.
- **National/sub-national** – most taxes are levied and collected by national governments. However, some taxes can be levied and collected at sub-national

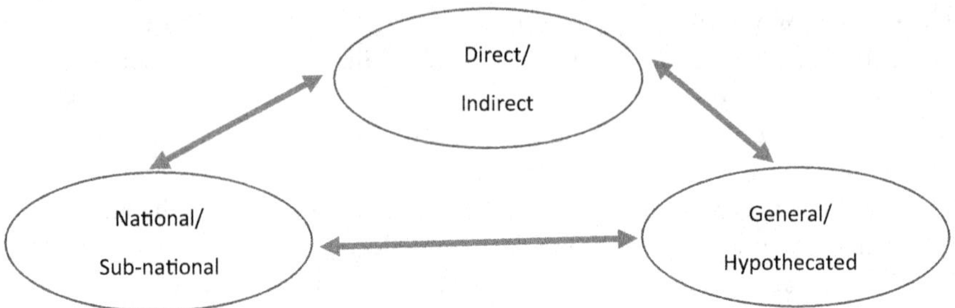

FIGURE 5.1 Dimensions of taxation

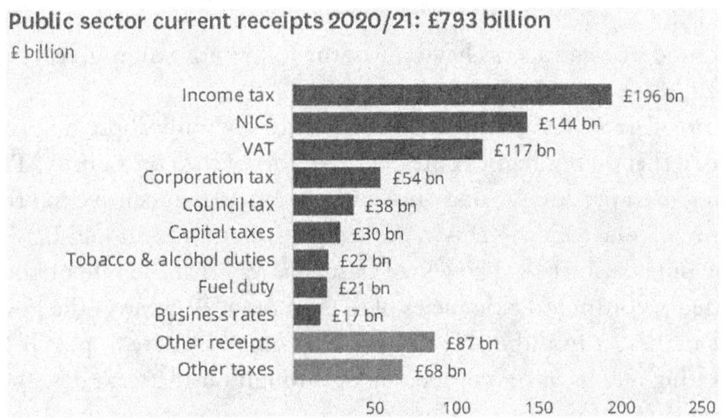

FIGURE 5.2 Mix of UK taxation

level. In the UK, the devolved governments have some tax-raising powers while local authorities collect council tax. Other countries make greater use of sub-national tax levies. For example, the Scandinavian health model is based on local municipalities or council taxes.

- **General/hypothecated** – a general tax means the proceeds of a tax go into a general pool and the government decides how the funds should be applied to deliver public services. A hypothecated tax means that the proceeds of the tax are "earmarked" for a particular purpose. Hypothecated taxes are hard to come by. National Insurance is often seen as a form of hypothecated taxation and is now used to finance some of the costs of the NHS, unemployment benefit, sickness and disability allowances, and the state pension. National Insurance is supposed to be "ring fenced", meaning the money raised is only used for these areas and won't be spent on things like education and defence. However, the government can borrow from the National Insurance fund to help pay for other projects. Another example, sometimes quoted, is the television licence fee, which provides most of the funds for public television, radio, and internet broadcasting by the BBC. However, as it is a flat rate amount it seems more like a charge than a tax. Suggestions are often made that the NHS and/or social care might be taxed by some form of hypothecated tax but this has never seriously been considered by governments other than the Welsh Government which has postulated a possible social care tax levied on the over 40s. Outside of the UK, many countries utilise what is termed a social insurance model to finance their health services. Although the term "social insurance" is used, this is really a form of hypothecated income tax.

Overall, it is probably fair to say that the tax situation in the UK is one where the vast majority of funding raised through taxation comes from direct and indirect taxes on income and consumption which are levied by central government and which are not hypothecated (House of Commons Libray 2021). However, this is not the situation in other countries and there is no fundamental reason why the UK position should not change its taxation approach. This will be discussed later.

Charges

Unlike taxation where the amount of tax paid by a person has no relationship to the volume of public services they receive, charges are linked to the services received. Hence, they might be referred to as user charges.

There are two main reasons why public service organisations might levy charges for services provided:

- To raise revenue for the organisation and defray the costs of provision.
- To influence the level of demand for public services. For example, levying charges for the weight of domestic waste collected might encourage greater recycling.

Charges levied for services can basically be of two types. The first is where the charge levied equates to the total costs of providing the services. The second is where the charge levied equates to only part of the costs of providing the services. The implication here is that there is some public subsidy to the service provided.

A range of charges are levied on users of public services for all sorts of services received. However, user charges represent only a tiny part of the funds available to finance public services although this does vary from sector to sector. For example, in social care provision, revenues from charges are significant and would need to be considered in any reform of social care finance.

Borrowing

Governments across the world borrow money to finance public services where there is a shortfall between government income and government expenditure. Such borrowed money could be obtained from a variety of sources such as citizens, citizens of other countries, other governments, and corporations. Of course, such borrowings attract interest charges and the borrowings ultimately have to be repaid perhaps years or even decades later.

Borrowing can be an acceptable method of finance for taxpayer equity, where the benefits of borrowing extend across cohorts of taxpayers, and it makes sense for the cost to be spread between taxpayers. Generally borrowing could be for three purposes:

- For capital investment where the benefits of the investment are achieved over a period of years.
- To cover cyclical changes in the economy between recession and recovery in order to smooth out those changes and prevent unnecessary economic disruption.
- To pay for a structural deficit between income and expenditure, but only where measures are being taken to eliminate the structural deficit and it is reasonable because of the period of time involved to spread the cost. Allowing structural deficits to accumulate without taking steps to eliminate them will be disastrous in the long term.

However, over the last decade, UK governments have borrowed significant amounts each year (which add to national public debt) but this has occurred during periods of economic growth that is not the traditional approach.

The funding situation pre-Covid

It is important to describe, first, the funding situation for UK public services prior to the Covid pandemic. We cannot cover all public services so we focus on a just a few.

Health

Starting with health, the reality is that the NHS needs additional funding each year to cope with the pressures of an ageing population and the introduction of new medical treatments and technologies that weren't previously available. For a 60-year period starting in 1958/1959, the NHS received, on average, real term growth in funding of approximately 3.9% per annum but with variations across different time periods (House of Commons Library 2020). The year 2010/2011 saw the start of what is now termed "austerity" with major changes being made to UK public spending levels. While some public service programmes suffered real term reductions in funding, the NHS (in England) was deemed "protected". This meant that the NHS in England would not suffer funding reductions but would get small amounts of growth of approximately 0.1% per annum (Nuffield Trust 2012) but these levels of growth fell far short of the historic levels referred to above. To keep up with demographic and technical changes it had been estimated that the NHS would need an annual real term increase of 2%. This level of increase made no allowance for contingency items or emergencies. The consequence was that over the period of austerity the NHS began to run annual deficits which had to be "plugged" by additional funds from the Department of Health. Subsequently those annual deficits turned into increasing levels of "winter crises" which gained additional funding, and by systematic underperformance against agreed performance targets. This made budgeting for genuine emergencies (like pandemics) virtually impossible, and the assumption was made through civil contingencies preparations that any national epidemic would simply be a severe form of existing seasonal issues that would require small-scale one-off funding.

Local government

> Local government has coped with a prolonged period of real-terms spending reduction which is without parallel in modern times. This large fall in local authorities' resources has been primarily caused by very significant cuts in central government grants.
>
> *(House of Commons Library 2019)*

In its evidence to the Housing, Communities and Local Government Select Committee, the Institute of Fiscal Affairs stated that local government had to adapt to significant reductions in funding. Between 2009/2010 and 2017/2018, spending on local services fell by 21% *in real terms.* Clearly, this is an average figure and the scale of reductions will vary according to different services and different parts of the country. Similar situations can be seen in the devolved administrations. In particular, it should be noted that local government is the provider of adult social care services, the demand for which (like health services) is affected by the ageing population. The potential impact of increasing demand for social care on local authorities was recognised over a decade ago with the "Barnet graph of doom" when the Chief Finance Officer for the London Borough of Barnet showed his members a graph which indicated that with the continuous growth of social care needs there would come a point when it would absorb the whole of likely future resources for the borough. Clearly this cannot happen but over time that situation has come much closer and attempts at coordination cannot disguise the issue of the balance between public and private funding for social care remains unresolved despite the recommendations of numerous enquiries. Several local authorities attempted to deal with the squeeze on their resources by utilising the exceptionally low interest rates to borrow from the Public Works Loan Board (PWLB) in order to purchase commercial property which will provide them with – they hoped – a regular stream of income to defray the increasing costs of local services. In the event, a number of these commercial developments have proved unprofitable (especially retail development badly affected by the Covid-19 pandemic and long-term trends towards online purchasing by customers). As a result, a few authorities are currently capitalising their losses, which postpones the issue of dealing with the long-term structural deficit, but which does not provide a permanent solution. With austerity came increasing restriction on the use of council tax for the local government. The central government now virtually controls the totality of resources for local authorities, and following the issues of poor commercial investments is increasing the level of restriction. For the first time since the authorities were set up, it becomes credible that one or more may yet go bankrupt and there is no policy to determine what will be done in such a situation.

Policing

Police services in England and Wales have had to adjust to large cuts in funding from the central government. In 2018/2019, £13.3 billion was spent on the police in England and Wales (excluding capital spending) which is 16% less in real terms than in 2009/2010 (IfG 2019). While police forces are making more use of reserves funding (this being money set aside for unforeseen spending) and have sold off capital assets, including police stations, neither is a sustainable source of funding. In terms of personnel, in March 2019, there were 123,171 full-time-equivalent (FTE) police officers (an increase of 0.6% on a year earlier) but this still left police numbers 14% below their March 2010 level (IfG 2019). The impact of these reductions has been such that a number of chief constables and police commissioners have made it clear that the police no longer have the resources to seek to cover all the demands that are made upon them and are consequently prioritising their responses. A low-level criminal activity such as burglary or car theft is regularly noted but not followed up – it being left to the insurance industry to cover the loss to the individual by means of redress. This has behavioural consequences and that individuals now regularly under-report criminal activity believing the police will not act upon it, a feature which shows up in the discrepancy between surveys of crime and the police recording of crime.

UK public finances

In 2009/2010, at the start of the period of austerity, UK public annual borrowing amounted to £158 billion (House of Commons Library 2020). Over the next decade through government measures, the annual borrowing requirement was substantially reduced but in 2019/2020, the UK was still borrowing £63 billion (ONS 2020). Borrowing only adds to debt outstanding and while UK public debt amounted to £0.5 trillion (or £500 billion) in 2006, it had risen by March 2021 to £2.2 trillion (£2224 billion; ONS 2021) which equates to 106% of the annual GDP of the UK. The trend is illustrated in Figure 5.3.

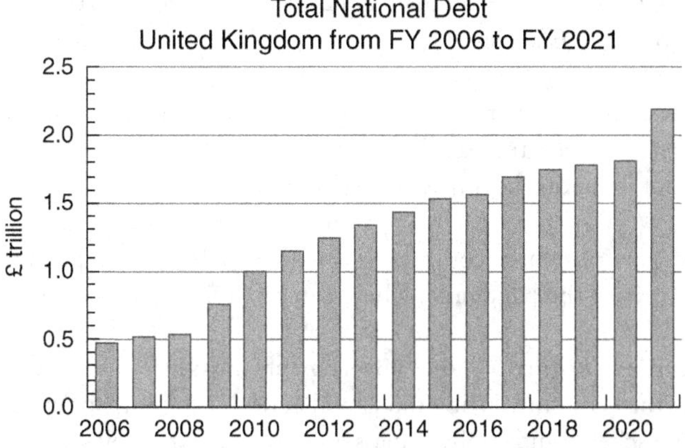

FIGURE 5.3 UK national debt

Following its election in December 2019, the Conservative Government announced ambitious expenditure plans for various purposes (e.g. levelling up the North and Midlands). This would add further to government borrowing and public debt. This is intended to cover capital investment which may be acceptable if the investments have a positive return. (See later chapter on economic development.) However, a great many investment projects generally overspend and deliver less than expected – Crossrail and HSR2 being clear examples.

While the resource situation in public services may have eased a little, in recent years, the reality is that, prior to the pandemic, many sectors were already struggling to cope with the impact of ten years of austerity and increasing service demands. Thus, the aim of this section is, merely, to illustrate that prior to Covid-19, UK public services were already financially stretched and yet UK public borrowing was still substantial and public debt had ballooned enormously.

The impact of Covid-19 on public expenditure

Covd-19 has played havoc with public finances in the UK and the rest of the world. We can identify a number of factors that will have implications for UK public finances.

The first thing to note is that the pandemic inevitably led to an economic recession as large parts of the UK economy have been shut down almost completely. During the first quarter of 2020 the economy dropped by 10%, the largest reduction since 1709, and despite recovery the second period of lockdown caused it to drop again by 2.9% in the third quarter. We are thinking here of sectors such as retail, hospitality, sports and leisure, all of which contribute large amounts to the country's economy.

We know, from experience, that economic recessions have two main impacts in relation to public finances:

- Tax revenues, both personal and corporate, will inevitably decline.
- There will be an increased demand for public services including social protection benefits, health and social care.

Already the government is committed to additional public expenditure to cope with the impact of the pandemic. These can be divided into two main themes:

- **Economic support** – the government introduced various schemes to support the economy during the Covid period including, for example, the job retention scheme and small business support. The Chancellor of the Exchequer indicated that these schemes would only be temporary in nature and they have largely been run down now. These schemes have meant the government has had to borrow huge sums of money. In the year 2020/2021, the first year of the pandemic, the UK government borrowed £299 billion, the highest figure since records began in 1946. The government is expected to borrow less in the current year, 2021/2022, though the figure could still be more than £200 billion (King 2021).
- **Public services** – health services have incurred major additional expenditure in relation to specific items such as personal protective equipment (PPE), increased ventilator capacity, and Covid testing; the development of Track and Trace alone is estimated at £37 billion to 2023. Additionally, the endemic nature of the virus will create ongoing expenditure on the preparation and administration of annual vaccine programmes. In addition, local government has increased expenditure commitments in relation to social care and other services. It is estimated (OBR 2020) that the costs to government of the Covid-19 epidemic will be approximately £133 billion with some additional costs being incurred by the devolved governments. However, for a complete fiscal year, official forecasts and government leaks suggest the overall impact on UK public finances could lie between £298 billion and £337 billion. At the time of writing Covid is still very prevalent and this will have further expenditure implications for government.

It now seems likely that the Covid virus will become endemic, and restrictions, partial lockdowns, social distancing, and annual vaccination programmes are likely to become the norm. In this it is likely to follow the pattern of the Spanish flu epidemic that followed the First World War. The initial phase of that epidemic took three years before it settled to a manageable level, and then variants of the same virus emerged significantly in 1933, 1957, and 2009 and are still part of the influenza virus groupings we see today. Although medical advances in vaccination improve our resistance to such virus infections, and advances in treatment reduce the morbidity, the fact seems inevitable that the Covid virus and its variants are here to stay for the long term.

Other longer-term expenditure pressures

There are also some other factors which are very likely to put significant pressures on UK public finances although the magnitude of cost can only be speculated upon at this stage.

Climate change

Apart from a few people on the other side of the Atlantic there is probably a broad agreement about the likely extent and causes of climate change and the existential threat that it poses to human societies. The likely public expenditure implications of countering climate change, over the next few decades, are exceedingly difficult to forecast.

Many developed countries in the world (including the UK) are signing up to an objective of having net-zero carbon emissions by the year 2050. We do not wish, here, to delve into the issue of whether this objective is sufficient or even achievable. Instead we would prefer to focus on the likely costs to the public purse. In doing this the following themes can be identified:

1 **Category 1**: The cost implications for public service organisations of reducing their own carbon footprint as an organisation. There would be costs involved in doing this but we do not think it would be too difficult to derive an estimated cost for achieving this.
2 **Category 2**: The cost of implementing preventative measures to mitigate the climate change and its implications. Of course, this category has a huge scope and would include all sorts of existing and future technologies. It is likely that there will be huge costs to government of increasing the supply of these innovations and also stimulating demand for their use. The supply side could include huge public investment in research and development of new technologies. The demand side could involve government financing of new infrastructure (e.g. charging stations for electric cars), financial incentives for people to use these new technologies, and incentives to retire outmoded existing technologies. A key aspect of climate change is the shift in energy sources from fossil fuels to renewables. This will not come cheap and the costs will be impacted by the pace of change. One researcher (Abdo 2021) has said "*A quick and unbalanced move towards a severe cut in fossil fuels would not come cost-free*".

At this stage it seems almost possible to put any figure on these costs but they are bound to be large. The costs of meeting category 1 and category 2 are likely to involve direct private expenditure as a result of government restrictions on greenhouse gas emission, such as prohibiting fossil fuel vehicles, and space heating, together with requirements to reduce the household carbon footprint through greater recycling, less waste, and energy conservation. These are likely to be coupled with "green taxes" to finance major public infrastructure investments, but aimed particularly at getting drivers to amend individual behaviours to bring them in line with climate change initiatives.

3 **Category 3**: The cost implications of having to deal with serious incidents (e.g. flooding, storms) which are a consequence of climate change. At the moment the incidence of these sorts of events does seem to be increasing but future trends cannot be predicted with any certainty not least because they depend on the success of the preventative measures in category 2. This makes forecasting the cost implications in this category an almost impossible task.

Meeting the costs of category 3 issues is not only highly variable but is inevitable. Even with vigorous attempts to mitigate the effects of climate change under category 1 and category 2 these will be insufficient to prevent a significant change in global temperatures. This is the consequence of years of the consumption of fossil fuels. So significant will be the change in climate and in other impacts of human behaviour that the period since 1950 has now been designated the Anthropocene by the international committee that adjudicates on geologic timescales. There is a debate as to whether this represents a stage, period, era, or aeon change (each being at a more significant level than the previous one) but that we have a new geologic period in which humankind is the greatest influence is now beyond doubt in academic circles. Although the changes in temperatures seem modest, particularly with reference to previous geological periods, it is important to recognise that humankind since its first existence has lived in a period of oscillations between ice ages and warmer interglacials. The temperature variation between these is only in the order of ±2°C. A failure to mitigate the effects of human behaviour on the planet which have been estimated at increasing global temperatures by up to 5°C would place us outside of the range of the world that we have inhabited since our existence, and into the temperature ranges of much earlier periods in the Miocene epoch. It would, for example, see sea levels some 15–22 m higher than current levels. This would see the inundation of many countries and parts of countries and would wipe out many of the world's greatest cities including a significant number of capital cities. The impact would also be felt in those parts of the world close to the equator which are currently subject to desertification. Those deserts would expand considerably and the temperatures in areas surrounding them would rise to levels of 40–50°C, making them virtually uninhabitable. The pressures that this would create in terms of competition for water, scarce resources, and migration are positively apocalyptic.

There are estimates of the costs of climate change but such estimates vary enormously. The UK government's climate change committee (CCC) has suggested a figure of £50 billion (CCC 2019) while the Stern Report (Stern 2006) suggested that 2% of a country's GDP would need to be invested in climate protection which equates to about £500 billion. The former Chancellor (Hammond 2019) has suggested it could be as much as £1,000 billion (BBC 2019). Clearly, the differences between these estimates imply variations in timescales, assumptions, etc. However, we can be reasonably sure that very large sums of money are inevitable.

Ageing populations

It is well known that, in line with many other countries, the population of the UK is ageing. This is a consequence of continuing declines in all-age all-cause mortality rates, meaning that more and more people are living into their 80s, 90s, and beyond. In addition, there is the phenomenon of declining fertility rates (and new births) which means that populations are becoming skewed to the older end of the spectrum.

Table 5.1 shows the impact of this for England only over a 25 years period.

It can be seen that over this 25-year period the population of England is projected to increase in total and for every age group. However, the overall balance of the population is changing with decreases in the percentage of those under 60 and percentage increases in every age band for the over 60s.Similar changes are expected in Wales, Scotland, and Northern Ireland.

The impact on the demands for public services as a consequence of the ageing populations is significant and is well known. Particularly in relation to health and social care the per capita service needs of the elderly (65+) and the very elderly (80+) are significantly greater than for younger members of the population.

It is expected that the ageing of populations will eventually level out but there is huge uncertainty about when this might happen. However, it seems unlikely that this will happen much before the end of this century.

TABLE 5.1 UK population trends

	2018	*2018*	*2043 (est)*	*2043 (est)*	*Change*	*Change*
Age band	*Numbers*	*%*	*Numbers*	*%*	*Numbers*	*%*
0–19	13241287	23.7	13336721	21.7	95434	−1.9
20–39	14833658	26.5	15235568	24.8	401910	−1.7
40–59	14678606	26.2	14830749	24.2	152143	−2.1
60–64	3044374	5.4	3614092	5.9	569718	0.4
65–69	2822593	5.0	3201433	5.2	378840	0.2
70–74	2724800	4.9	3372728	5.5	647928	0.6
75–79	1863126	3.3	3153288	5.1	1290162	1.8
80–84	1403756	2.5	2085488	3.4	681732	0.9
85–89	865702	1.5	1519953	2.5	654251	0.9
90+	499276	0.9	1037497	1.7	538221	0.8
Totals	55977178	100.0	61,387,517	100.0	5410339	0.0

Source: ONS.

TABLE 5.2 Improving health system resilience

Key components	*Other components*
• Hand hygiene education programmes • Contact precautions and testing • Environmental surface cleaning and decontamination • Anti-microbial stewardship	• Immunisation programmes • Hospital ward closures • Waste management • Real-time reporting tools

Source: Caeiro and Garzon (2018).

International health protection

There are international treaties designed to minimise the chances of a virus moving between countries. However, compliance with these treaties is incomplete and consideration needs to be given to what needs to be done to strengthen compliance with existing treaties. This probably means investment in health systems in low-income countries to make them more resilient. Caeiro and Garzon (2018), suggest that the measures needed in such countries are relatively straightforward and are summarised in Table 5.2.

However, the authors also note that only a handful of low-income countries are capable of doing all of this.

Although difficult to quantify, it does seem that the level of investment needed to strengthen health systems in low-income countries, although significant, is not likely to be great in terms of global public expenditure. However, it is probably beyond the means of low-income countries themselves. Hence, for their own self-protection, it would seem desirable for high-income countries to fund such investment in a similar manner to Marshall Aid after the Second World War. Such investment would reduce the threats to countries like the UK of future pandemics being caused by lack of disease-containment approaches in poorer countries.

Mass forced migration

According to the UNHCR the world currently has 79.5 million displaced people who may be refugees, asylum seekers, internally displaced people, etc. Consequently, in recent years, we have seen large-scale population migration in various parts of the world and dealing with this has required large-scale expenditure by the accepting countries.

Collier and Betts (2017) have argued that it is much more economical to provide support to refugees within their own region rather than them travel to distant lands for support and protection. They note that the world spends $75 billion a year on the 10% of refugees who make it to the West, and $5 billion on the other 90% who remain in developing countries. This represents a spending ratio of $135 per refugee in the developed world to every $1 per refugee in the developing world. In the light of this differential, it becomes clear that the refugee policy cannot focus solely on asylum or resettlement, but must also consider developing policies that would help all refugees secure what the three needs of refugees are: rescue, autonomy, and a route out of limbo.

Future forced mass migrations seem likely in the future as a consequence of war, climate change, water shortages, etc. and so further large-scale public expenditure may well be required especially by high-income countries, whatever approach is adopted. The significance of climate change drivers has already been mentioned.

Public finance futures

The discussion above indicates that the UK (and many other countries) faces formidable challenges in deciding how to finance public expenditure in the medium to longer term. This section considers options that are open to UK governments to respond to the situation described above.

Economic growth

This has already been discussed and it was shown that the huge expansion in public services that took place in the 20th century was funded largely by the proceeds of economic growth. Earlier in this chapter, we outlined why we believe the UK economy is unlikely to generate the levels of growth that it has received in the past. In the immediate post-war period annual growth rates were in the order of 2.2% a year. Of the difficulties of the 1970s the new (or rather old, since it was a reversion to earlier economic thinking) economic regimes aimed at maximising growth but only resulted in a halving of the growth rate to 1.1% per year. Since the onset of the three crises – financial, pandemic, and climate change – the rate of growth has dropped even further; estimates place it at only 0.5% a year for the foreseeable future. At that lower rate, although it may have positive effects on total global consumption and therefore be an advantage in facing climate change, it will be too small to deal with social issues, demographic change, and wealth and income inequalities braking pressure for policies of distributional change.

Tax increases

There is an old adage that the UK population expects Scandinavian standards of public services on US levels of taxation. This is clearly impossible to sustain and we believe there need to be some significant increases in tax levels, although the composition of those tax increases is debateable. While there may be some scope in relation to corporate taxes this seems limited because of the ease with which multi-national companies avoid paying UK corporation tax. Redressing the balance between the business and the personal taxation is considerably undermined by several countries (including the UK) promoting "tax havens" within their jurisdictions as a way of attracting a greater proportion of international business. It is particularly lucrative for small nations without significant raw material resources or access to global markets. Dealing with this issue requires a global solution – particularly hard to come by in a world increasingly dominated by a resurgence of nationalist interests. However, the recent proposals by President Biden about changes in the international taxation regime of multi-national companies look of interest but we must wait to see what happens.

Hence, it seems that the bulk of taxation rises may have to fall on individuals and the choice therefore comes between direct and indirect taxes. Indirect taxes are notoriously regressive and can have deflationary effects on an economy so it seems that tax rises must involve taxes on income and wealth. In terms of income, the UK has the seventh most unequal income distribution of 30 countries in the developed world. While the top fifth of the population have nearly 50% of the country's income, the bottom fifth have only 4% of the income (Equality Trust). Wealth is even more unequally divided than income. In 2018, the ONS calculated that for the period 2016–2018 the richest 10% of households hold 44% of all wealth. The poorest 50%, by contrast, own just 9% (ONS 2018). Thus, there does seem scope for significant increases in both income and wealth taxes to fund future public expenditure.

However, there are two snags:

- Politicians believe (and perhaps they are correct) that the electorate is very much opposed to increases in direct taxation and to do so would be electoral suicide. However, proposals to raise additional tax for specific purposes, such as the NHS, often command popular support. Perhaps that is the case that people are prepared to pay tax if they can see and appreciate what it is being spent on, and that concern about bureaucracy, waste, corrupt dealing, lack of transparency, and general obfuscation is a contributory factor in undermining public trust in politicians – currently at a very low ebb. Because of this, politicians may be unwilling to "test the waters" because they fear how the public might react to better information.
- The globalised world we live in means that there are many ways for individuals and companies to avoid direct taxes and this can only be overcome by international tax collaboration.

Although desirable, it seems unlikely, in the current economic and political climate, that there will be effective collaboration between countries to curb tax avoidance.

Taxation and regional governments

At the moment, both the Welsh and Scottish governments have certain limited tax-raising powers. These involve land transaction tax, landfill tax, and the ability to vary aspects of income tax. In other developed countries, regional governments have much greater tax-raising powers as well as powers to borrow funds for investment purposes.

Consideration might be given to extending tax-raising powers to UK regional governments within a structure of devolved government across the UK. There are certain possible advantages to this.

- **Location** – the tax revenues raised in a region would by definition be spent within the region where they have been collected rather than, at present, disappearing into a large Exchequer pot in London. The fact that people would know that any increases in taxation would be spent in their region might improve transparency and reduce the hostility to increasing tax levels.
- **Hypothecation** – opinion polls suggest that increases in hypothecated taxation are more likely to be acceptable to the electorate than general taxation. In Wales, proposals have been made to introduce a hypothecated tax to finance future needs for adult social care but whether such an approach is ever introduced remains to be seen (Holtham 2018). In addition, proposals to introduce a UK hypothecated tax to support the NHS have been mooted. Again, increased hypothecation, at the regional (or national) level, might also reduce the hostility to increasing tax levels.

There is a snag here though. As already noted, the negligence of governments of all parties to the regions of the UK has led to huge social and economic inequalities between the South and the North. Thus, in the short/medium term, there is no possibility of regions outside the South East being able to raise sufficient revenues, locally, to finance their public services. This may be an aspiration for the longer term when the UK economy is more evenly balanced (see Chapter 6) but this is some way off. Hence for the foreseeable future the bulk of tax revenues will still need to be raised at national UK level and re-distributed among regions. However, the process for distribution of these nationally collected financial resources must be done in a manner that is transparent and one which bases the distribution of resources, between regions, according to need, however measured. The regions of the UK did not ask to be poor compared to London and the South East and this is a consequence of government neglect of regional economies by all political parties. Therefore, it is only fair that the UK government provides the resources needed by regions to develop their own economies. The recent announcement of the decision to keep the HS2 line from London to the Midlands but cancel the HS2 link to Leeds and cancel the trans-Pennine line is a clear example of such unfairness. The latter two developments are key to developing regional economies in the North while the HS2 is a London-centric vanity project and this decision is a classic example of London-centric thinking.

Charges

Changes could be made to the extent and magnitude of user charges. The political and administrative problems associated with them mean this is not likely to be a major source of additional revenues. However, it should be noted that charges could be useful in redirecting public behaviour, e.g. charge the drunks who constitute 30% of A&E users at peak time or charges to reduce the amount of domestic waste people create. In addition, countries like Sweden charge for visits to GPs when a practice nurse could have provided the same or better advice.

Curtailment and transfer

One approach to finance the new demands for public expenditure outlined in this chapter would be by transferring funds from existing public services. Clearly, this means reducing or curtailing these existing services and there is a difficulty in getting governments to face up to this issue.

There would be difficulties in releasing funds from major domestic public services such as schools, health, social care, and roads. However, there are other services where such reductions might seem more palatable such as defence and international aid. In Table 5.3, we show the situation of the UK compared to other comparable countries in Europe with regard to these two services.

It can be seen that, in the past, the UK committed more of its GDP to these two services than any of the other countries shown. In the UK, merely by moving back to the average for all the countries shown would release significant amounts of public funding for other public services. Such reductions would be hugely controversial and would be strongly opposed as was seen when the UK government announced it will be scaling back international aid to 0.5% of GDP, a decision which has now been reversed.

TABLE 5.3 Comparative analysis of UK public spending

Country	*Defence spending as a proportion of national GDP*	*International aid as a proportion of national GDP*
UK	2.1	0.7
Germany	1.3	0.6
France	1.9	0.4
Spain	0.8	0.2
Italy	1.4	0.2
Ireland	0.3	0.6
Holland	1.3	0.6

Source: Various.

Additional borrowing

Table 3.2 shows historic trends in UK public spending as a percentage of GDP. Two things were noticeable:

- The regular upward path of UK public spending as a percentage of GDP over a 110-year period.
- The two huge peaks of public spending represented by the costs associated with the two world wars.

During times of war, the need for public spending on armaments. was so great and so urgent that the only option available to governments was to borrow huge sums of money. These borrowings had to be repaid and it took until 2014 for the UK to repay, fully, debts incurred because of the First World War.

Thus, it seems this is the route the UK government will adopt in a similar manner to the way major wars were financed as the Covid-19 outbreak seems to have a wartime feel about it. Many political commentators are calling for the UK government to finance additional expenditure by more borrowing on the basis that interest rates are currently at a historic low. Thus, whatever happens in relation to taxation, it seems likely that governments in the UK and elsewhere will resort to additional borrowing and debt burdens will be greater than what would have been seen as acceptable ten or even five years ago. This whole debate seems to ignore the fact that loans have to be repaid or replaced and interest rates may rise.

How far can the government go with this debt strategy? Well essentially when it increases debt long term it is expropriating the assets owned by the public and private sectors because it effectively mortgages the value of these against the repayment of the debt. However, at present the public sector balance sheet after years of privatisation is net negative. That is the government owes more in debt than it owns in public assets. So, it must turn to the private sector for the mortgaging of assets. The private sector owns in total around 400%–500% of GDP. Theoretically, the government could go up to that level and simply expropriate all private assets. However, before it got that far it will begin to discover that the interest on debt repayment for the future plus the unavoidable costs of public service provision exceeded its ability to tax – a position with several the southern European countries were getting close to during the euro crisis. It would find as it approached such a level that the interest rate that it was charged for being able to fund that debt rose dramatically – as was the case in Portugal, Italy, Spain, and Greece. The general feeling is that at present the government can borrow at exceptionally low interest rates but if it started to borrow too much and those interest repayments rose to something of the order of 7%–10% then we will be in a serious long-term trouble. It could get the position we would never be able to reduce the principal on the debt. It is that constraint rather than the expropriation of total private assets which is likely to be binding. At present the government can borrow at incredibly low rates. An indication of how the market thinks that it's going in terms of future debt can be seen by looking at the way interest rates rise differentially between different countries.

However, many other countries will probably take the same approach and the global public debt burden will also grow. In 2019, global public debt amounted to a staggering $69 trillion ($69,000 billion) (Desjardin 2019), three quarters of which is held by just eight countries (including the UK). If the levels of Covid-related and other public expenditures discussed above were repeated, in these eight countries (which does not seem unrealistic), it does not seem far-fetched to imagine global debt could increase by a further15%–20%. These sums involved are astronomic and there are two dangers to consider:

- A global public debt crisis
- Inter-generational equity

Global public debt crisis

At present, many governments, including the UK, seem relaxed about further large-scale borrowing. Some economic commentators are also relaxed by the growing size of global debt and believe it to be manageable. However, others including the authors take a different view and see great dangers here. We take the view that many politicians and monetary economists have cavalier views about the size of public debt in terms of both individual countries and globally. The following claims are often made:

- Interest rates are currently very low and so we can borrow cheaply. This is true but, in years to come, interest rates may have risen and low interest rates will have to be replaced by higher interest loans which raises issues of affordability.
- Inflation in an economy will reduce debt levels in real terms. This is also true but ignores the fact that inflation hits the poor dis-proportionately.
- Economic growth will generate additional government revenues and allow debt to be repaid. However, it is not clear where this economic growth will come from particularly in an era where climate change must constrain economic growth.
- We can undertake quantitative easing to increase the money supply. This is true but there are no guarantees about its impact and it may debase a currency.
- Borrowing (as a percentage of GDP) currently falls below acceptable limits. This is true but it appears that what is termed "acceptable limits" keeps being raised. Surely, there must come a point where such borrowing levels are not acceptable and become unaffordable.

Writing for the World Economic Forum, Alcidi and Gros (2019) state,

> With very low interest rates, it is tempting for governments to spend more. However, while risk-free rates hover around zero in the euro area, high-debt countries face considerable risk premia that can lead to a feedback loop in which high-risk premia lead to higher debt, which in turn leads to ever higher risk premia.

Illustrative calculations by Alcidi and Gros show that under realistic assumptions, a debt ratio of 130% of GDP constitutes a critical threshold, where the line between sustainability and unsustainability is very thin. With a debt ratio above this "reference value", a government might struggle to cope with the cost of debt. The UK debt ratio of 2019 is now over 100% and will continue to rise substantially in years to come as outlined above. Before long, we may be approaching this threshold of sustainability.

Moreover, it is not just a question of the debt of an individual country but of the world as a whole. Faced with mounting global debt, international investors may increase their risk premium requirement still further. In such a situation, existing loans, when they mature, may have to be replaced with higher interest loans at significantly higher cost.

Given the levels of debt involved, some governments may come under pressure to reduce debt burdens and must, therefore, tread one of three broadly defined paths:

1 Pay back the borrowing through future increases in taxation. One possible way of avoiding the impact of additional borrowing and debt will be to impose a Tobin tax on international financial transactions which would have the additional benefit of acting to damp down global asset price booms which have been a feature of financial and economic stability in the past 30 years. The proceeds of this tax could then be used to help offset the costs of climate change as suggested by Piketty in his book *Capital and Ideology*.
2 Decide not to pay, or agree with creditors to pay less than they owe – history shows that countries that go down this track do not fare well.
3 Wait it out, rolling over their debts while hoping that they shrink relative to the economy over time. This involves either continued rapid economic growth (which seems unlikely given the threat of climate change) or rising inflation that will reduce the level of debt in real terms. However, higher rates of inflation will have very negative impacts on poorer parts of society and increase inequalities still further.

Moreover, if enough high-debt countries started to have difficulties in servicing or repaying their debt, this could lead to a global debt crisis on a scale not seen before in history.

Inter-generational equity

In all of this, an important factor to be borne in mind is that of inter-generational equity (IGE) or fairness between generations (Prowle and Klumpes 2013).

Many of the so-called "baby boomers" had the advantage of free university places, a free NHS, and a final salary pension scheme. As they get older, they will be placing increasing financial burdens on the health and social care system and extracting pensions well above what they have contributed to the state schemes. These benefits will, of course, be financed from the tax contributions of younger generations (who will, themselves, never receive the sorts of benefits received by older generations) or by government borrowing.

At the same time, older generations are sitting on a mountain of wealth in terms of property, savings, pension funds, etc. While this wealth may eventually pass to their children this is unlikely to occur before their children turn 60 and will be unevenly spread across the population. A further suggestion of Thomas Piketty (2014) is that a wealth tax could act to deliberately distribute wealth from an older generation who have accumulated it and give it as a grant or bonus payment to young people to enable them to acquire property or start a business.

Forecasts suggest that future generations will be far less affluent than current generations due, in part, to the need to address climate change. It is already the case that current levels of public borrowing and debt will be leaving future generations with the problem of servicing and repaying this debt. Increasing the debt to the levels discussed above will make this even more of a problem for future generations.

Laurence Kotlikoff is an American economist who served as economic advisor to President Ronald Reagan. Kotlikoff has written extensively on the issue of government debt and inter-generational equity. He once described American economic policy in the following terms:

> The Bible enjoins us to do better unto our children than we would do unto ourselves: "From generation to generation." But, in much of the developed world, our economic faith for the past six decades has been quite different: "Taketh from the young and giveth to the old".

Governments in the UK (and elsewhere) gleefully pile up debt without any consideration of how this is to be dealt with by future generations. Comments are often made that "*economic growth will solve the debt problem*" (which seems unlikely) or that "*debt is cheap at the moment*" (which seems to ignore the fact that ultimately this debt will have to be repaid or replaced by new debt at a higher rate of interest).

Now not everyone might agree with Kotlikoff's colourful language but the reality is that he is highlighting a major issue which is hardly ever discussed inside or outside government circles in any developed country. There seems almost a conspiracy of silence about such a major issue affecting future generations.

Conclusions

In the UK and globally, public expenditure can be expected to increase dramatically because of Covid-19 and other factors. The current situation seems to have parallels with that of the World Wars and governments can be expected to finance this new expenditure through additional borrowing, which, in turn, will raise national and global public debt to astronomical levels.

While there may be an argument, in the short term, for lowering taxes, to help the economy recover from the Covid pandemic, in the longer term, the UK tax burden must rise. These large increases in borrowing, in the UK, must be offset by significant increases in taxes on income and wealth. However, this does not seem likely to happen. Instead, governments will pursue vast amounts of borrowing which will add to national and public global debt with severe consequences for future generations.

However, there is something of a possible irony here. If the path of high borrowing does lead to a global debt crisis, as described above, then a possible consequence of this is that, to achieve some degree of stability, the lenders may be required to accept a "haircut" (meaning a write-off of some of the debt). This is what took place to resolve the Greek debt crisis which commenced in 2010 onwards but would be on a much bigger scale. Although different in magnitude and impact, this "haircut" might be seen as having some equivalence to a wealth tax described earlier but with far more dramatic consequences.

Dealing with the debt overhang is not a new issue. In his book *The Economic Consequences of the Peace*, John Maynard Keynes outlined the need for the combatants in the First World War to write off significant amounts of debt between countries in order to stabilise their economies for peacetime. The failure of the countries at the Versailles conference to see the importance of this, and particularly the reluctance of the United States to take a lead as the principal creditor nation, led to individual countries seeking to secure their debt position. The consequence was a boom in the United States in the 1920s and inflation created by excess monetary input recessions in the UK, France, and, above all, Germany (as France attempted to recover its debt position by transferring the cost to Germany in reparations). Subsequently, the Wall Street crash turned the recessions in the combatant nations into depression which became a material factor in the rise of fascism, but also provided an essential economic boost as the nations geared up for the inevitable war that followed.

Overall, this looks a daunting agenda for the next few decades but it need not be. All that needs to happen is for our social and economic problems to be addressed rationally and without ideological baggage. Fundamentally, it does also require fundamental and far-reaching reforms to the way in which the UK state is organised and functions but that is a topic for another day.

References

Abdo, H. (2021), COP26: paying for the transition to sustainable energy, https://www.nottingham.ac.uk/vision/cop26-paying-for-the-transition-to-sustainable-energy?mc_cid=f0ba4eff2e&mc_eid=3c2a29f27b

Alcidi, C. and Gross, D. (2019), Public debt and the risk premium: a dangerous doom loop, semantic scholar, https://www.semanticscholar.org/paper/Pub-lic-debt-and-the-risk-premium-%3A-A-dangerous-Alcidi-Gros/3c0e883b1119ab333baf61c83d-9655fb9218bbae

Caeiro, J.P. and Garzon, M.L. (2018), Controlling infectious disease outbreaks in low-income and middle-income countries, https://pubmed.ncbi.nlm.nih.gov/32226321/

Collier, P. and Betts, A. (2017), *Refuge: Rethinking Refugee Policy in a Changing World*, Oxford University Press.

Desjardin, J. (2019), $69 Trillion of world debt in one infographic, visual capitalist, https://www.visualcapitalist.com/69-trillion-of-world-debt-in-one-infographic/

Equality Trust, The scale of economic inequality in the UK, https://equalitytrust.org.uk/scale-economic-inequality-uk

Hammond, P. (2019), Climate change: emissions target could cost UK £1trillion warns Hammond, *BBC*, 6 June 2019.

Holtham, G. (2018), Paying for social care, an independent report commissioned by the welsh government, https://gov.wales/sites/default/files/publications/2018-11/paying-for-social-care.pdf

House of Commons Library (2019), Local government finance and the 2019 Spending Review.

House of Commons Library (2020), The structure of the NHS in England, June 2020.

House of Commons Library (2021), Tax statistics: an overview, October 2021, https://commonslibrary.parliament.uk/research-briefings/cbp-8513/

IfG (2019), Police performance tracker, institute for government.

King, B. (2021), How much is Covid costing the UK and how will we pay? *BBC*, 22 June 2021.

Nuffield Trust (2012), Briefing on the health committee: public expenditure inquiry, October 2012.

ONS (2018), Total wealth in Great Britain: April 2016 to March 2018, Office for national statistics, December 2019.

ONS (2020), Public sector finances, UK: April 2020, Office for National Statistics, April 2020.

ONS (2021), UK government debt and deficit: December 2021. Office for National Statistics, December 2021.

Piketty, T. (2014), *Capital in the Twenty-First Century*, Harvard University Press.

Prowle, M.J. and Klumpes, P. (2013), *What Lies Beneath*, Public Finance December 2013.

Smith, A. (1776), *The Wealth of Nations*, W. Strahan and T. Cadel.

Stern, N. (2006), *The Economics of Climate Change*, Cambridge University Press.

PART C

Public policies and public services under a regional government model

6

REGIONAL ECONOMIC DEVELOPMENT

Roger Latham

Introduction

The first chapter in Part C of this book concerns regional economic development. In many ways, this is the most important chapter, since a robust and buoyant economy is essential for every region in order to generate prosperity for its residents and funds for its public services.

We have already discussed the huge economic imbalances across the UK that have existed for many decades and which have largely been ignored by governments of all parties in favour of maintaining a buoyant economy in London and the South East. In the light of such failures of economic development policy, we now see it as essential that regional governments have the power and capacity to develop their own economies freed of outside interference.

In this chapter we will be looking at the thinking that lies behind the policies of economic development, the current issues that it faces, and how our proposals for regionalisation would bear upon those issues.

In making our assessment, I have utilised my personal experiences of working for many years in local economic development as well as some new research. In addition to document reviews, I have undertaken a number of interviews with those in the devolved UK nations working in this area, and with individuals involved in regional economic development in key countries identified by the EU as having a substantially federal as opposed to a unitary structure, referred to in Chapter 3.

The chapter is structured as follows:

- The nature of economic development
- Economic development policies – unitary versus federal states
- Why regionalism?

DOI: 10.4324/9781003201892-9

- Regional economic development policy and strategy
- Potential blockages

The nature of economic development policy

So, what exactly constitutes economic development policy? At its heart it consists of public sector interventions in the modern market economy to address:

- Activities to encourage business investment and innovation
- The provision of common infrastructure to support economic activity, and, particularly in more recent times, actions to deal with issues of externalities (where a particular economic activity has impacts, financial or otherwise, which lie outside the enterprise undertaking the activity)
- Issues of geographic, income, and wealth inequalities that have social implications
- The "tragedy of the commons" where individual activities utilising a common resource overuse that resource to its ultimate destruction (be that physical resources like water, mineral resources, or animal resources like fishing)

The kinds of policy initiatives utilised in economic development include:

- The prohibition of certain economic activities like child employment or slavery
- The use of taxation policy to encourage certain kinds of economic activity and discourage others – such as capital allowances for research and development and innovation
- The giving of grants, loans, and subsidies to encourage economic decisions to be taken in ways which meet the physical and social objectives set in government plans
- Steps to encourage savings and the provision of adequate private sector liquidity as a resource for corporate investment
- The provision of common physical infrastructure
- Taxation and subsidies aimed at reducing inequalities
- The use of permissions, authorities, and approvals to shape the pattern of economic activity
- Regulatory bodies that can control excessive competition concentration, or to support consumers against oligopolistic or monopolistic markets which might otherwise act to their detriment
- Activities, such as privatisation, that aim to control the overuse of the "commons" by handing them over to the private sector, or regulate, by use of licences, extraction of resources by private sector operators

These are a wide range of possible initiatives, and new ideas such as enterprise zones or free ports can commonly be introduced to see if they will achieve overall economic objectives. But on the whole economic development function is set within an explicit set of government objectives. In recent years, issues of inequality have begun to exercise many governments with ideas being canvassed to help the "just managing" or to "level up" those who have been "left behind" within the developing economy. However, in the past, technology and innovation has been a specific government objective with the "white heat of technology" the cliché of the day in the 1960s, or with concerns being expressed about the relative lack of productivity in the UK economy compared to its continental rivals. A developing area of economic development policy is concern to "green the economy" and to achieve "net zero carbon" in response to the developing climate change crisis.

We must recognise that the economic development function of public services is not one whose validity has been universally recognised by all parties. Indeed, at several points in the past Government Ministers with responsibility for economic development policy have questioned whether they should be doing anything at all with their department or in their service area. Sir Keith Joseph, one of the principal architects of the Thatcher revolution, questioned whether the Department of Trade and Industry should exist at all, and more recently the current Business Minister, Kwasi Kwarteng, has suggested that the traditional activities of the economic function should be redirected. In both cases they are responding to an economic orthodoxy that has become dominant since the 1980s.

Recently, Mark Carney (2021) in his book *Values* has drawn attention to three commonly held views about the market economy: (1) the market always clears; (2) the market always reflects values in the price; and, what he considers to be the most deceptive four words in the English language, (3) *this time it is different.* History, he maintains, shows that these three statements are false. The market does not always clear – significant resources are unemployed; prices do not reflect the values society attaches to activity – health and care workers are highly valued but poorly paid, whilst the common view of bankers is reversed; worst of all we do not seemingly learn from economic disasters – instead, we tell ourselves that "this time it will be different". Part of the reason for this is that many politicians, business leaders, financiers, and entrepreneurs remain wedded to outdated economic thinking.

> The power of economic theory is greater than is generally imagined. Indeed, the world is ruled by little else. Practical men of affairs, who believe themselves to be quite immune from its influences, are usually the slaves of some defunct economist and madmen in authority who hear voices in the air are distilling their frenzy from some academic scribbler of a few years back.

So, wrote John Maynard Keynes in the preface to his 1935 "General Theory", and he never said a truer word! So, despite the fact that the current economic theory is a matter of great contention, in this chapter we will be looking specifically at the question of whether a more regionalised structure would be likely to deliver better and more sustainable economic development strategies aimed at achieving key objectives such as "levelling up", improving productivity, and achieving "net zero carbon" economies.

Economic development policies – unitary versus federal states

In Chapter 3 we referred to the view of historians that the "glue" that held together the UK in the past had been "Protestantism, Empire, and war", noting that each of these three elements was now much diminished in significance. We also noted the dominance of England, where the unitary central authority, dominated as it was by London, still exhibits a hangover of the imperial attitudes expressed by politicians and the Executive who hanker after an often mythical past a period of power and a desire to "take back control" and re-establish political independence. This attitude becomes very apparent in looking at the way that economic development policies are both formulated and implemented in the UK.

In England, in 2010, regional economic development agencies were abolished and the idea of economic regions was effectively made non-existent. Such local economic planning as exists is strictly on a small scale. Most of the significant economic policies continue to be determined and delivered at West minster/Whitehall. There is some degree of autonomy in respect of directly elected Mayoralties, and this is most significant in London, but even their local policies are subject to overall national approval and there is no independence of funding.

The devolved governments of Scotland, Wales, and Northern Ireland have discretion over their own economic development polices but the funding for these policies must be drawn from the block grant, receivable from the UK government, to finance all of the public services for which they are responsible. Hence, any additional spending on economic development must, by definition, take away resources from health, schools, etc. In other words, there is an opportunity cost involved. Furthermore, the devolved governments have no control or influence over the key economic issues of fiscal policy, monetary policy, and trade policy. These are the province of the UK government.

In the past, when the UK was part of the EU, the support for economic development, regionally, was through the European Regional Development Fund, but even then plans had to be approved centrally, and the central government resented any direct discussions between regions under the EU either locally, or through the numerous local European Regional Development Offices established by Brussels. With the departure of the UK from the EU, the European funding is to be replaced by a national fund, and any suggestion of local autonomy has been further reduced by the decision of central government to control this funding itself. This pattern of over-centralisation of planning and funding seems, however, to be a function of a unitary government, for in Wales the independent Welsh regional development agency was also disbanded and taken into the arrangements of the Welsh Government, thus showing that the tendency to centralise can operate at a devolved as well as a national level. This tendency of national governments to bypass devolved administrations in respect of economic development was also clearly seen in the response of the UK government to the threat of a second Scottish referendum on independence where significant investment plans were agreed at a central government level without reference to the devolved administrations.

This "Imperial" attitude of the central government in the UK extends to Northern Ireland which oscillates between an unstable devolved administration and a direct rule from Westminster but it is also a feature of other unitary states. The Republic of Ireland has arrangements for regional organisations to meet EU requirements, but it is quite clear that they exist in name only, and that all planning must be approved at national government level as does the necessary funding arrangements.

Contrast this with the varying federal arrangements that exist elsewhere in the EU. What emerges as a key feature is that the arrangements in federated states do not follow any kind of uniform pattern, but are highly influenced by the culture and history of the nation. So, for example, the Spanish federal system must recognise that the nation is largely composed of separate statelets which have shown functional, social, and linguistic differences. It is essentially a national central state built of separate federated states. In recognition of this the arrangements federally vary from region to region. Some areas such as Catalonia, the Basque country, Navarre, and Galicia have a high degree of autonomy in terms of economic development and its funding. Other areas are more subject to central economic development planning and funding, whilst some areas, like Andalusia, have negotiated an intermediate status. Within Spain there is a constant tension between the pressures for greater levels of independence and the integrity of the national state, and these are reflected in economic development functions and powers, reflecting that connection between economic development functions and other public services.

The situation in Belgium is quite different. Here the linguistic, cultural, and historical differences between French-speaking Wallonia and Dutch-speaking Flanders have been the subject of some violence and conflict even in recent times. The federal arrangements that have therefore developed give a high degree of autonomy, and especially economic development autonomy to the various regions, and the federal regional arrangements are overlain by linguistic cultural arrangements in addition, giving an overlap of functions between the national government, regions, and linguistic groups. The degree of economic development independence gives rise to considerable pressures with the increasing economic dominance of the Flemish regions putting pressure on the stability of the state in the longer term.

Different arrangements apply in Germany, which was unified (along with Italy) relatively late in the 19th century and was dominated for many years by Prussia (just as Italy was dominated by the Piedmont/Lombardy region). Within

Germany the regional groups, the Laender, have considerable autonomy and the federal system is very much an amalgamation of the powers of the individual regions. Within a bicameral system, changes to the federal law must be approved both by the national parliament and by a council of the regions. In terms of economic development, Laender have considerable autonomy and the financial competence to carry through their individual policies. After being dominated for such a long time by Prussia the German arrangements militate against the over-dominance of one region, and this can lead to a slow response to issues of structural regional imbalances or national issues within a globalised economy.

Why regionalism?

With such a variation in the arrangements for economic development within federal states it is reasonable to ask why this book is promoting the idea of a federal/regional arrangement for the UK. The matter is even more complicated when you look at some of the arrangements for existing unitary states within the EU. Poland, for example, is regarded as a unitary state but it provides a significant degree of autonomy to its regions on economic development matters. Austria is similarly a unitary state, but it is able to bring forward regional development proposals that are acceptable to all its regional groupings. Where regions have been introduced they are not always free from controversy. France introduced a significant regional element having been one of the most centralised of unitary states in the past (a position which is now probably held by the UK), but in doing so it failed to sort out the arrangements between the existing department and the regional level for economic development. Consequently, something of a "turf war" has developed. So why regionalism for the UK?

We identified from our research these four key reasons:

- Replacing the glue
- Greater democratisation
- Promoting the powerhouse rather than the victim
- Achieving greater integration

In saying this, one point needs to be made clear from the beginning. In promoting regionalism, we are not promoting the idea of the breakup of the UK into its constituent units. Quite the opposite. We see the development of regional federal arrangement as being the only way the UK can remain united. This is a theme that runs through the whole book.

Replacing the glue

If the glue which held together the UK during the imperial past is no longer relevant or effective, the danger is always that the different historic, social, and cultural differences between the various parts of the UK, and within England between London and the rest of England, will lead to pressures to assert that independence politically and economically. The greatest danger is that of a democratic deficit where people lose their trust in politics and politicians and seek instead to determine their fate for themselves. It is a truism of management theory that if people have not been involved or consulted in making a decision they do not own that decision and its implications. In a situation where the imperial attitude of the Westminster government results in the imposition of economic policies that worsen regional economic inequalities, this will lead to tensions which will damage the Union. The work of John Rawls (1971) clearly indicates that for stability in society it is essential that the weakest are protected and that there is genuine equality of opportunity. One of the fundamental points of equality of opportunity lies in education, which is grossly unequal at present and depends critically on the income of parents, and thus perpetuates income and wealth inequality in long-term. It is even more critical because there is a clear link between the overall level of education and skills in a community and its ultimate productivity in economic terms. A greater equality of opportunity in education is in the interests of all. In the mid-Victorian period the upper and middle classes realised that improvements in public health for the working classes also benefited themselves through the reduction of endemic infectious disease. Perhaps 21st-century societies need to learn the same lesson in respect of universal, and equitable, education – to the highest levels.

Greater democratisation

This involves, effectively, acting as a means of protecting the weakest which starts at all levels. Whilst shareholders who provided capital for enterprise need to have their interests safeguarded, they cannot be at the expense of those who work for the enterprise, or for the greater community within which the enterprise functions. So, democratisation of the individual enterprise through worker councils, membership of boards, and the development of alternative types of enterprise into social enterprises and cooperatives is a step forward. Such initiatives have been operating since the Second World War in German and Nordic countries, and although not perfect, the criticism that this approach impacts on productivity and exacerbates wages to an unreasonable share of the enterprises surpluses has been shown to be false.

Powerhouse or victim?

All the recent talk of government about "levelling up" or "the left behind communities" or individuals who are "just managing" recognises the inequalities which often go back to a great many decades and the consequences of successive economic revolutions from the Industrial Revolution to the current changes in nanotechnology, artificial intelligence, and DNA technologies which have been described as the "Fourth Industrial Revolution". Such changes, according to Joseph Schumpeter (1942), are episodes of "creative destruction" whereby older technologies are destroyed in favour of the development of new technologies. With this inevitably go changes in employment with older jobs and skills being lost, often before new skills and employment are created. But for those areas where older technologies are now to be made redundant the replacement does not take place in the same geographic area. All the heavy industries of the North that were prominent in the 19th century were not replaced by technologies based on electricity and internal combustion engine which were instead based in London and the South East, close to their critical consumer markets. In the past the adjustment to such changes has been made by way of emigration, but this often leaves behind the less economically mobile, and generally older population. The phrases being used of such communities often look at them as if they were victims, and they often feel that they are victims. There is an underlying sense of resentment on both sides as a result. It was this sense of resentment that was a driving force behind the Brexit referendum decision when regions in England outside of London (which voted Remain) voted Leave and helped to create the tensions that now exist between England and Scotland, and Northern Ireland (both of which voted Remain) and a developing mood for independence in Wales (which supported Leave, but only marginally). But in a federal regional system it would be possible to change that victimhood into one of developing local unused potential. Instead of becoming the helpless casualties of change, a regional economic development plan could seek to utilise and redevelop natural resources so that they were a net contributor towards national income, rather than people who were subsidised from more economically prosperous areas. In the past this has been described as "powerhouse", but more often that has been a hollow and pretentious phrase rather than a reality. The classical economist David Ricardo (1817) in developing his thinking about the economy introduced the concept of trade through comparative advantage, showing that even if a nation had an absolute advantage in all areas, it still profited from the global outcome if each country traded in the area to which it had the greatest absolute productivity and efficiency. The same is true for a region as well as a nation. By trading on comparative advantage – whatever that might be – a region could develop its own, independent, functioning economy. An example can be taken from the United States where the town of Rochester, Minnesota is home to the Mayo Clinic – a complex of medical and hospital facilities that have an international reputation. The comparative advantage here was that the Mayo brothers were physicians who were born there. But from that small beginning the whole area has now got a sustainable economy based on health specialists and research. Historically in Victorian times towns often had entrepreneurs who placed their businesses there because they lived there. That might not be the case for all regions and areas, but the idea of comparative advantage and the utilisation of local unused resources would be a powerful and different approach to economic development regionally, and one that would benefit the whole nation. The alternative is to look at each region as being in competition with every other region. The competitive model is not particularly helpful. A past critique of the regional development plans submitted to the central government for approval was that they were remarkably similar – almost identical. They tended to concentrate on the same key developing technologies and growing industries and saw themselves as competing with other regions to gain a share of a limited market of inward investment. Such approaches rarely created new economic enterprise, but often only resulted in the displacement of activity from one area to another, often heavily subsidised from the public purse. In a centrally run economic development approach, such as we have in the UK at present, proposals to regenerate an area are often based on heavy investment into infrastructure, which is nonetheless almost always deficient in the improvements demanded by an over-dominant capital city region, and by having new designated initiatives aimed at creating a competitive advant age – such as enterprise zones, free ports, and the like. More often than not these only serve to displace activity from one region to another, and the benefits rarely go to the individual enterprises within such designated zones but tend to be shared with local property developers. Ricardo also introduced the concept of rent as a deadweight on economic enterprise and growth, robbing the economic system of profit and liquidity to enable it to expand and develop. The concept of "rent seeking" – the manipulation of the economy to maximise a share of economic surplus – was his idea also and becomes a significant issue in such initiatives.

Greater integration

As discussed later there are strong linkages between economic development planning and other public services. A regional/federal structure would allow a degree of greater integration between education, health, physical environment, housing, and even cultural public services. What is extremely difficult to create at the top of a hierarchical pyramid of control becomes much easier if the task is split up between regions which are responsible for pulling together and integrating their local economies with the necessary public support services. But to do so there is one important necessary condition – regions must have the ability not only to develop their economic plans independently but also to have the flexibility to deliver those plans by being financially competent. This means the ability not only to raise taxation but also to finance development by issuing debt independently backed by taxation resources. In some federal states the competence of regions financially is constitutionally guaranteed. The German regions have an agreed share of taxation, even though this taxation might be set at national level and collected there. They can also raise debt independently, but with the understanding that each region must produce a balanced set of accounts and a net zero balance sheet each year. There may be variations at year end but taking one year with another the accounts should balance. This was the principal control exercised in the UK of local authorities when they still had the ability to raise funds independently – and it is a highly effective one. It means that no region could entertain deficit financing, and such issues of macroeconomic policy remain at national level – albeit that any changes need the approval in their bicameral system of a Council of Regions.

One of the more problematic areas in national economic policy concerns monetary policy. One of the standard criticisms of the UK system is that such policies are decided, independently of government, by the Monetary Policy Committee of the Bank of England. However, this is dominated by members from London and the South East who are more heavily influenced by the needs of the City of London as a finance centre, though its consequences for interest rates may have significant effects on industrial investment in regions outside London. As Alexander Hamilton noted when proposing a single currency for the new USA, the need for a single currency binds the individual regions/states together. There cannot be a nation that has separate monetary policies for the regions. But in Germany this difficulty is partly overcome by me ensuring that each region has representatives on the decision-making body of the Bundes bank – an arrangement that could be copied. One of the inevitable consequences of giving regions financial competence is that the individual regions do not start off from an equal position. Indeed, a substantial part of the current difficulties comes about because regional inequalities are substantial and have been growing in the recent past. So, some form of financial arrangement between regions to redistribute funds more equitably seems inevitable. The problem here is that such arrangements tend to become too rigid and fixed. In the UK the Barnett formula was established in the late 1970s as a means of ensuring a distribution of funds towards Wales, Scotland, and Northern Ireland. The formula has proved almost impossible to shift, even though circumstances have changed. The same problem, we found in our interviews, exists in Germany where there is a formula that distributes the taxation proceeds between regions. Whilst this helps with planning for the public services in each region, and variations in the pattern of taxation between direct and indirect taxation are accounted for by the formula, shifting it significantly has not been possible. In part this comes about because the actual level of "free" resources available for redirection within such formulas is generally small – typically less than 5% of the total – the rest being taken up with existing commitments. In the past in Germany only significant issues such as the need to "level up" the former East Germany within a unified German state saw an agreement to vary the formula over time. The ability of a single region to argue for variations in the formula is usually counter-productive, as this can usually only be achieved at the expense of other regions. The design of any distributional formula, within a regional federal arrangement for the UK, would need to consider not only the shifting pattern of inequality between regions but also the impact of distributional policy. If a comparative advantage approach is adopted, one of its measures of success will be that each region would receive a declining level of central subsidy – even if that agreement comes through a federal council of regions decision.

Regional economic development policy and strategy

In the UK, Wales, Scotland, and Northern Ireland there are already established economic development functions. However, England has no regional economic infrastructure and so English regions would have to start developing regional economic policy from virtually a zero base.

In this section I consider the main issues concerning economic development policy within a regional government. The situation is summarised in Figure 6.1:

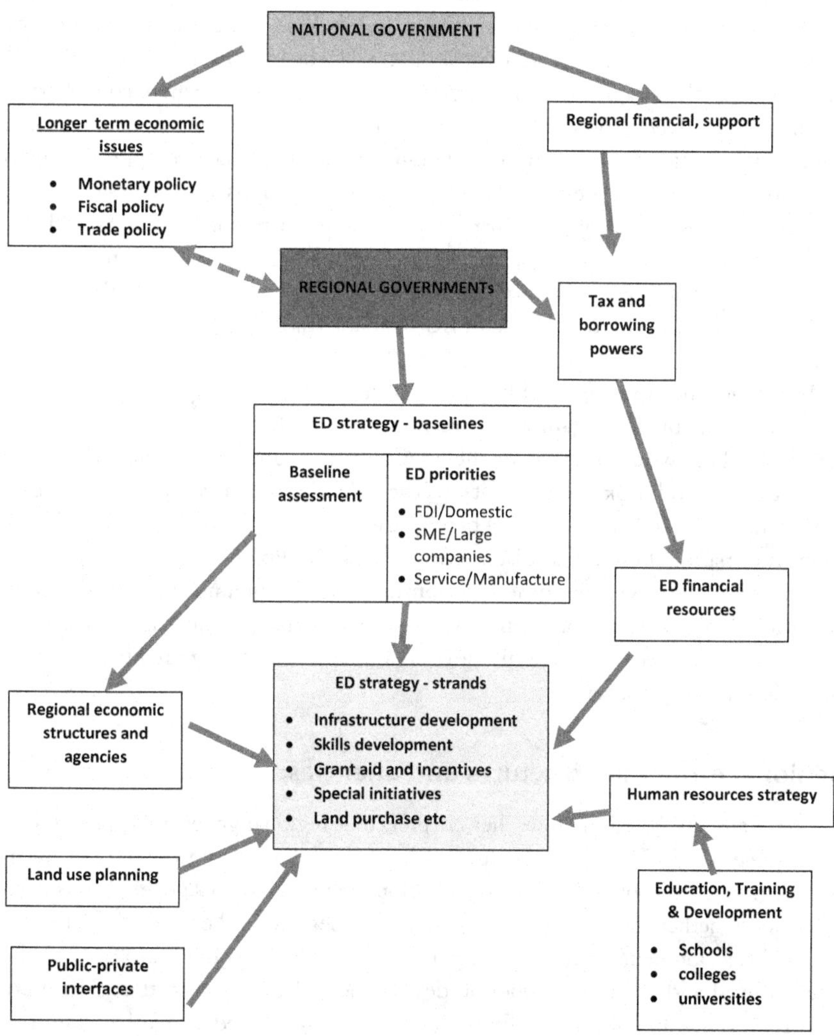

FIGURE 6.1 Regional economic development

Longer term economic issues

There are three specific issues which have major implications for regional economic policy. These are:

- Monetary policy
- Fiscal policy
- Trade policy

The UK is a nation state and, thus, it is inevitable that policy in relation to these three issues is the province of national UK government. However, it is important that policy formulation in these three areas takes place in the context of the regional economic situation across the UK and not just the London economic situation. As the diagram illustrates, there needs to be a formal consultation mechanism between the UK government, the Bank of England, and regional governments regarding any policy changes. Indeed, it may be appropriate to have some regional representation in these matters. This is something which happens in other developed countries and we see no reason why it should not happen here. Indeed, some countries go even further and regions may have a veto on, for example, trade policy. In 2016, lawmakers in the small Belgian region of Wallonia voted to block an EU-Canada trade deal which then required renegotiation.

In relation to these three policy areas, it may be also thought appropriate to alter the remit of the organisations responsible for these policies (e.g. Bank of England). This would be that in their deliberations and in making their decisions, they should look at the equity of their decisions across the UK as well as the overall UK national picture. There is always a balance to be struck between growth in national GDP and distribution of that GDP growth.

There may also be some other economic matters which need to be addressed at national level. This could include regulatory matters such as competition policy and financial services regulation. Again, appropriate regional involvement is needed in these matters.

Regional economic structures and agencies

We have already noted, in an earlier chapter, that regional governments should be responsible for deciding the structure of local government and other agencies in their region. This applies to economic development and regional governments need to decide whether there should be separate agencies (along the lines of the former regional development agencies) or a part of regional government itself. Also, the roles of local authorities in economic development should be clarified. These are important issues. In our research for this book, we have learned from other countries that failure to clarify these issues early on can lead to problems decades later.

Regional economic strategy – baselines

As there is with any form of strategy, there are a number of baseline tasks which need to be done. These include:

- **Baseline assessment** – there is a need to undertake an honest and robust baseline assessment of the state of a regional economy including its strengths and weaknesses. There are many issues to cover including the following: transport infrastructure, telecommunications infrastructure, skills base, financial resources.
- **Priorities** – it is impossible to try and cover all possible dimensions of a regional economy in the same time period and choices about priority areas need to be made. This is often politically difficult and it may be that some attention will need to be given to all areas of activity with a greater emphasis on just a few areas.

Economic development resources

The implementation of a regional economic strategy will require significant financial resources. In the longer term, it is to be hoped that regional economies will improve to the stage where local tax-raising powers will be sufficient to fund public finance requirements including that for economic development purposes. However, in the medium term, the scale of economic inequality in the UK means that this will not be possible and regional governments will need financial support from the federal government drawn from centrally levied taxation. However, these funds will need to be distributed between regions in an *equitable and transparent manner* which is not, as has already been noted, the current situation.

Economic development strategy – strands

The economic development strategy of a region will inevitably comprise a number of diverse but interconnected strands. The composition of these strands will vary from region to region, as a consequence of different regional circumstances. This is a large part of the rationale for a regional government whereby policies are based on locally defined needs and not on a "one size fits all" approach from the national government. Just a few examples of the sorts of strands which might be found in a regional economic development policy include:

- Infrastructure development in relation to transportation, buildings, telecommunications, etc.
- Skills development to meet the workforce needs of the economy in the future

- Grant aid and incentives – financial incentives to current or prospective companies to make investments in the region
- Special initiatives – projects such as science parks and business parks
- Strategic land purchases where additional land is felt to be needed, at sometime in the future, for economic development purposes

Land use strategy

There are a number of other influencing factors which impinge on economic development strategy and must be considered alongside it. The first of these concerns regional land use.

The UK has a large population located on a relatively small land mass. Thus, land as a resource is often scarce in many parts of the country, particularly in urban areas. There is often much competition for this scarce land from the needs of housing, recreation, public services, parklands as well as various business needs. Thus, land use must be a key aspect of regional economic development strategy and economic strategies must take account of the future needs for and availability of land to support its economic objectives. This land use strategy will form part of the overall strategic physical planning of the region and will consider a variety of issues such as land purchases, land divestments, re-designation of land for specific activities, and clearance of derelict land. Under a regional government arrangement, the existence of regional planning law and policies will facilitate the development of local land use strategies which are more relevant to the needs of the region and are not constrained by national controls.

Human resource strategy

The second factor concerns human resources. Ensuring that the region has the numbers and types of human resources needed to support its businesses is a key task for the regional government. Attempts must be made to forecast the skill needs of the regional economy for (say) the next decade and the likely shortfalls and surpluses if no actions were taken. The human resource needs of the business economy are, of course, just part of the larger task of human resource planning in the region as it is also an important task in relation to public services. Thus, human resource planning must be an integrated task for the whole region. The issue of regional human resource planning is discussed further in Chapter 12.

However, whilst there are various approaches at attempting to get the required volumes and types of skills needed in the region a key factor is the role of various education training and development organisations within the region. This encompasses schools, colleges, universities, and private training providers.

Public-private interfaces

Public services and the business economy in a region are inextricably linked and this must be recognised. Business development and investment may often need to be supported by the existence or development of public services such as roads, buildings accommodation, and training. However, public services also need to keep in mind the role they play in relation to regional businesses. A key aspect of this concerns public procurement and the attitude of public services towards local businesses. The possibility and potential role of public-private partnerships (PPP) in relation to economic development also need to be kept in mind. In some parts of the UK, such approaches are frowned upon from an ideological standpoint but we suggest that a pragmatic approach to such possibilities should be taken by regional governments.

Potential blockages

Whilst we believe the reasoning behind moving towards a federal arrangement for the UK is unassailable and would have big advantages, we also recognise that it is going to be extremely difficult to achieve. We anticipate blockages and difficulties which would need to be addressed. These are as follows:

Contradiction of economic thinking

There are often inherent contradictions in economic thinking. The incoming Conservative Government in 2020 made it one of their priorities to "level up" the "left behind" "Northern powerhouses", and this heaping up of clichés is perhaps indicative that whilst it's the government's intent to do so, then it may find actually achieving this rather more problematic for the following reasons:

- Despite its immediate attempts to reverse the public expenditure and investment cuts of a decade of austerity, its new proposals do little to repair the long-term damage. They certainly do not do anything like as much as would be required to undo all the years of austerity – at best they put a stop to the continuing rot of public services.
- The current government remains committed to a long-term process of debt reduction as a percentage of GDP, and it will find it difficult, if not impossible, to deliver this objective at the same time as "levelling up" the income and investment deficiencies of the traditional northern regions. There is an inherent policy conflict here unless they are prepared to reduce resources going to London and the South East.
- There is a potential policy conflict in that the Brexit process that might create some recessionary impact on the UK, in the short term, and to the loss of manufacturing and service bases in the UK. The impact of this will be

most keenly felt in precisely the regions which the government now wishes to "level up".

- The impact of the pandemic has set back any actions to deal with inequality very significantly. Not only was the impact greater in many of the "left behind" communities, but the differentials in education, the availability of IT support for students, the differential impact on employment prospects for young people – particularly in entertainment and hospitality industries – all have tended to exacerbate existing inequalities, making the government's target harder to achieve without some incredibly significant changes.
- The intergenerational inequalities are becoming particularly acute as the impacts of the climate change crisis become more evident. For every year in which the collective failure of willpower, to address the changes needed, this means that future generations face a harder and harder time of transition to promote a liveable environment.

There remains a strong possibility that these levelling up policies will be "too little, too late" with the possibility that there may be a considerable voter backlash, and potential exit to populist minority parties, born out of dashed expectations.

So, we argue that notwithstanding these policy initiatives, the changes that the government is proposing do not meet the two issues that fundamentally need to change – the abandonment of the policy of neoliberal economic thinking, and a concerted effort towards greater democratisation. Without the former the government will be saddled with an economic theory that exacerbates regional inequality and leaves the most vulnerable open to the impact of poorer public services and greater globalisation. Without the latter there is the risk of greater disenchantment with the political process, since it is a well-known management dictum that where people are not involved in taking a decision in a meaningful sense, they do not own the decision that is subsequently taken.

Release of power

The second blockage will be the difficulty experienced by the existing UK central government in giving up power. In this book, we envisage not an addition to the existing governance system, but as Chapters 3 and 4 have indicated a significant slimming down of the existing national government and the distribution of its powers to the regions. We do not see this as happening easily. The centralising tendencies of the present government are well known but we must remember that previous governments (of all political parties) have all had strong centralising tendencies, to a lesser or greater degree and we do not see this changing. A future government might, for example, re-instate regional development agencies (abolished in 2010) but this would be pointless if these RDAs were still subject to close central control from Whitehall and have limited powers of action, as was the case prior to 20201 by a Labour government.

The history of other European countries shows that changes such as we describe have been achieved but this has usually been as a consequence of war, invasion, revolution or a combination of these. In the UK, none of the above seem likely or desirable. Hence, we are looking for a process of peaceful and democratic change as took place with the 1999 devolution changes.

As noted throughout this book we see little chance of any of these changes taking place because of the dominance of many and varied powerful vested interests in London (see below) which would resist such changes. We would love to be proved wrong but we don't think this will happen. In the light of this we foresee three things could happen:

- A failure of the populist agenda to deliver the promises being made could result in a complete collapse of trust and a loss of face, with a public demand for a major reversal of policies – possibly with community violence involved as occurred in Belgium in the 1970s.
- A series of uncontrolled crisis points that could include a potential breakup of the UK, or an existential crisis of climate change, where the central administration was simply unable to cope and by default localised solutions involving the transfer of power took place.
- A catastrophic collapse, followed by a deliberate intention to ensure that the disaster "never happened again", such as occurred in Germany and Italy following the Second World War, and the re-democratisation of Spain after the fascist regime of Franco.

This is drastic, but a sober reflection on what could be the worst-case scenario but it might just promote a sea change in attitudes on the key issues of managing the economy to meet the values of the community, and the defence of democratic values.

Dominance of London

The third blockage concerns the issues of the dominance of London and the South East in economic development terms. A regional federal system works best when the regions are roughly balanced in economic terms. In other countries the dominance of a single region always creates something of a difficulty – as in Italy, Germany, or Spain – in the UK the issue would be the dominance of London and the South East. Whilst the lowering of the national government profile and the redistribution to the regions would help, part of the success of such a regional approach will be to lower the pressures on London in terms of infrastructure, housing, and population. Such a transition would inevitably result in the alienation of certain assets, particularly housing and other property assets, which are at unsustainably high price levels which create an internal London market of debt dependence on which would have serious consequences if asset prices were to fall significantly. Some care would have to be addressed to the transitioning arrangements of a significant constitutional change.

Political competence

The final issue that needs to be addressed is political competences as it has been experienced in Germany and would likely be repeated in the UK if it adopted a similar federal arrangement. It is perhaps inevitable that politicians look to the short term, being dominated by an election cycle, but there is also the danger in a regional arrangement that local politicians become exceedingly parochial which means that at a national level the approach to global issues such as tax havens, the impact of globalisation, and climate change will have a tendency for them to be ignored, or the response to them significantly delayed. However, it is also the case that within the existing devolved regions local policies have been set on key issues like climate change and intergenerational issues so that it is not necessarily the case that these issues do not get addressed – the issue may be one of national coordination rather than indifference.

Conclusion

The basic messages of this chapter are threefold.

The first is that successive UK governments, over many decades, have failed in the task of rejuvenating regional economies outside the South East, in order to reduce the large inequalities across the UK. Whilst this comment is true of all political parties, one might suggest that Labour governments are most at fault for failing to rejuvenate the economies of the North of England and Wales, this being their traditional areas and the places where their electoral strength lay. As they say, "chickens come home to roost" and we have seen the impact of this failure in the breaching of Labour's "red wall" in the North of England. One wonders how, in 2018, a hundred Labour MPs could vote to construct a third runway at Heathrow Airport with a cost in excess of £50 billion. A fraction of the money spent on this vanity project for the South East could have revolutionised the transport infrastructure and economic performance of large parts of the UK outside of London.

Second, improvements in economic output in English regions will have positive implications for the prosperity of residents and their ability to better fund public services in those regions.

Third, elected regional governments in England should have economic development powers in line with those of the current devolved governments. However, these powers need to be significantly enhanced beyond what is currently found in Wales, Scotland, and Northern Ireland to bring them in line with what is found in regional governments in other large European countries.

Finally, regional governments need to develop effective strategies for the development of their economies, making full use of the powers granted to them.

References

Carney, M. (2021), *Value(s)*, Harper Collins.
Keynes, J.M. (1935), *The General Theory of Employment, Interest and Money*, Wordsworth.
Rawls, J. (1971), *Theory of Justice*, Harvard University Press.
Schumpeter, J. (1942), *Can Capitalism Survive*, Harper Collins.
Ricardo, D. (1817), *On the Principles of Political Economy and Taxation*, Dover Publications.

7

HEALTH AND HEALTHCARE

Malcolm J. Prowle

Introduction

In all parts of the UK, the state of the NHS is almost always one of the top two issues which concern the population (particularly at election time) where it jockeys for top place with other issues like Brexit, the economy and immigration.

Leaving aside pensions and welfare benefits, which are essentially just transfers of cash from governments to individuals, expenditure on health is by far and away the largest public service in expenditure terms as shown in Figure 7.1.

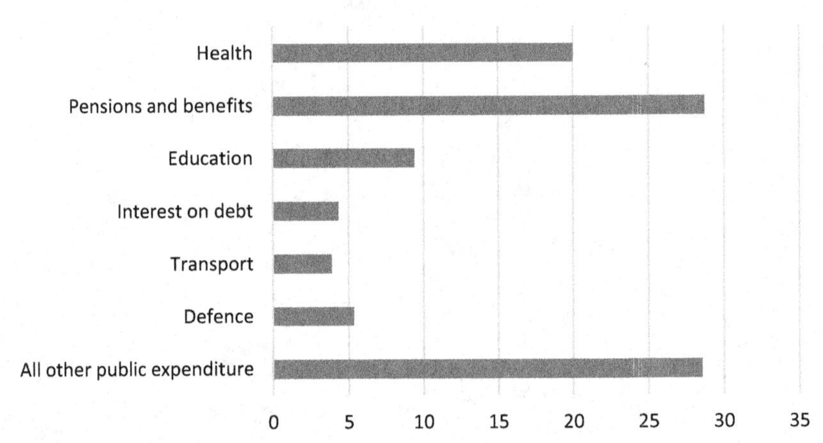

FIGURE 7.1 Analysis of UK public expenditure
Source: UK Public Spending https://www.ukpublicspending.co.uk/breakdown

DOI: 10.4324/9781003201892-10

Prior to the 1999 devolution settlement, health services were the province of the UK central government, for the whole of the UK, but from 1999, responsibility for many elements of health was passed to the devolved governments of Scotland, Wales and Northern Ireland. Consequently, in the UK, it is often said that there are four health systems in operation which comprise the NHS (England, Wales, Scotland and Northern Ireland).

This chapter is concerned with the development and implementation of policy for health and healthcare in a regional government setting. At the outset it is important to draw a distinction between the two terms, "health policy" and "health care policy", since they are not synonymous. This is discussed below.

Structure of chapter

This chapter is structured as follows:

- Health and healthcare
- The relevance of global health issues
- UK health policy – a case of over-centralisation
- Consequences of over-centralisation
- The impact of devolution on health and healthcare
- Health and healthcare under a federal structure
- Health and healthcare in a regional government
- Coordination of health policy across regional public policy areas
- Some key health policy themes for regional governments
- Population and public health
- Organisation of healthcare services in the region
- Delivering effective and efficient healthcare – the need for a new culture
- Conclusion

Health and healthcare

There are a number of issues to consider under this heading:

Health and healthcare – the distinction

At the outset, it is important to draw a distinction between the terms "health" and "healthcare". The term "health" concerns the overall health status of an area, as measured by a range of indicators such as mortality, morbidity, well-being and the wide range of factors which can influence that health status. The existence of health inequalities has led to a growing awareness that many health issues are determined by social and economic factors. Healthcare services can help in reducing levels of morbidity and mortality in society but economic, environmental and social factors can shape people's risk of getting ill, their ability to prevent sickness or their access to effective treatments. Thus, it can be seen that while the delivery of healthcare is an important aspect of public policy, it is just one of the factors which impact on health status. Indeed, many would argue that the other factors such as, for example, lifestyles, housing and the environment have a bigger impact on health status than the delivery of health services. Indeed, the history of UK health services shows that the biggest gains in health status came from public health policies like clean water and effective sanitation rather direct healthcare services to patients. These factors are discussed in the next section entitled "Determinants of health".

As the title suggests, the term "healthcare" concerns the way in which healthcare services are delivered to the community and individual patients, primarily through primary care practitioners and in hospitals.

Determinants of health

The Dahlgren-Whitehead rainbow model remains one of the most effective illustrations of health determinants, and has had widespread impact in research on health inequality and influences and is illustrated in Figure 7.2.

We see a series of concentric circles illustrating the different factors which impinge on health status of individuals and communities. These circles are as follows:

- **Inherent factors** – these are factors such as age and sex which impact on health status. There is little that governments can do to alter these.

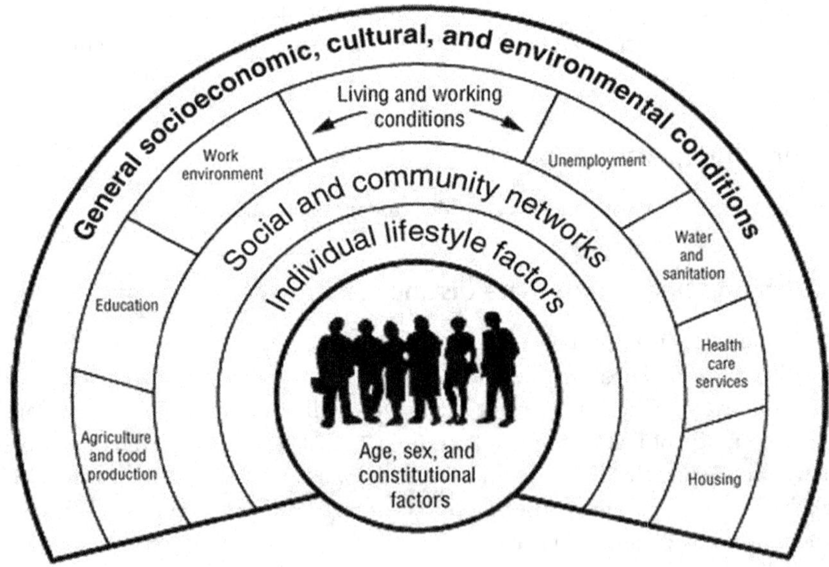

FIGURE 7.2 Determinants of health

- **Individual lifestyle factors** – these are factors which can impact, positively or negatively, on the health status of an individual. Many of these are well known such as cigarette smoking, obesity and excess alcohol consumption. Clearly, it is possible to introduce measures to encourage people to change their lifestyle leading to improvements in health status.
- **Social and community networks** – individuals live, work and socialise in a variety of communities. The nature of their involvement in these networks can also have an impact on the health status of an individual, particularly mental health, and it is suggested that developments in this area can improve individual health status.
- **General socio-economic, cultural and environmental conditions** – this is a very broad group of factors which concern the external environment in which individuals exist. Thus, it includes factors such as housing and working conditions.

In the light of this, it can be seen that health policy goes well beyond healthcare policy and, ideally, requires a health dimension to almost every other aspect of public policy such as housing, the environment, education and community development.

Nature of a health system

The World Health Organization (WHO) defines health systems as being responsible for delivering services that improve, maintain or restore the health of individuals and their communities. This includes the care provided by hospitals and family doctors, but also less visible tasks such as the prevention and control of communicable disease, health promotion and health workforce planning. Other important factors are improving the social, economic or environmental conditions in which people live but many would argue this falls outside of a health system.

Around the world a wide variety of health systems can be found with as many histories and organisational structures as there are countries. As with other social institutional structures, health systems are likely to reflect the history, culture and economics of the states in which they evolve. Implicitly, countries must design and develop health systems in accordance with the needs of the population and the resources available, although common elements in virtually all health systems are primary healthcare and public health measures. In some countries, health system planning is distributed among market participants, while in others there is a concerted effort among governments, trade unions, charities, religious organisations or other coordinated bodies to deliver planned healthcare services targeted at the populations they serve.

In the UK, the health system of an area will probably comprise all of the following elements:

- Primary care covering medicine, dentistry, ophthalmology and pharmacy
- Intermediate care delivered at a patient's residence

- Secondary hospital care – covering a wide range of medical and surgical specialities
- Tertiary hospital care – specialist hospital care usually at a university teaching hospital
- Ambulance and paramedic services
- Population and public health

In addition, a further key element of care is that of social care which is delivered, in the UK, by a local authority but working in collaboration with the NHS. This is an important matter which is repeatedly mentioned throughout this book.

Challenges facing health systems

This book has referred many times to the challenges facing public services in the future. Some of these challenges apply equally to all public services while others are more health specific.

At the time of writing, the main challenges facing health systems in the UK would seem to concern:

- **Ageing population** – in an earlier chapter, the issue of ageing populations was discussed. This factor has a huge impact on healthcare services. Linked to this is the fact that the needs and costs of healthcare tend to rise as individuals age.
- **Medical Science and Technology** – at the time of the creation of the NHS, there was a belief (subsequently proved wrong) that all the government needed to do was to pump more money into health services which would reduce the demand for healthcare and the need for expenditure would flatten out or even reduce. Clearly this view was incorrect and looks rather naïve in hindsight. It took no account of the developing ability of medical science and technology to treat conditions that previously were untreatable. Since the creation of the NHS in 1948, there have been many new approaches to diagnosis and treatment and these have fuelled demand for these services. Let us take just one example to illustrate this point which is surgery to insert an artificial hip joint. Modern hip replacement surgery really dates back to the 1960s and prior to that treatment options were limited including pain relief. Today there are 160,000 such procedures performed, each year, in England and Wales alone. The costs of undertaking these procedures would amount to several billions of pounds for a service which was unavailable 70 years ago. Looking ahead, there seems no end to the stream of new medical science and technology developments that will fuel new demands and costs.
- **Societal changes** – this concerns broad societal changes such as family breakdown, loss of the extended family and the numbers of persons living in one-person households. Such trends have, over the last few decades, had major implications for many public services, including health, and seem likely

to do so in the future. Also, to be noted are increased public expectations of what public services will deliver and an enhanced sense of "entitlement" which probably has its origins in the "choice" agenda of the under the Blair/Brown governments.

- **New threats** – the last couple of years have seen the Covid-19 pandemic with unprecedented health and economic impacts across the globe. It is too early, as yet, to predict the final outcomes of this pandemic but there are already some significant health implications which will need to be dealt with by the NHS. These include dealing with patients suffering from Long Covid, mental health problems consequent on lockdown and a large backlog of elective work which was deferred during the pandemic. There are also concerns that other variants and other pandemics could emerge without warning which implies a need for preparedness absent at the start of the Covid pandemic.
- **Resources** – the financing of the NHS in the UK is always a political football with political parties competing with one another regarding pledges to spend more on the NHS. As we have discussed in Chapter 5, in the real world, there will always be constraints on how much can be spend on healthcare services and these pressures are likely to increase in the future. However, it is not just about finance. At the time of writing both the NHS and social care have major difficulties in recruiting staff and retaining existing staff. The existence of Covid has increased this pressure.

The relevance of global health issues

It has already been mentioned that health is an issue relevant to local, regional and national levels of a country. But, it must also be recognised that UK health services cannot operate in a vacuum since they must take cognisance of the international forces at work which will affect domestic health. Indeed, the UK is a signatory to a number of international health treaties.

The Covid pandemic has clearly indicated this, since the coronavirus appeared in China but quickly spread to almost every part of the globe. Even though the UK is a set of islands, the movement of people and goods resulted in the virus arriving in the UK and very quickly spreading to all parts of the country.

However, Covid is only a part of the story. A recent UNEP (2020) report noted that 60% of known infectious diseases and 75% of emerging infectious diseases are transmitted from animals (zoonosis). Over the past 30 years more than 30 epidemics or pandemics of zoonotic diseases have been recorded. These include variants of the influenza virus, HIV/AIDS, SARS (Severe Acute Respiratory Syndrome), Ebola and now the coronavirus. All countries are now vulnerable to infectious diseases due to the increase in global travel. While passenger numbers fell dramatically during the pandemic, a National Geographic article (Rosen 2017) noted that according to the International Air Transport Association in

2016 there were 3.8 billion air journeys, which were forecast to rise to 7.2 billion by 2035.

The rise in zoonosis reflects a failure to recognise that human and animal health are interdependent and bound to the health of the ecosystem at a global level. The SARS and Covid-19 most probably passed between animals and humans in markets selling animals for human consumption. Influenza pandemics are most often attributed to human contact with farmed animals and birds. But an equally serious threat to health arises from the misuse of antibiotics in farming, which is one of the main causes of the declining effectiveness of antibiotics for the treatment of human infections.

Thus, any country, including the UK, must recognise the risks posed by infections which originate in other parts of the world. I suggest there are a number of important issues here:

- The need for the UK to take greater action to protect ourselves, as far as possible, from infectious diseases (that have originated elsewhere) entering and spreading through the country.
- The need to ensure that the UK is prepared to counter the spread of, and treatment for, infectious diseases originating from outside the UK. This was clearly lacking in relation to Covid-19.
- The need to assist developing countries to reduce the chances of infectious diseases originating and spreading throughout the country of origin and elsewhere. This goes beyond just strengthening their healthcare systems but could involve such things as improved water and sewage systems, and cleaner environments. This will require large-scale investment for developed countries.
- International co-operation is also required to detect the emergence and spread of infectious diseases by testing and developing resources to treat and immunise those at risk. National and global investment in health systems capacity is necessary to prepare and share reserve resources for pandemics.
- There is a need for international action to support the World Health Organization and the United Nations Environmental Programme (UNEP) in addressing the challenges of global and planetary health. Whatever their perceived faults, both agencies have been shown to be chronically underfunded and underpowered to address the immense challenges the world now faces. Kristalina Georgieva, IMF Managing Director, has suggested that the coronavirus pandemic could cost an estimated $28 trillion in output losses over the next five years, while the WHO budget is some $4.5 billion.

UK health policy – a case of over-centralisation

As is well known, the National Health Service (NHS) was formed on 5 July 1948 by the post-war Labour Government and replaced a somewhat ramshackle system of healthcare provision. The NHS had at its heart three core principles:

1 It meets the needs of everyone.
2 It be free at the point of delivery.
3 It be based on clinical need, not ability to pay.

Prior to 1999, health in England and Wales was the responsibility of the UK Department of Health but between 1948 and 1999, the health systems of Scotland and Northern Ireland were managed by other UK government departments, namely the Scottish Office and Northern Ireland Office respectively. In 1973, in Northern Ireland, the NHS was merged with the broader social care system and called the Health and Social Care (HSC) system rather than the NHS. In 1969, the Welsh NHS was separated from the English NHS, and put under the control of a separate UK government department, the Welsh Office thus bringing it into line with Scotland and Northern Ireland. Thus, during this period, health policy and health services remained the responsibility of the UK central government albeit through geographically based government departments not the Department of Health. In 1999, devolution was introduced and health services of Scotland, Wales and Northern Ireland were no longer the province of UK government departments but passed to the Scottish Parliament and the National Assemblies for Wales and Northern Ireland and these bodies then became responsible for health policy and health.

In the other chapters in Part C of this book, issues of policy in relation to various public services are discussed in some depth. In particular, a common criticism is the over-centralisation of policy making by UK governments, of all political parties, often accompanied by mixed messages. It is the same with health policy and over many years, there has been much criticism of health policy as being far too centralised by the UK government. Just a few of many examples of this can be quoted to illustrate the point.

Back in 2002, a report by the Kings Fund on the Future of the NHS commented:

> over-centralisation is evidenced in the continuing dominance of national priorities over local issues in driving change. Over-centralisation hinders improvement because it stifles appropriate, locally sensitive innovation, and limits local responsibility. The NHS is compromised and over-burdened by an excessive number of frequently conflicting objectives. As a result, staff can become disillusioned and, as a consequence, the process of modernisation may not meet public expectations or Government pledges.

In 2014, the incoming chief executive of the NHS, Simon Stevens, gave an interview at which he commented on various aspects of the state of the NHS. Among his comments were:

> The NHS must end mass centralisation and instead expand its local services to treat people in their own communities. He added "many health services

in western Europe were already successfully serving their local communities without centralising everything".

More recently, the problems of over-centralisation of health policy came to the fore with the Covid-19 pandemic and many stories were reported in the media of local health officials having to wait for permission from Whitehall to impose restrictions on local areas, which they knew were urgently needed. Writing during the Covid lockdown period, one academic commentator (Stoddart 2020) stated:

> England's over-centralisation isn't just a governance issue now – it's a public health emergency. The concentration of power at Westminster and Whitehall has long frustrated those of us who engage closely with the structures of governance and compare it to decentralised norms across much of Europe. Now, as with so many facets of the Covid-19 crisis, the pandemic has exposed national vulnerabilities and left us grappling with the consequences. The grip on initiative that rests in SW1 is one such weakness, which is impacting how our system is responding to the virus, in turn perpetuating the public health emergency we find ourselves in.

Many similar examples and commentaries could also be cited which give a similar message. To quote a well-known saying "*if it looks like a duck and walks like a duck, it is probably a duck*". It is the same with centralisation.

Consequences of over-centralisation

We believe there are a number of consequences of over-centralisation which can be identified.

Core principles

First, if we go back to the core NHS principles described above, we would argue that there is a strong case for saying that these principles have not been adhered to under a heavily centralised health system.

- **Meets the needs of everyone** – this is a contentious principle. It is clearly the case that many patients have to wait months or even years to receive the treatments they need and so their needs are not met, as and when they require them to be met. Also, it is undoubtedly the case that in some medical specialties, because of waiting times, some patients will die before receiving treatment. Yet other patients choose not to wait and attend a private hospital for treatment.
- **Free at the point of delivery** – it is well known that this issue caused consternation in the Labour Government of Clement Atlee and led to the resignation of Aneurin Bevan in 1951. As early as 1952, prescription charges were introduced and since then charges have been introduced for other services, such

as eye tests and dental treatment. Many of these charges were, subsequently, abolished by the devolved governments as discussed below. However, it would be fair to say that the vast bulk of NHS services (but not social care services) are free at the point of delivery but if services are not available, people may revert to paying for treatment, effectively nullifying the free service principle.

- **Based on clinical need, not ability to pay** – again this is contentious. It is clearly the case that for most patients, decisions about treatment are made on the basis of clinical need not ability to pay. However, ability to pay does give some people the opportunity to take up private care rather than wait for NHS treatment.

Large variations across the country

In 1945, the then Minister for Health (Aneurin Bevan), when considering how the NHS should be established, stated that "*We have got to achieve, as nearly as possible, a uniform standard of service for all*". This was seen as the rationale for establishing an NHS controlled, from the centre, by the UK government, as opposed to an alternative of placing health under the control of local government.

While this aim of Bevan was laudable, 70 years later the NHS is nowhere near achieving that ideal and the reality is that the centrally controlled NHS shows large healthcare variations of many kinds across the UK (Kings Fund 2011), resulting in notably different life expectancies. While some variations in different parts of the country can be described as "warranted" because of differences in demography, geography, morbidity, etc., there are other large variations which are not warranted.

Policy uniformity

Almost by definition, healthcare policy in England is developed by the Department of Health and NHS England, for implementation by NHS organisations on a national English basis. The degree of local discretion available to those local NHS organisations implementing national policy is debatable but many in the NHS would say local discretion is limited. The thrust of this book, and of this chapter, is that English regions are large enough and diverse enough to be capable of establishing their own health policies, tailored to meet local needs and priorities, rather than having to rely on a uniform national policy which tends to have a London and South East orientation to it.

The impact of devolution on health and healthcare

As already noted, in 1999, responsibility for health services in Wales, Scotland and Northern Ireland was transferred to the relevant Assembly/Parliament. Henceforth, the UK Secretary of State for Health and the Department of Health were no longer responsible for the vast bulk of health policies and delivery of health services in the devolved areas. Furthermore, decisions about funding the NHS became the responsibility of the devolved governments which would decide what proportion of the block grant received from HM Treasury will be applied to the NHS in their area of jurisdiction.

Over the ensuing 22 years, we have seen a number of deviations in health policy in the devolved areas compared to health policy in England. The following deviations from the English model are recognisable:

- **Overall NHS organisation** – in England, the separation of the NHS commissioner and provider functions has been maintained, in one form or another, since 1991 although the configuration of both commissioners and providers has changed over time. In Scotland and Wales, subsequent to devolution, the commissioner and provider functions were merged into integrated health boards.
- **Private healthcare provision** – there are two aspects of this. First, within the English NHS, there is a significant degree of healthcare provision delivered by private healthcare providers, but funded by the NHS. A key aspect of this is the independent sector treatment and diagnostic centres set up to deliver care funded by the NHS. Second, some English NHS hospitals treat private patients in dedicated private beds. Such policies are almost completely absent in Wales and Scotland.
- **Financing** – importantly, devolved governments can prioritise health spending according to their own assessments of need, albeit within the parameters of the grant provided by the UK government. Specific examples of devolved financial initiatives in Wales and Scotland relate to prescriptions and hospital car parking which (in NHS owned car parks) are free whereas in England most adults have to pay a prescription charge currently standing at £9.35 per item and car park fees at the behest of the private provider. While this means a loss of income to the NHS in Wales and Scotland, it makes access to these facilities more affordable to poor people and confirms to the original principles of the NHS discussed above. Also, it recognises that Scotland and Wales have many deprived areas and can tailor their health policies in the light of such deprivation. This is not the case in many regions of England which also suffer deprivation.
- **Capital spending and PFI** – the NHS in Wales and Scotland has largely eschewed the use of PFI as a means to finance new hospitals and other facilities. Consequently, they have avoided situations found in the NHS in England of certain PFI funded assets becoming unaffordable by an NHS Trust.
- **Public health** – as noted later, there are considerable variations in the organisation of the public health function across the UK.
- **Other** – this covers differences in the organisation of primary care and different approaches to drug prescribing policies and initiatives as a means of addressing inequalities in health.

In previous chapters of this book, there are often suggestions made that the devolved governments did not make sufficient use of their new powers, in various areas of public policy, to make more changes to the policies they inherited from the UK government. Similarly, it is also a debatable point as to whether the devolved governments fully utilised their new powers sufficiently to reshape health services to make them more appropriate to the needs of their population.

Health and healthcare under a federal structure

Although there are many issues of operational detail, some public services such as schools and some aspects of social care can be seen as inherently simple in nature with local services being delivered to local recipients by locally based staff. Some of these services will utilise local buildings (e.g. schools, residential homes) while others will be delivered at the recipient's home (e.g. domiciliary care).

However, health and healthcare services are far more complex. While some health services might be seen as basically a local service (e.g. GP visit), other health services will have implications at community, local, regional, national and international levels.

Hence, it is important to recognise that, under a regional government arrangement across the UK, while much of health policy and health services will rest with regional governments there are some aspects which will sit under the federal government level. The precise division of these responsibilities would need to be negotiated but Figure 7.3 gives a broad idea of the split.

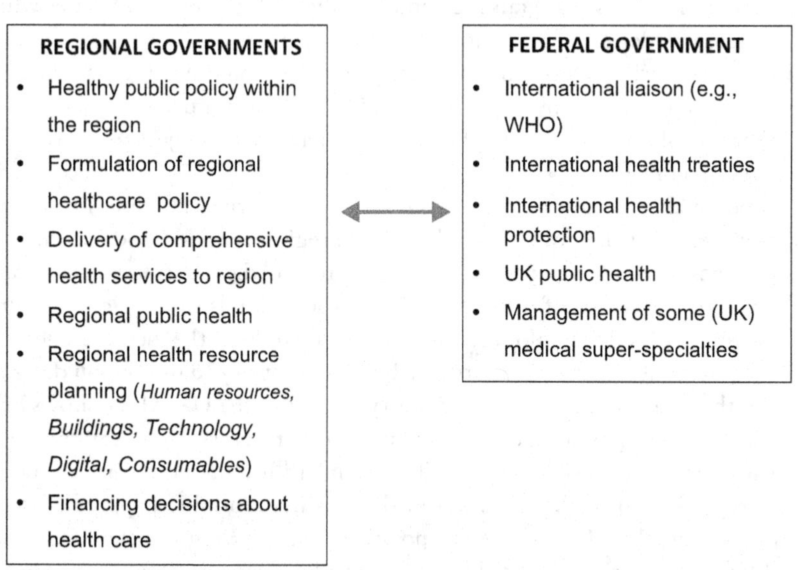

FIGURE 7.3 Division of health responsibilities between governments

It must be emphasised that the relationship between the federal tier and the regional tier is not one of superior/subordinate but one of collaboration. In discussion with the federal government tier, regions may agree that some functions are best undertaken at the federal level but this is based on an agreement not a diktat.

Health and healthcare in a regional government

The introduction of regional government in relation to health produces a liberation of English regions from top-down controls allowing them to set regional healthcare policies and to plan and manage healthcare services which meet local needs and demand, in the same way as Wales, Scotland and Northern Ireland, but without constant interference from Whitehall. This would bring decision-making for health closer to communities across the UK and encourage innovation in policy making to match the potential of medical and information technology to further transform healthcare delivery, creating the fully engaged society which will be essential for sustainable healthcare funding.

However, there are concerns that some regions might abuse these freedoms and make changes that would run contrary to the founding ethos of the NHS. Hence, there may be a need for some form of NHS "constitution" which set down some founding principles for the NHS focusing on the rights and obligations of citizens to health and care services, measures to protect public health, equity of funding across the UK and global issues affecting the determinants of public and planetary health. Nowhere are we suggesting regional government equates to a breakup of the UK. We are talking about a realignment of responsibilities which ensure strong federal government, strong regions and strong localities. These are not mutually exclusive objectives. These principles would need to be agreed by all regions not imposed by federal government and it is a debatable point as to whether they should be enshrined in law and therefore be subject to court action for perceived breaches.

As noted above, the case for elected regional governments rests strongly on the argument that the government based in a region is better at identifying the health needs of its regional population and addressing them correctly, than policy makers many hundreds of miles away. The expectation is that regional governments are more likely to tailor their health policies to meet the identified needs of their region rather than have to utilise a blueprint developed in London designed to meet the needs of the whole of a country the size of the UK which shows huge variations in health, wealth, culture and many other factors. Hence, in this chapter it is clearly not possible to prescribe a standard health and healthcare policy for all regions. This is the weakness of the existing centralised approach which tries to do just that. Instead, health policy is a task for regions themselves and the different policy approaches by the devolved governments, to the pandemic, within the overall framework of a UK approach, demonstrate both the desire and achievability of a more decentralised system.

What we do in this chapter is to identify and discuss the various themes which constitute health and healthcare policy and would need to be addressed by a regional government. It must also be mentioned that it is not necessary, or desirable, for all aspects of regional health and healthcare policy to be dealt with by regional governments acting alone. Five models present themselves:

- Aspects delivered by a regional government acting alone
- Aspects delivered by two or more regions acting collaboratively
- Aspects delivered by regional government(s) and federal government collaboratively
- Aspects delivered by a federal government alone
- Aspects delivered internationally be several governments

In practice there are bound to be limitations to the ways in which regions will deliver healthcare services to its population on a unilateral basis and these options will need to be considered.

Coordination of health policy across regional public policy areas

Earlier in this chapter, it was noted that there are many determinants of health status other than healthcare. Health status can be affected by issues such as housing, environment and education. The Ottawa Charter for Health Promotion (WHO 2012) identified building healthy public policy as one of the main policy areas for improving health. This could combine diverse but complementary approaches, including legislation, fiscal measures and organisational change. The policy also requires the identification of obstacles to the adoption of healthy public policies in non-health sectors and the development of ways to remove them.

In a devolved system, regional governments will have responsibility for ensuring coordination of public services in such a way as to improve health status in the region. As most of the relevant public services including housing, environment and education would fall under the regional government, this is a key policy area. Intuitively, it would seem easier to achieve effective coordination of this kind in smaller regional governments than try to achieve it in the larger UK arena through monolithic government departments with only limited experience of doing this.

Some key health policy themes for regional governments

The NHS delivers a large and comprehensive range of healthcare services which can be classified in a number of ways:

- By medical category (e.g. orthopaedics, urgent care, paediatrics)
- By population group (e.g. children, older people)
- By location of service delivery (e.g. primary care, "at home" services)

It would be impossible in a book such as this to discuss all aspects of health policy in any sort of detail and, in any case, much of the policy decisions at this level will be strongly influenced by approved professional practice applied within a framework of clinical governance. What I would like to do is just highlight a few policy areas which regional governments would need to act on fairly promptly. These are summarised as follows:

- **Long Covid** – this is the term used to describe patients who have ongoing symptoms, often unpleasant, as a consequence of contracting Covid-19. This condition is not fully understood, or even if it is one or several conditions, its longer-term prevalence and impact cannot be accurately predicted at this time.
- **Mental health** – mental health has often been described as the Cinderella of the NHS in terms of priority and resources. There were serious concerns about NHS mental health services prior to the onset of Covid-19. The impact of Covid has been to magnify these concerns and there is the possibility of a sea of Covid-19 generated mental health problems among adults and children.
- **Older people** – the impact of ageing populations on health and social care has been frequently mentioned in this book. This is an issue which is not going to disappear and which must be addressed.
- **Integrated care** – we have addressed the relevance of this several times in this book. Under devolved arrangements, regional governments would be fully responsible for *both* health and social care and have the opportunity to accelerate integrated approaches and better coordination of services.
- **End-of-life care** – this is the term used to describe the support and medical care given during the time surrounding death. It is something which has changed hugely over time (Davidson and Gentry 2013) and is a matter which is one of great sensitivity and resource intensiveness. It is a difficult issue and one which regional governments must face.
- **Health inequalities** – this book has emphasised the scale of health inequality between different regions in the UK. There are, of course, also significant health inequalities within regions and between different segments of the population. Under regional government arrangements, it is clearly the responsibility of regional governments to address these issues.

Population and public health

This topic deals with the patterns of health and illness in groups of people, rather than in individuals. The terms "population health" and "public health" are often used interchangeably since both disciplines monitor health trends and examine the determinants of health and they also propose interventions at the population level to protect and promote health, and provide options for delivering these interventions. There are, however, some distinctions between population health and public health (Colleaga) which we can ignore for the purposes of this discussion. Population and public heath can be considered at an international, national, regional and local level. At the international level the obvious example of this is the World Health Organization to which the UK contributes and participates in its activities.

At the national level, we see that Public Health England was expected to advise on national UK public health issues and to participate in efforts to address threats to global and local health threats including the fear of an Avian flu pandemic. But while it has played a leading role in the science of global health, it has not been given the budget or support needed to take practical action at the national level. This was revealed by the 2016 Exercise Cygnus, a simulation, which showed the need for action to prepare for a pandemic. This clearly demonstrated the need for a reserve of items such as Personal Protective Equipment (PPE) and capacity to deal with a surge in the need for hospital capacity, the steps needed to act on the problems associated with Covid-19 which were not funded or taken in time. In April 2021, Public Health England was abolished having been blamed (perhaps harshly) for problems regarding the Covid pandemic and especially the fiasco of the track and trace system. Hence, in the context of regional governments, with their own public health functions, there would still be a need for a national UK public health function to deal with those issues which are best dealt with at national level. Following the demise of Public Health England, the UK government created the UK Health Security Agency which could fulfil that role for the UK.

Regional governments could also coordinate public services and community organisations to address issues that enhance public health and well-being within the region. For example, social care that can help support struggling families and improve the health of their children, education that can guide the development of health behaviour, policing that can work with health services to address drug and alcohol issues, and housing that enables healthier community living.

In England, 2013 saw the transfer of the public health function from the NHS to a combination of local government and Public Health England (PHE) and it was one of the most significant extensions of local government powers and duties in a generation. Thus, local authorities in England have clearly defined functions in relation to public health. The Act also established Health and Well-being Boards to act as a forum at which representatives of health and care systems could work together to improve the health and well-being of their population. However, cuts to government grants led to a 17% fall in spending on public health from 2009 to 2019. However, in Wales, Scotland and Northern Ireland, different arrangements are in place with stronger links with the NHS.

Once again, there is no definitive view as to what is the best approach. Consistent with other chapters, we posit that the differences in circumstances between regions of England suggest it is a major issue for each region to reflect on and decide for themselves. The best public health arrangement rather than apply some form of national blueprint.

At the local level it will be essential to fully engage communities not only in improving their own health but also in the changes to lifestyle necessary to preserve planetary health. UK regional governments must bring public health and well-being, healthcare, social care and all other public services together, to work with communities to improve health and well-being. This is discussed further in Chapter 14.

Organisation of healthcare services in the region

The various organisations concerned with the delivery of healthcare services can be considered as follows:

Commissioners and providers

In England, for many years the NHS could be broken down, organisationally, into two groups – commissioners and providers.

- **Commissioners** – these were responsible for assessing the health needs of an area and for defining the health services that needed to be provided to meet those needs. In turn, commissioners let contracts with provider organisations for the actual service delivery. In England the arrangements for commissioning healthcare have changed many times, largely, in response to perceived failures of the commissioning process. The number of changes exemplifies the failures referred to earlier of focusing on structures and not the actual processes of commissioning.
- **Providers** – these are the organisations which are responsible for the actual provision of healthcare services in line with contracts agreed with commissioners. They can be listed as follows:
  - Primary care providers
  - Intermediate care providers
  - Secondary care providers
  - Tertiary care providers

As already noted, not all parts of the UK adopt this process of organisationally separating commissioners from providers. In Scotland and Wales, the NHS is organised around a series of health boards which integrate the commissioning and providing aspects of healthcare into a single organisation. It is debatable as to whether the separation of commissioner and provider functions into separate organisations adds any value and probably, the answer to the question is that it depends on the nature of local circumstances concerning matters such as demography, geography and health needs – one size doesn't suit all. Hence, it is a clear role for regional governments across the UK to decide what is the most appropriate model they wish to adopt concerning the commissioner and provider functions.

Composition of healthcare providers

The bulk of healthcare services are provided by organisations which are part of the NHS. However, some healthcare services are provided by organisations which are part of the third sector or the private sector.

The involvement of the private sector in the delivery of publicly funded healthcare services is a very sensitive political issue. We must emphasise that the private sector has always had, and always will, have a large involvement in the NHS. The NHS purchases vast quantities of drugs and medical supplies from private companies as well as maintenance contracts for buildings, equipment, etc. In England, over the last two decades, the private sector has had a growing and significant involvement in the delivery of NHS services through initiatives like the PFI and the Independent Sector Treatment Centres. In addition, there are a variety of local arrangements between the NHS and local private hospitals, private laboratories, etc. to provide services to patients.

However, it is in the area of the private sector directly delivering health services to patients that sensitivities appear. In particular, in the devolved areas, the involvement of the private sector in direct delivery of services is much lower than in England. In some cases, there may be good economic and managerial reasons for not utilising the private sector to deliver such services but in other situations the decision is very much a political one.

Nevertheless, we see it as a key plank of regional health policy to decide what should be the involvement of the private sector in the region in delivering healthcare services. I suggest a pragmatic approach is needed here. If there is a strong financial and service case for using the private sector in specific activities then this should happen. If there is not a strong case then it should not happen.

Such decisions should take account of the needs of patients, their geographic location and the availability of sufficient private sector providers to avoid a monopolistic situation occurring.

The third sector is already a significant provider of health services and this role is set to continue and even expand in years to come because of the pressure on statutory services. In Chapter 14 of this book we talk at some length about the potential future role in public service provision for the third sector.

Financing healthcare services

Chapter 5 of this book discusses the general aspects of public service financing and so this section focuses more specifically on the way health services might be financed under a model of regional government.

The grounding principle of the NHS was that healthcare should be free at the point of delivery. While this principle is not 100% applied, since there are a variety of user charges applied in the NHS, it broadly holds true and should continue to be the case even under a regional model of health policy and provision. If we consider the funding of health services, it is important to identify two aspects of this:

- Funding of ongoing running costs of healthcare services
- Funding of non-recurring capital expenditure needs of healthcare services

Funding of ongoing running costs

With regard to the funding of ongoing running costs, the options available to regional governments would be as follows:

- Proceeds of charges for services
- Funds provided by federal government via nationally levied taxes
- Funds obtained from any regionally levied taxes

It does not seem likely that the proceeds from charges for services can be hugely extended or contracted by an individual region but they may want to consider this.

Regions will receive an allocation of funds from the federal government derived from nationally levied taxes such as income tax and VAT. It would then be up to regional governments to decide how much of those funds should be applied to healthcare services.

One further option would involve regional governments having some regional tax raising powers. The scope for this would be limited by the small tax base of some regions consequent on economic inequalities discussed earlier. Progress could only be made on this with sufficient re-balancing of the UK economy outlined in Chapter 6. For the purposes of health services, regional governments may also wish to consider the possibility of a regional hypothecated tax with the proceeds dedicated to healthcare services

Funding of capital expenditure

Healthcare services require ongoing expenditure on capital items such as buildings, equipment or vehicles because existing items are worn out and/or need replacing with more technologically advanced items. Traditionally, funds have been provided by national governments for this purpose and this seems likely to continue under a regional government model whereby regional governments would set aside part of their available funds for capital purposes. However, we suggest that this is not a very flexible approach that meets local needs for capital expenditure and so consideration might be given to regional governments having borrowing powers for capital expenditure purposes. In this way, funding could be obtained on the basis of a robust business case for the proposed investment.

Service collaboration and integration

As noted, frequently, in this book a vitally important issue is that of integrating the planning and provision of public services. This can be considered from two standpoints:

- Integration of healthcare services with other public services
- Integration of the elements of healthcare

The first of these standpoints concerning the integration of healthcare services with other public services is considered in significant detail in Chapter 13. In that chapter, it is argued that the key to better collaboration and integration does not lie in government proscription of structures of collaboration but in the three "mutuals" of mutual understanding, mutual gain and mutual trust between the partners in the collaboration.

The second standpoint concerning the integration of the elements of healthcare is perhaps not so widely discussed but the failures of integration in healthcare are often observed in practice. Integrated care is a worldwide trend in healthcare reform and new organisational arrangements focusing on more coordinated and integrated forms of healthcare provision are being pursued. Integrated care may be seen as a response to the fragmented delivery of healthcare services being an acknowledged problem in many health systems. Integrated care covers a complex and comprehensive field, and there are many different approaches to and definitions of the concept. WHO (2008) gives the following definition:

> [T]he organization and management of health services so that people get the care they need, when they need it, in ways that are user-friendly, achieve the desired results and provide value for money.

Integrated care involves different ways and degrees of working together and three important aspects of this are along the spectrum of autonomy, coordination and integration. While autonomy refers to the one end of a continuum with least co-operation, integration (the combination of parts into a working whole by overlapping services) refers to the end with most co-operation and coordination (the relation of parts) to a point in between. Distinction is also made between horizontal integration (linking similar levels of care like multi-professional teams) and vertical integration (linking different levels of care like primary, secondary, and tertiary care).

Continuity of care is often subdivided into three components:

- Continuity of information (by shared records)
- Continuity across the secondary-primary care interface (discharge planning from specialist to generalist care)

- Provider continuity (seeing the same professional each time, with value added if there is a therapeutic, trusting relationship)

Integrated care seems particularly important to service provision to older people who often become chronically ill and subject to co-morbidities and so have a special need of continuous care. We believe improved integration within the NHS is something regional governments could be well equipped to achieve.

Healthcare resource planning

In Chapter 12, the issue of resource trends and resource planning in public services was discussed in some detail covering the following resources:

- Human resources
- Buildings
- Technology
- Digital
- Consumables (e.g. drugs)

These matters apply as much to health and healthcare as to other public services and we see these as responsibilities to be, largely, addressed by regional governments and not the federal government. There will be arguments that matters like digital and consumables should be undertaken at the federal level in order to achieve "economies of scale". However, we do not accept this and suggest the "economies of scale" argument is one of many myths of classical economic theory (e.g. P2P Foundation 2012). We would suggest that the current staff shortages facing the NHS are a consequence of inadequate HR resource planning at the national level. While some aspects of HR planning, such as medical staff, might best be addressed at the federal level, we believe other aspects are best dealt with at a more local level where there is a clearer idea about what is needed and how it can be made available.

Delivering effective and efficient healthcare – the need for a new culture

An important issue for regional governments is how healthcare services are to be delivered in an effective and efficient manner. In considering this, a number of terms come to mind as being important including being flexible, integrative, holistic and innovative. Achieving this is not easy and is very much reliant on achieving significant culture change within the NHS.

The problem is that the NHS is often referred to as a bureaucracy. However, caution is needed as the term "bureaucratic" is often used, pejoratively, by health professional staff to describe NHS managers who they see as being too numerous. Bureaucracy is not the same as management and bureaucracy can be described in a number of ways. Bureaucracy can mean a system of human organisation in which activities and relationships are governed by fixed, rational rules rather than by personal decision or tradition. The prime characteristics of bureaucratic organisations include:

- Formalistic impersonality
- Rigidity of response
- Proliferation of "offices";
- hierarchical appointments usually requiring precisely defined, formal qualifications.

This led Sir Stuart Rose, the former chief executive of Marks and Spencer, to conclude that "*the NHS is drowning in bureaucracy*" in his review of NHS leadership published in 2015. The problem is that bureaucracy makes it difficult to be flexible, integrative, holistic and innovative and it is worth mentioning a few examples. Take innovation: the NHS is constantly encouraged to be innovative and to take on board recent innovations. However, there is a constant stream of evidence (Castle-Clarke et al. 2017, Darzi 2014) to suggest that the NHS is slow at taking up innovations and bureaucratic structures are to blame. Another issue is the integration of services both within healthcare and between health and social care. I can remember this being an issue for the NHS 40 years ago and it seems that limited progress has been made.

In this book, we have strongly emphasised that while organisational structures are an important issue for the delivery of public services, including health services, they are not be all and end all of the issue. Theory and practice of management, in both public and private sectors, clearly show that structure should follow process (or form should follow function). What this means is that before settling on organisational structures one needs to be clear what the organisation is expected to do and how it should do it. Civil servants and politicians rarely seem to grasp this simple concept and persist in approaching organisational issues by starting with structures and then hoping these structures would work. No wonder we see so many examples of public policy failure leading to yet more structural re-organisation. This is a very important issue and one which central government seems unable to resolve. We can only hope that smaller and more focused regional governments can address this more successfully.

Conclusion

In his memoirs, former Chancellor of the Exchequer, Nigel Lawson, stated that "*the NHS is the closest the English have to a religion and that they treat the medical profession as a priesthood*". While this may be seen as a bit "*over the top*" by many people, it does indicate the degree of importance and even love that most UK people have for the NHS. However, this may be balanced by concerns about some of the failings that do take place. The impact of Covd-19 on the NHS might be described as traumatic and it is still with us. The longer-term impacts on staff and morale are yet unknown.

However, what Covid has done is to highlight some major weaknesses in the NHS which have always existed but which have now been amplified and are the consequence of a system which is vastly over-centralised and over-bureaucratic. Hence, the arguments in this chapter for a more regionalised approach to planning, organising and delivering health services and health policy must be coupled with a change in culture and behaviours both within the NHS and between it and its partners.

References

Castle-Clarke, S., Edwards, M. and Buckingham, H. (2017), *Falling short: why the NHS is still struggling to make the most of new innovations*, Nuffield Trust.

Colleaga, How does population health differ from public health? https://www.colleaga.org/article/how-does-population-health-differ-public-health

Darzi, A. (2014), The NHS does not use innovation effectively, *The Guardian*, March 2014.

Davidson, S. and Gentry, T. (2013), *End of life evidence review*, Age UK London.

Kings Fund. 2011. Variations in Healthcare. https://www.kingsfund.org.uk/sites/default/files/Variations-in-health-care-good-bad-inexplicable-report-The-Kings-Fund-April-2011.pdf

Kings Fund, https://www.kingsfund.org.uk/sites/default/files/field/field_publication_file/future-of-the-nhs-framework-for-debate-discussion-paper-kings-fund-january-2002.pdf

Rose, S. (2015), *Better leadership for tomorrow: NHS leadership review*, Department of Health and Social Care.

Rosen, E. (2017), As billions more fly, here's how aviation could evolve, *National Geographic*, Washington DC.

Ruche, A. (2012), *Economies of scale are a myth*, P2P Foundation.

Stevens, S. (2014), https://www.theguardian.com/society/2014/may/30/nhs-england-mass-centralisation-simon-stevens

Stoddart (2020), https://inlogov.com/2020/05/22/englands-over-centralisation-isnt-just-a-governance-issue-now-its-a-public-health-emergency/

UNEP United Nations Environment Programme and International Livestock Research Institute (2020), Preventing the next pandemic: zoonotic diseases and how to break the chain of transmission, Nairobi, Kenya.

WHO (2008), Integrated health services - what and why? Technical brief No 1.

WHO (2012), Ottawa charter for health promotion.

WHO Health Systems, https://www.euro.who.int/en/health-topics/Health-systems

8

SOCIAL CARE

Tony Garthwaite

Introduction and context

Finding an answer to the "social care problem" has emerged as seemingly one of the greatest unsolved mysteries of 21st century public policy. Successive UK and devolved governments have promised, and failed to deliver, a social care system that can sustain a robust response to the big challenges of the day, primarily those of meeting ever-increasing demand from an ageing population, coping with limited resources to do so, ensuring it works seamlessly with the NHS and other partners, and resolving how to do so in a way that is financially credible and sustainable. It is undoubtedly the latter which dominates the thoughts of politicians and regrettably the "social care problem" is now a phrase that is synonymous with the question of how best to finance the care system. This reinforces a basic misconception that the way a service is paid for can be determined separately from a clear understanding of what that service is and how it needs to be formulated in the light of ever-changing circumstances.

The Covid-19 pandemic has brought social care to the public's attention like never before and has increased public understanding of its value as a key public service. Patience for the Westminster government to "sort it out" is running out with the head of the NHS in England pronouncing on the 5th of July 2020 his hope that within a year, "we have actually, as a country, been able to decisively answer the question of how are we going to fund and provide high-quality social care for our parents' generation" (BBC 2020).

In September 2021 the UK government passed legislation to raise national insurance contributions and dividend tax to form a ring-fenced annual £12 billion health and social care levy for the whole of the UK. They also announced that there would be a cap of £86,000 on the amount people will have to pay for care in England over their lifetime. At his press conference which accompanied

DOI: 10.4324/9781003201892-11

his announcement the Prime Minister disappointingly framed his support for the investment in social care within his desire to support the NHS, stating that "we cannot now shirk the challenge of putting the NHS back on its feet, which requires fixing the problem of social care" (Johnson 2021). First reactions from the social care sector were to welcome any additional funding but express concern about it being far too little and that a joint health and social care levy will mean the priorities of the NHS, particularly the acute sector, will again take precedent. Evidence of these fears is that the social care element represents only around 15% of the total package, some of which, in England at least, presumably will be devoted to achieving £86,000 cap. Moreover, the fact that a sum of money is earmarked in Whitehall doesn't mean that the money will find its way to the "coalface" of social care. Once again, social care is presented as a "problem", the irritatingly annoying child holding back the progress and success of the star pupil, the NHS, and the crux that problem is all about money.

The new funding is included in "Build Back Better", a new UK government plan for health and social care (HM Government 2021). This plan is strong on rhetoric and light on detail. It is certainly not the cohesive strategy necessary to reform social care and basically reiterates the unfilled promises of long-term financial stability for the sector, a more stable workforce, greater integration of health and social care, and more consistent quality in terms of delivery. It provides little reassurance for the millions of unpaid carers, usually family members, on whom the country depends to sustain social care. How the promises will be achieved, we are told, will be included in a future White Paper on social care reform. So, still no significant proposals to debate yet, I'm afraid, and it will be interesting to see whether the additional funding will be sufficient to stimulate the existing devolved governments into their own reform proposals. Inevitably, the focus of any national review of social care when it arrives will be on structure and finance, no doubt generating the usual clutch of arguments for a national care service, merger with the NHS, and all sorts of taxation and insurance ideas. Once again, therefore, form is likely to be inappropriately put ahead of function.

Nobody would contest the fact that "sorting out" social care is an extremely complex and difficult task and I fear that the review, when it arrives, will miss the opportunity to take a deeper look at the role and function of social care as a critically important modern public service. We need to consider carefully how social care should be regarded within the overall health and care system. Where do issues like improving well-being and preventing the escalation of need – central to many government policies – fit as key responsibilities of social services agencies? Where should individual responsibilities for personal care end and state intervention begin?

These are some of the important questions that need answering before structural solutions are arrived at. Only then can we determine the right way of organising finance, the workforce, and the role of unpaid carers and partner agencies within the third and independent sectors. Only then can we properly understand the case for a devolved system of social care. In this context, it is worth noting that given the individual nature of social care need, it is inevitable that social care must remain a locally delivered service, in or close to people's homes. Other than a relatively small number of specialist placement facilities, centralised resources are rarely used by social care commissioners yet funding for services has increasingly moved away from local authority control to top-down governmental grant-based financial support. Social care, therefore, is a prime case study in any discussion about regional government.

In this chapter, I take a step back to look at the core role of social care in today's society in order to develop ideas from a different base for its organisation, resourcing, and delivery for the next decade and beyond. In doing so, it is necessary to trace the development of social care and social services since the advent of the welfare state, following the Second World War. It is important to note why the focus of this chapter is on social care as it applies to adults. The reasons for not also covering children's social services do not relate solely to restrictions of space in a single chapter of this book. The law applying to children's services is different and access to services for children is not means tested as it is for adults. Social care is not a universally accepted expression to describe the work done to meet children's needs, safeguard them from harm and abuse, and support families. Moreover, the social care "problem" that has perplexed politicians for decades has largely been presented as relating to adult social care, namely the challenge of tackling demographic changes, relieving pressures in acute health settings, avoiding people having to give up assets to pay for care, and working out a fair and equitable system of funding. To illustrate the point, the 2011 Dilnot Commission report on social care funding, which has dominated the debate about funding for the last decade, did not address the issue as it affected children's services, and the Johnson government's 2021 announcement of additional funding for social care referred to children only in the context of building five new children's hospitals.

In saying this, I would not wish to diminish the importance and relevance of children's services in any discussion on social care. Considerations of adult social care must bear in mind the relevance of families and households as whole entities, when determining and responding to people's needs in terms of care and support. In this regard there are many who still dispute the advantages of the breakup of social services departments in England into separate children's and adults' services departments between 2003 and 2008 following the report by Lord Laming into the death of Victoria Climbié. There is undoubtedly a UK wide funding gap in relation to children's services, attributable in part to increased social pressures, child poverty, and the identification of children with complex needs. The number of children looked after by local authorities has risen exponentially, and the cost of individual specialist placements can, in some cases, be counted in the hundreds of thousands. There are particular challenges of funding and support when children transition into adulthood. Overall, therefore, there are also many so-called "problems" that need to be resolved in respect of providing care and support for children that also need to be borne in mind when considering how best to organise and deliver an effective social care system.

Whilst commenting on how different aspects of social care policy are applied across the UK, this chapter does not attempt to appraise or compare current performance in social care by the four UK nations. Implicitly, therefore, social care is taken to mean social care that is capable of being delivered to a good quality. Neither does it offer a simple solution – the complexity of the subject matter deserves greater consideration than that affordable to a single chapter in a book. Instead, it sets a basis for further debate, centred on the notion that social care policy in England is not best formulated at central government level and should be devolved to appropriately sized regions, following the pathway set by the existing devolved nations. It promotes the argument that form must follow function in determining the future shape and governance of social care; therefore, the function of social care must be better understood in terms of its wider application to ensure it is not considered solely as an extension of the NHS, and that the challenge of funding social care should not inhibit ambition in determining how best to strategically plan and deliver it sustainably.

As we consider solutions for the social care "problem", we must keep in mind the primary challenges we are looking to resolve. Many, but not all, are linked to bridging the funding gap. These include:

- the need to invest in a poorly paid workforce in order to resolve significant recruitment and retention problems;
- ensuring that the care market is sustainable;
- adopting charging policies that are not punitive to the service recipient;
- enabling new models of care to be introduced safely whilst disinvesting in those that are outdated.

Others changes, however, are less dependent on funding. These involve making policy choices about the balance of care provision amongst public, private, and third sectors; placing an emphasis on prevention; and working co-productively to match people's expectations and allow them to exercise a large degree of voice and control over the services they receive. There are many other more detailed and nuanced issues that face social care agencies on a daily basis that the regional administrations of the future would need to face. Whilst the funding-related challenge would need a fundamental shift in government policy around taxation and benefits systems to be resolved, the others could get off to a flying start through more devolved autonomy building on the local intelligence that already exists.

What exactly is adult social care?

Smith et al. (2019) suggest the term "social care" emerged in both official and academic publications in England in the 1990s but has not been defined in legislation. They note that whilst the element of "personal care" has been present in the range of descriptions of social care, the policy context has changed dramatically, affecting the broader debate about priorities in public support for vulnerable adults. They also argue that the meaning of social care as a policy has changed over time and this confirms the relevance of undertaking a historical review to determine where we are today. My intention in this chapter, however, is not to attempt to create a new definition of adult social care that is relevant to meeting today's public policy challenges but rather to provide a deeper understanding of social care on which to base an argument for a more devolved regional approach to its governance.

That said, it is worth establishing a baseline of understanding of the fundamentals of social care and to do this I refer to two descriptions, both cited in Smith et al. (2019), being excellent account of the indeterminacy of the concept of social care. The first, by the Law Commission in 2011, saw social care as including

> older people, people with learning disabilities, physically disabled people, people with mental health problems, drug and alcohol misusers and carers. Adult social care services include the provision by local authorities and others of traditional services such as care homes, day centres, equipment and adaptations, meals and home care. It can also extend to a range of so-called non-traditional services such as gym membership, art therapy, life coaching, personal assistants. emotional support, and classes or courses. Adult social care also includes services that are provided to carers-such as help with travel expenses, respite care, and career advice. Finally, adult social care also includes the mechanisms for delivering services, such as assessment, personal budgets and direct payments.
>
> *(paragraph 1.5)*

The second description, in the 2012 White Paper on reforming care and support in England, placed adult social care in the context of overall care and support which it referred to as enabling

> people to do the everyday things that most of us take for granted like getting out of bed, dressed and into work; cooking meals; caring for our families; and being part of our communities. It might include emotional support at a time of difficulty or stress, or helping people who are caring for a family member or friend. It can mean support from community groups and networks: for example, giving others a lift to a social event. It might also include state-funded support, such as information and advice, support for carers, housing support, disability benefits and adult social care.
>
> *(HM Government 2012, p.13)*

Both these descriptions allow us to begin to understand that social care is certainly not one-dimensional, and it follows that planning for its effective delivery is inevitably going to be a complex task. The term "social care" is often used synonymously with "social work" and "social services" even though they are clearly different elements within the care system – social care generally being thought of as relating to the practical components of personal care, social work the more professional interventions, and social services the overall package of services that are the responsibility of local authorities. In this chapter, I am not overly concerned with these differences and am happy to embrace the widest interpretation of social care as a concept that embraces all of these elements, the reason being that in discussing social care as an area of public policy, it is impossible to avoid simultaneously considering the statutory duties of social services authorities and their social work function. The narrative that follows, therefore, will contain references to all three expressions.

Learning from history

In many ways, understanding social care is synonymous with understanding social welfare in general. At the heart of it, historically, is the philosophical division of individualism and collectivism, the former assuming that people are individuals responsible for their own well-being devoid of any state intervention, and the latter based on emphasising the role of the state in assuming some responsibility for supporting people because of the social conditions in which they live and the impact on the quality of their lives. The beginning of attempted reforms of the Poor Laws at the start of the 20th century and the 1911 National Insurance Act heralded new approaches that would eventually lead to the creation of what we now refer to as the welfare state. It is worth noting that there remain ingredients of individualism and collectivism in the current approaches to social care in that there is a strong emphasis on today's care agencies promoting independence and encouraging people to recognise their own strengths in maximising their levels of self-sufficiency.

An interesting insight into some of the origins of social services can be found in the early writings of Clement Attlee who, as Labour Prime Minister from 1945 to 1951, led his government in founding the welfare state. Jonathan Dickens (2018) at the University of East Anglia helpfully reminds us of the relevance of these writings. It is often forgotten that Attlee was a social worker prior to becoming a politician and he wrote in 1920 that social work was formerly done "for" the working classes but was now done "with" them. He argued that social work needed to move from its basis in ideas of charity to a "social service idea" grounded in social justice and citizenship. He was even so enlightened as to lay down a pathway to what we now call co-production by referring to social workers and those who received their services as "fellow workers" in creating a better society. This is probably a timely reminder that we should always regard developing trends in social care and social work in the context of historical events.

Attlee further helped us understand the foundations of social care and social work by arguing that social workers should be pioneers in social reform, tracking the results of new policies and legislation and campaigning for change. He also argued for good working conditions for social workers and recognition of their value alongside stockbrokers or lawyers, demonstrating how little some debates have changed in over a century.

The main reference point for understanding modern social care for adults, however, is the 1948 National Assistance Act. Before the Second World War, the only publicly funded social care for older and physically disabled people was through the Poor Law, named Public Assistance following the Local Government Act, 1929. The Poor Law was abolished by the 1948 Act which required local authorities to provide residential accommodation for older and disabled people "in need of attention which is not otherwise available to them". Unlike the NHS where services were free at the point of delivery, local authorities could levy means-tested charges for residential and community services as well as commissioning fee-charging independent services. Thane (2009) notes that the boundary established in the Act between health and social care was far from clear and could not easily be identified for older and disabled people, another preview into current discussions about the need for greater health and social care integration.

The 1960s saw further legislation, via the National Assistance Act 1948 (Amendment) Act 1962 and the Health Services and Public Health Act 1968 which widened the role and powers of local authorities. These included providing meals, recreational workshops, and day centres for older and disabled people and providing care services including making adaptations to homes and providing domestic help. Thane (2009) comments on the growing concern, in the 1960s, about the lack of co-ordination of health and social services which led to the appointment of the Seebohm Committee on Local Authority and Allied Personal Social Services. This reported in 1968 stating that the development of domiciliary services needed to enable older people to stay in their own homes had been slow partly due to the shortage of trained social workers. The Seebohm report led to the 1970 Local Authority Social Services Act, establishing a single social services department covering services to both adults and children. As this was when I began my own career in social services, I want to pause our historical journey for a moment for some personal reflections on how the organisation and delivery of social services looked and felt at the time. Significantly, "social care" was not part of the professional vocabulary. Instead, "personal care" was the common way of describing those functions that related to actual bodily contact, undertaken by staff known as "manual workers"; "social work" reflected the professional aspect of providing support, undertaken by qualified staff; and "social services" was the umbrella phrase covering the whole dimension of social care provision, exemplifying the fact that the emphasis at the time was very much on providing services to people rather than working with them to co-productively find solutions to their difficulties.

The 1970 Act had emphasised the need for a coordinated approach to social care which involved detecting need and encouraging people to seek and receive support. It was followed by the Chronically Sick and Disabled Act of 1971 which required authorities to register disabled people and publicise their services. A major reorganisation of the NHS and local authorities ensued in 1974 and certain functions, such as psychiatric social work, transferred from the NHS to local government. Depending on the political views of local councillors, the priority was to place the safety net for people in need quite high, exemplified in my own authority by a generous provision of free telephones to those regarded as generally housebound, a liberal approach to providing disabled car badges, and a refusal to charge for home care and many other services. It is very much felt, however, that support was still being done "to" people in that people were often fitted into available services rather than the other way around exemplified by relatively strict regimes of mealtimes and bedtimes and a lack of menu choice in residential care homes.

It was possible in the 1970s and 1980s to understand social care through a simple matrix of services, with one axis containing the different population groups – then referred to as the elderly, the physically and mentally handicapped, the mentally ill, and children and families – and the other the services available to them: home care, residential care, day care, and the protection and family support provided by social workers. This, of course, is an oversimplification and does not do justice to the range of complex skills and tasks staff employed on a daily basis in helping to support people. Nevertheless, it is a useful illustration of how both the language around social care and the approaches followed today have evolved. The elderly are now generally referred to as older people; learning difficulties is now deemed to be a more appropriate expression to describe people formerly regarded as being mentally handicapped; and safeguarding is now the preferred way of describing that aspect of service formerly known as child protection. A proper acknowledgement that adults also needed safeguarding from harm and abuse came much later.

Arguably, the most fundamental shift in late 20th century approaches to adult social care, however, came with the NHS and Community Care Act of 1990. A decade of Thatcherism had seen unprecedented cuts in public services and a big shift to downsize the state in favour of privatisation of services. The White Paper which preceded the Act had stated the government's expectation that local authorities would make use whenever possible of services from voluntary, not-for-profit, and private providers to maximise cost effectiveness. Much of social workers' activity moved into what became known as assessment and care management where their primary function was to assess people's needs and commission services to meet those needs. Many social workers argued that this de-professionalised their contribution to people's well-being, taking them away from undertaking the skilled interventions for which they'd been trained. Effectively the commissioner/provider split in the functions of social services had arrived with the 1990 Act.

A central aim of the Act had been to shift the balance of care away from institutions like care homes and hospitals to care in the community but the absence of increased funding to support this inhibited its progress. Inevitably, services became more and more targeted at those in greatest need and whilst the logic of prioritising those people is undeniable, the true value in terms of preventing the escalation of need through relatively low-level services like cleaning, shopping, and even lighting house fires in some cases became lost. There isn't time here to debate the alternative argument that such services added to feelings of dependency and inhibited independence.

Thane (2009) suggests that services at the time were highly variable across authorities. Interestingly, in the context of this book, there was some local and regional resistance to the national prescription. Thornicroft (1994) reported that Southwark Council, for example, had proposed to spend a different proportion of transferred funds for residential care from social security budgets than prescribed in Department of Health guidelines because of a fear of starving some groups of services. Another example saw the predominant position in pre-devolution Wales following the Act still being the direct provision of social services by local authorities. These simple examples demonstrate that in such a complex area of service such as social care, where so many local circumstances vary, it is naïve to suggest a single central government policy can be universally applied.

The final stage of our journey through history brings us up to date by examining what has happened since the Great Recession of 2008. The Coalition Government began a programme of austerity and pronounced in 2010 that social care in England should not be solely the responsibility of the state and that communities and wider civil society should be set free to run innovative local schemes and build local networks of support. This was accompanied by Prime Minister Cameron's vision of the "Big Society". Supporters of small government welcomed this and the approach also found favour in some professional circles if it resulted in fewer people being inappropriately drawn into the care system. An alternative view was that this was a cynical attempt by central government to divest itself of some of the burden of financing social care by passing responsibility for care and support back to individuals and local communities under the guise of giving them voice and control and consciously keeping people out of the system through raising eligibility criteria. It forced a re-think of the balance between the individual and the state in terms of personal responsibility for well-being.

Similar debates began in the devolved nations as they too faced the prospect of what was to become a decade of spending cuts. The period 2010–2020 saw increasing recognition of the importance of social care in an integrated health and social care system. Unfortunately, this has been accompanied by references to it being in crisis and as a problem that needed resolving. This crisis is based not only on the mismatch between the needs of an ageing population and reduced public expenditure but also on the relative lack of value placed on social care workers, the insecurity of the care home market, and a lack of any cohesive strategy by government to tackle the issues in the short, medium, and long term. Significantly, the funding crisis in particular is regarded by the devolved nations as one that is preferably sorted at the UK level because of its close links with the benefits system. As the First Minister of Wales declared in May 2021,

> What I'm not prepared to do it commit to spending large sums of money that come to Wales to deal with the responsibilities that we have only to find all that money taken back to the Treasury through the benefits system.
>
> *(BBC 2021)*

He also confirmed, however, that Wales would go it alone if the UK government failed to produce a plan in the near future. This is a further example of the relevance of social care as a central topic in any debate about the merits of a more devolved approach to government in the UK and it will be interesting to see how the devolved governments react to the September 2021 decision to increase UK wide funding but still without a detailed plan for reform of the system.

The same period also saw the creation of significant legislation and initiatives across the UK. The 2014 Care Act facilitated a framework in England for determining when an adult was eligible for care and support. It has been described as the most significant change in social care law in England for 60 years through its objectives of reducing reliance on formal care, promoting people's independence and well-being, and giving people more control over their own care and support (Hunter et al. 2020). The Social Services and Well-being (Wales) Act 2014 has similar objectives and places an emphasis on preventing the escalation of need, working collaboratively across agencies, and recognising the improvement of well-being as an outcome for people needing care and support. In Scotland, the Public Bodies (Joint working) (Scotland) Act of 2014 requires the integration of local health and social care services. In Northern Ireland, where joint health and social care organisations had been in place for over 40 years, the Transforming Your Care Programme led to the creation of a national strategy called "Health and Wellbeing 2026: Delivering Together" which seeks a more holistic approach to health and social care.

Policy comparisons across the UK

In any discussion that favours further devolution, it is tempting to begin with a strong case exposing how the devolved nations have used their discretionary powers widely to improve services through innovative and tailored policies. The search for differences in the approaches to social care, however, must begin with similarities. All four nations believe the current arrangements are struggling, if not failing, to meet its declared intentions and all four continue to operate a means test (of different generosity) to determine eligibility for state funded care and support for at least some services. The search also reveals that fundamentally all four nations are adopting similar objectives in that they are looking to:

- create person-centred care where the individuals are able to work co-productively with commissioners and providers of care in exercising voice and control over the care and support they receive, increasingly through the use of direct payments;
- prevent people needing to enter the care system through being encouraged to recognise and use their strengths and access good community support;
- ensure that agencies work collaboratively in planning and delivering services.

These similarities are not surprising in that, notwithstanding the individual nature of people's needs and circumstances, it is difficult for governments to justify wanting different outcomes for the population as a whole. Moreover, all four nations' flexibility is constrained by the size of the public purse. Their reliance on a central government funding system, with its control of taxation and social security benefits, limits the ability of devolved governments and local authorities to exercise discretion where costs are involved. This challenges the extent to which they can be ambitious for people in terms of state support and the methods used to fulfil that ambition, but there is evidence that they have pushed the boundaries of their discretion whenever possible. Although there are different priorities given to different needs at given points in time, the main differences amongst the four nations tend to relate to the structures, methods of delivery, and charging policies that apply, which in turn affects their spending patterns. For example, we have already noted the separation of adults' and children's social services in England but not elsewhere. There are also different means of achieving collaboration with the NHS which reflect the different health service structures across the UK. The generosity applied to means testing varies, with most personal and nursing care being free in Scotland following an assessment, and charges for home care in Wales being capped at a maximum amount of £100 per week at the time of writing. Wales also operates a much higher threshold for disregarding assets in respect of how much people pay for residential care. Nobody over 75 is charged for home care in Northern Ireland.

These variations are significant in themselves but may appear relatively marginal in terms of resolving the so-called social care problem especially when one considers the centrality of the shortage of funding to the difficulties governments face. For example, those seeking more frugality in public spending point to the subsidisation of care as simply adding to the problem. Jones (2020) contrasts the increasing central government shaping and regulation of the personal social services with the greater decentralisation in other countries and notes the "significant differences of emphasis and horizons" between the devolved administrations of the four UK countries. Importantly, the variations represent part of different overall policy frameworks and political approaches to matters of public services and social welfare. They display sufficiently differing intent to demonstrate the potential for a much more radical approach, if finances permitted. In other words, where discretion has been possible, it has been used and this suggests both an appetite and benefit in having more.

Year 2021 saw the report of a major study by the Institute for Government into how each of the administrations of the UK have made different choices about how much to spend on public services and how to manage them. This confirmed that all four nations shared a set of aims but revealed that they provide different levels of adult social care, with all three devolved governments spending more on care than in England. Some of the other significant headlines from this report are that the gap in spending between the devolved nations and England has widened in the past ten years. Interestingly, however, spending is similar for working-age adults but a lot less in England when it comes to spending on older people. In Wales, spending on residential care is reported to have risen in the past few years, possibly due to the more generous threshold for disregarding assets, and in Scotland the free personal care policy is highlighted as the likely reason for an increase in care in the community rather than in care homes.

These examples illustrate how policy choices affect not only spending patterns but how outcomes for people are managed. The policy comparisons across the UK, therefore, enable some valuable learning about the challenges facing social care but also, more importantly, about some of the possible remedies, as they evidence that there is a direct correlation between political choices, public spending, and service configuration. Unfortunately, the report also concludes that the impact of social care on people's well-being and safety is difficult to measure and it is hard to judge the consequences of cutting state-funded social care. It posits that it is not possible to say from the data which social care system in the UK performs best. The report does acknowledge, however, that the number of people accessing care has not kept up with demand in any of the four nations with the number receiving home or community care falling sharply in England after 2008 more than in any other country. The report succinctly concludes that "squeezed budgets have resulted in squeezed services in all four nations".

The funding dilemma

Given the centrality of the debate about funding, it is appropriate to now reflect on the suggestions offered to date for resolving the problem. I have already referred to the 2021 announcement of £12 billion per annum for health and social care, only £1.8 billion of which is earmarked specifically for social care. The Institute for Fiscal Studies points out that the additional £1.8 billion per year is equivalent to around 9% of what councils spent on social care services in 2019–2020 but that as a result of the big spending cuts in the early to mid-2000s, adult social care spending per person was 7.5% lower in real terms in 2019–2020 than in 2009–2010. They conclude that

> it is clear that the extra funding will not be sufficient to reverse the cuts in numbers receiving care during the 2010s. Thus, while more people will become entitled to financial support as a result of the reforms planned, many people with care needs not considered severe enough will continue to miss out.
>
> *(see Johnson et al. 2021)*

Although the additional funding will be statutorily ring-fenced, there is no guarantee that councils, under pressure to support other important services like education, will not see it as an opportunity to divert funds in those directions that were otherwise earmarked for social care. The funding must also be seen within the context of the gap in funding between what is needed for adult social services and what is available. The Health Foundation (2021) estimates the gap in England for 2030/2031 to range from an additional £6.1 billion needed to meet

(a) future demand to £14.4 billion to meet (b) future demand, improve access to care, and allow local authorities to pay care providers more to improve the quality of care people receive. These estimates do not include additional funding needed to protect people against the high costs of care, i.e. the cap on total individual lifetime spending. Unsurprisingly, the Health Foundation's response to the UK government's September 2021 announcement is less than complimentary. It describes the additional funding as being "well short of what is needed to stabilise the current system and the comprehensive reform so desperately needed" and that the government had "parked decisions on wider funding and reform".

The King's Fund (2021) point to a number of options for reforming social care funding, "all of which have advantages and disadvantages". These include reform of the means test, a cap on care costs, and an improved preventive offer to support people with lower levels of need. The King's Fund rightly argue that

> reform to funding and eligibility must go hand in hand with wider system reform of social care that sees quality improved, reforms to improve the operation of the social care market, better integration with the NHS, and a strategy for expanding and supporting the workforce.

Two previous reports on funding of social care are worthy of mention. The first is the 2011 report by the Dilnot Commission which referred to tighter rationing of services and rising levels of unmet need. Dilnot's brief was limited to addressing funding and he recommended, amongst other things, a cap on lifetime care costs of between £25,000 and £50,000 and a raising of the threshold in the means test for disregarding assets to £100,000. The costs of implementing the proposals were estimated at the time to be around £1.7 billion, rising to £3.6 billion by 2025/2026. He went further, however, in also making recommendations about improving the integration of health and social care, and establishing national eligibility criteria. The Dilnot report created much debate and was generally well received, with the King's Fund commenting that the question was "not whether we can afford the Dilnot proposals but how can we afford not to". No government action followed!

The other notable report, commissioned by the Welsh Government in 2018, was by Professor Gerald Holtham who recommended creation of a social care insurance fund, drawing on funding from a "reasonably moderate" tax on incomes or increase in basic income tax. This would possibly be a contributory scheme if practicalities and administrative costs allowed. Holtham also favoured making tax contributions dependent on age cohort as well as income in the interests of inter-generational fairness. The subsequent inaction on this must be seen in the context of Wales's First Minister's reluctance to act prior to greater fiscal clarity from the UK government.

So, there appears to be a limited range of choices available to government(s) to increase funding for social care, all of which have potential consequences either at the ballot box or for public finances and the economy in general. The fundamental choice is whether to accept social care as an important public service deserving of financial support comparable to that given to the NHS or to continue with the means tested system and maximise the income from service recipients through increased charges (or, of course, a combination of both). The September 2021 decision to increase national insurance contributions and dividend tax makes some attempt at the former but is woefully short of what is required and the social care element is much less than allocated to the NHS. In respect of the latter, local authorities have seen their budgets slashed for over a decade, mostly in England, and councils have been under unprecedented pressure to maintain services and keep council tax increases at reasonable levels. In any case, the extent to which council tax can meet the funding gap in social care is very restricted.

Notwithstanding all of this, we must bear in mind that currently, funding for social care services is determined by a number of factors including:

- the amount of funding "notionally" determined each year for social care by the UK government;
- the incorporation of that funding with other elements of the local authority revenue support grant and the way that funding is distributed amongst local authorities;
- the decisions local authorities take about using their allocation of revenue support grant (and council tax proceeds) and the amount they allocate to social care;
- the income from charges levied by the social care authority.

Thus, whatever announcements are made by national government about changes in social care funding levels, the amount allocated to a particular social care service may be very different – too many other factors are at play. This is a complete breach of accountability by the UK government which identifies a "notional" amount for social care funding but does not have to deal with the consequences if the actual amount received by local authorities is inadequate.

Under a system of English regional government, each region would likely receive a block grant from the UK national government and would decide how much of that grant could be assigned to social care. This is currently the case with the devolved national governments. Greater devolved powers to all parts of the UK, however, would free up devolved governments to become more economically self-sufficient and capable of levying their own taxes to finance public services. More innovative fund-raising schemes should follow, one example, as already mentioned, being the establishment of the proposed hypothecated tax in Wales, the proceeds of which would be applied to social care.

Integration

Before moving to conclusions about the future of social care, I want to briefly explore a policy that has been become something of a Holy Grail for successive governments for decades – the integration of health and social care. In Chapter 13 of this book we explain some of the features of integration in the context of collaborative working and its relevance to a devolved system of governance. In this chapter, I comment on the relevance of integration to the effective delivery of a whole system approach to health and social care.

When one considers the determinants of ill-health, e.g. poverty, poor housing, obesity, smoking, alcohol misuse, it is clear that the NHS, as currently configured, plays a relatively small part in their prevention. Many of the services that affect public health – housing, leisure, environmental health, education, social care – fall within the remit of local authorities, and it is not difficult to arrive at the logical conclusion that the better the collaboration between these different agencies and the NHS, the more likely there will be better social and health-related outcomes for people. Similarly, the more joined up aspects of health services can be – primary, secondary, and public health – the better too. True integration goes much further and can be simply encapsulated by the phrase "health and social care integration".

One objective of the NHS is to ensure people do not require treatment in hospital settings unless absolutely necessary, and, following treatment, they are able to leave hospital as soon as possible. Achieving this is often dependent on social care: first playing an effective role in helping to prevent admission to hospital, and second being able to support people when they are discharged. In recent years these functions have fallen under the term "reablement" and are generally provided or commissioned by local authorities as part of domiciliary care services. The degree to which this approach succeeds in practice is dependent on all the factors already mentioned – finance, workforce, etc. – but perhaps more importantly on the respective agencies having a shared purpose and common values.

When care and support is truly integrated, the tensions that exist between agencies, professionals, and practitioners dissipate. Solutions are discovered via conversations rather than procedures. Leaders display qualities of trust and joint direction. Territorialism and sovereignty become secondary to shared accountability. All four nations are placing a priority on achieving integration, albeit through different approaches. Whilst the evidence to support integration as a policy remains patchy, the Bill "reflects the conventional wisdom that the solution to the pressures….is integrated care" (Williams 2021).

Possibly the biggest initiative in achieving integration is currently underway in Greater Manchester where, in 2016, control of the region's £6 billion combined health and social care budget was handed over to local leaders as part of the first devolution of its kind. Key features include multidisciplinary neighbourhood teams, population health management, and community-focused models of care that centre on community and primary care and minimise hospital use. The Greater Manchester Health and Social Care Partnership claims to have made a "significant improvement in the quality of social care" through personalising care and support, raising pay rates and standards and improving leadership and management skills. They support their claims with statistics. However, a new report by the centre-right think tank, the Centre for Policy Studies (2021), provides data to suggest that with some exceptions, health and social care outcomes in the region are "generally significantly worse" than would have been expected. The report compares its performance against that of the West Yorkshire and Harrogate Health and Social Care Partnership, which it argues is more typical of what the ICS model will look like across England. In this region, performance is considered to be "slightly better" but that "the picture is one of limited change". The report acknowledges that the evidence is preliminary and that it could take over a decade for an ICS to bed in. Perhaps most significantly, in the context of this book, the report questions the top-down approach contained within the new Bill and advocates one which "recognises that integration is a matter of local collaboration and trust, developed over time through persistent working relationships. It cannot be willed into being by bureaucratic fiat" (Williams 2021). Despite inconsistent performance evidence, integration as a common UK policy is unlikely to disappear. Chapter 13 promotes the argument that the reasons for the inconsistency lie more with problems of implementation than concept and principle.

Organising social care for the future – understanding the key ingredients

In considering the best way to plan, organise, and deliver social care services in the future (the form), it is essential first to fully understand the concept and purpose of those services (the function). We have learned from our examination of some of the descriptions of adult social care, its history, its current shape and form, its policy diversity, its funding crisis, and its future strategic policy direction, that there are features and characteristics which help us understand what social care means today and on which we can base our thinking for the future. For ease of reference, I'll refer to a ten-point template for doing this.

1. Social care is essentially a highly personal, and increasingly personalised, service. Whilst many services are universally applied amongst those in need of care and support, the nature and circumstances of individual need means services will always need to be personally responsive and tailored if they are to be fully effective. Where services are delivered in a shared environment, e.g. in residential care homes, the emphasis is still on operational arrangements that respect people's dignity and individual needs and preferences.
2. The vast majority of social care is delivered locally, often and where possible in or close to people's own homes. Decisions about how to respond to people's needs are best made with the person, not for them, and therefore at the most local level possible. Individuals can be supported to properly articulate their needs through third parties like advocates.
3. A wide range of activities are included in social care, from providing some simple functional aids to complex interventions, each playing a different and complementary part in responding to people's needs and improving

their well-being. Actions to safeguard people from physical, emotional, and financial harm are a fundamental element of social care. Assuming social care merely relates to those domiciliary care functions that help relieve pressure on the NHS therefore does it a major disservice.

4 The value of social care is as much about preventing need as reacting to it. New models of care are constantly being developed to facilitate people's independence. Social care is central to ensuring and improving people's well-being. It plays a key coordinating role in protecting people from harm as well as in harnessing the roles of other agencies like housing and education to maximise people's potential and live fulfilled lives. It is, therefore, a major contributor to the welfare state and societal change.

5 The statutory responsibility for the delivery of social care rests with local authorities (except in Northern Ireland which has joint health and social care boards) whose role has shifted over time from being direct providers of services to commissioners. Social care is commissioned to be delivered by agencies within the private, independent, and third sectors as well as still being provided, in fewer cases, by the public sector. There are thousands of employers operating in the social care market including individuals themselves via direct payment schemes. That market is therefore very fragmented and does not operate as freely as others in commercial terms because commissioners have a powerful role in determining price.

6 Successful delivery of social care is dependent on maintaining a sufficient supply of competent workers. Those workers employed on the front line of care are characterised as being low paid and unqualified. There is a shortage of workers in social care, and social care employers find it difficult to compete in the employment market for staff, especially with the NHS and the retail sector. The size of the social care workforce means it is an important component of the UK economy.

7 The demand for social care has increased and is still increasing as people live longer and benefit from technological and clinical advances in health services. Resources available to social care agencies have not kept pace with this demand. The funding gap is measurable in billions and is increasing.

8 Unlike the NHS, social care services have not historically been free at the point of delivery but are subject to charging regimes that are based on means testing individuals' ability to pay through their financial assets. This is still the case in most instances although charges vary as a result of different political decisions by both the devolved national governments and local authorities, even to the extent of care now being free in some cases.

9 Social care agencies are obliged by law to work collaboratively. Different systems and legislation for achieving an integrated way of organising and providing care between the NHS and social services authorities and agencies operate across the four UK nations. The overall aim, however, of having integrated care throughout the UK is a common one and is unlikely to change as public policy in the foreseeable future.

10 The stated objectives of meeting people's needs for care and support are fundamentally the same throughout the UK. Differences across the four nations, although generally confined to structural arrangements and charging and spending policies, are significant in recognising the appetite and potential for exercising more regional and local discretion. This, however, is inhibited by central government's control of taxation and social security benefits.

Each of these issues presents options for policy makers and this reminds us of the absurdity that a single policy approach by the UK central government can ever be a viable proposition. The discretions used by the current devolved governments and local authorities, highlighted earlier, provide insight into some of the considerations which could be triggered by greater autonomy. There have been enough public pronouncements from ministers in the devolved nations to be confident about predicting the changes which would then occur in respect of charging policies, the balance of private/public provision, the impetus on greater collaboration, and better pay and conditions for the workforce. Moreover, there is no rational argument that suggests changes that are predictable in Scotland, Wales, and Northern Ireland would not be equally attractive in the English regions. Indeed, there is probably more scope in English regions because of their generally larger size.

However, the antithesis of this regional diversity is characterised by UK national politicians' apparent pursuit of a "one nation" state where the dreaded "postcode lottery" of uneven distribution and quality of service has become anathema. This is particularly evident at the time of general elections when issues of regional inequality become measures of governmental attitude and performance. Achieving equity is a noble ambition but proponents of the case for a one nation approach to ensuring equity of service provision and opportunity only have to look at the inequality of life expectancy in different regions of England to realise the invalidity of their argument. The irony here in the context of social care is that successive governments have epitomised the value of localism by promoting the concept of individual choice and control by the user of services as being central to their policy direction at the same time as tightening eligibility criteria and starving local authorities of the funds needed to implement radical change. The law also allows discretion to local authorities to set eligibility criteria and charging levels albeit within the overall financial envelope afforded to them by central government. In this regard, Lewis and West (2014) note that the Association of Adult Services in England had reported that the government's austerity programme from 2010 saw £2.68 billion savings made in adult social care, 20% of net spending, yet the government still denied the existence of a funding gap (and unmet need) and saw no reason to tighten eligibility thresholds. This reinforces claims that government's pursuit of personalised care is motivated more by opportunities to reduce public spending and the role of the state rather than altruistic attempts to improve outcomes for people.

Resolving the "social care problem"

We can use the features and characteristics in our ten-point template to re-assess what is meant by "the social care problem" and ensure it is not simply translated into "how do we adequately fund social care without having to raise all the revenue through taxation and/or charge people receiving care beyond their real means?" A more appropriate question that successive governments have failed to address properly, never mind answer, might be:

What is the best way to organise and sustain this highly personal invaluable public service, which is complex in nature, and covers a range of different tasks and functions, that are:

- *strategically planned and commissioned by local authorities but largely dependent on central government funding;*
- *subject to ever-increasing demand from demographic changes, especially an ageing population;*
- *suffering from an acute gap in funding that is measured in £billions;*
- *delivered predominantly by low paid and often unqualified workers, who work mainly for thousands of different private sector employers, and are in short supply; and is*
- *critically important in playing a major part in preventing ill health and hospital admissions, and supporting rehabilitation and independence?*

Finding a solution to the funding issue is, of course, central to addressing all the challenges facing social care but it is not the only issue. Achieving an integrated approach that produces beneficial outcomes is equally important. Policy decisions over the last 70 years have resulted in today's position where delivery of a crucial public service is dependent on a fragmented network of private employers who operate in a market that has been described as "unequal and inefficient" (Lewis and West 2014). The benefits of a mixed market of care in terms of stimulating choice for users through competition are compromised by the fact that prices are controlled by the purchasers (local authorities) not the suppliers (care providers) and that those purchasers' financial flexibility is controlled by the funding they receive from the central government. The logic underpinning this arrangement is at least dubious if not entirely flawed. Add to this the fact that the purchasers are effectively third-party agents acting on behalf of those whose care needs they have assessed and the lack of logic becomes even more pronounced. It has resulted regrettably in an oversimplified representation of the debate as being whether social care should be delivered by private or public sector bodies. This misses the point. The real issue is that if the government creates a system through policy, it should be obliged to ensure that the system can work effectively in practice.

I began this chapter by stating that "sorting out" social care is an extremely complex and difficult task and deserves greater consideration than that affordable to a single chapter in a book. The King's Fund (2021) point to the numerous failed attempts to find a way forward as including 12 white papers, green papers, and other consultations in England alone plus five independent reviews and commissions. Add to these works done by the devolved governments and you'll see what I mean. Social care has been bedevilled by the experience of the last 30 years in terms of government policy decisions that were as much to do with political philosophy and economic priorities as they were about meeting people's needs, coupled with too many quick fix ideas. I for one am not going to compound that felony. Deciding policy means making choices and managing the consequences. The review of social care we are still waiting for must not be another addition to the list of previous reports. It should be embedded in the mantra that "form should follow function" and take into account the views of not only current stakeholders but also as diverse a range of opinions from outside the sector as possible.

I'll conclude by reflecting on a couple of key facts which always return to mind when thinking of these hugely complex issues. The first is that we are content that our welfare system should provide social care, in its various forms, that is free for children – in some cases up to the age of 25 – and that healthcare should be free for people of all ages. Yet we perpetuate a system of means tested social care for adults and create a system to sustain that philosophy that involves complex bureaucratic procedures to facilitate a mixed market of care with inadequate resourcing. Furthermore, we support the idea of integration at the same time as operating policies and procedures, some of which are based in legislation and regulations, like Continuing Health Care and Funded Nursing Care, that hinder integrated working because of arguments about who is responsible for paying for care. The old joke when seeking a destination of "If I were you, I wouldn't start from here" rings true but hopefully we are now clearer about where "here" is.

Postscript

Stories are often the best way of getting a message across, no more so than when they relate to social care. Let me finish with one about Joyce and John. They had been happily married for nearly 50 years when John, then in his late 60s, was diagnosed with peripheral artery disease – blockages in the arteries which were no doubt a consequence of a toxic blend of tobacco, alcohol, and poor diet which plague many working-class people. Successful major by-pass surgery sorted John's problems out and his long-term post-operative treatment amounted to not much more than an aspirin a day.

Throughout his 70s John's health gradually deteriorated and eventually led to a diagnosis of vascular dementia. This affected both his cognitive and physical abilities and it was at this point that the local social services department was able to provide practical help via some household aids including the installation of a stair lift. Joyce provided any personal care that was needed and the couple's independence was preserved.

It was clear, however, that a journey towards greater intervention by social services had begun and over time, John's needs progressed to a stage where he could no longer get upstairs safely even with the stair lift. He also developed other problems associated with dementia like incontinence and communication difficulties. The NHS provided a specialist bed downstairs; social services arranged for the home to be further adapted in the form of a downstairs bathroom (John and Joyce contributed to the cost following a means assessment) and other access aids, and home care workers attended four times daily to help John get up in the morning, go back to bed in the evening, and meet his personal needs. The primary duty of care and support, however, continued to fall on Joyce who refused to view it as a burden and more a matter of love and responsibility. She was determined not to allow the obvious increasing impact on her own health and well-being to get in the way of caring for John but she did access some support as a carer in the form of occasional periods of respite care for John.

Throughout this period, John was able to attend a day centre regularly, facilitated by the availability of a mixture of council and third sector transport schemes. His care at home was complicated by his insistence on being cared for by male staff of which there was an acute shortage. Joyce was invited to consider having a direct payment to organise John's care and support directly rather than receive it from the council but she rejected this as she did not want the additional responsibilities of becoming an employer of personal assistants nor deal with the associated financial issues. He also underwent a Continuing Healthcare Assessment which deemed his primary needs to for social care not healthcare.

Eventually, John's disease became a life-threatening problem when he lost the blood supply to his leg. The medical advice amounted to a choice between him having to go through a series of dangerous surgical interventions, including amputation, or being enabled to live his short remaining days at home. On the advice of a sympathetic GP, and with the support of community nurses, the latter course of action followed and an end-of-life pathway was triggered, which included pain control. Not long after, John passed away at home with his dignity intact.

What can we learn from this story about how the health and social care system works?

- Many of John's health problems were preventable had he adopted a different lifestyle, but he was happy when he smoked, he ate what he liked the most, and he enjoyed and benefitted from the friendship engendered by a regular drink down the pub. His feeling of personal well-being, therefore, was good and this illustrates how elusive well-being is as a concept to be considered alongside good health.
- John's initial health and well-being needs were best met by the NHS but for the vast majority of the time, it was social care which he needed most. That care and support included liaison with health practitioners but required no structural or organisational changes amongst the agencies. Social care prevented John's needs escalating and, therefore, the need for expensive NHS interventions was avoided. However, that wasn't the driver for John's support package. It was about meeting his needs and there was no question of

him needing hospital treatment. Social care stood up on its own two feet, not as an extension of the NHS.

- John and Joyce benefitted from a relatively generous means testing system which capped the amount they were charged weekly for their home care. This took away any immediate financial worries they had.
- Joyce did not want a direct payment and its associated responsibilities. She was also glad to receive support directly from local authority staff, via John's social worker, the home care workers, and the team, at the day centre. She felt less secure when staff shortages meant different agency staff needed to be deployed.
- The biggest issue affecting the quality of John's care and support was undoubtedly the shortage of care workers, especially male care workers. This affected both the time John received support and its continuity.
- The end-of-life pathway necessitated close collaboration and integrated agency working involving the GP, community nurses, social worker, and domiciliary care service. It illustrates the point that integration works best when there is a clearly shared purpose.

By the way, John and Joyce were my parents.

References

BBC (2020) Social care reform needed within a year - NHS England boss, 5 July 2020 https://www.bbc.co.uk/news/uk-politics-53297312

BBC (2021) Election 2021: Wales 'ready to go' alone on social care reform, 9 May 2021 https://www.bbc.co.uk/news/uk-wales-politics-57048911

Department of Health (2010) *A Vision of Adult Social Care: Capable Communities and Active Citizens*, November, London: Department of Health.

Dickens, J. (2018) Clement Attlee and the social service idea: Modern messages for social work in England. *British Journal of Social Work*, 48, 5–20. https://doi.org/10.1093/bjsw/bcx025 Advance Access Publication April 21, 2017.

Health Foundation (2021) Social care funding gap: Our estimates of what it would cost to stabilise and improve adult social care in England, https://www.health.org.uk/news-and-comment/charts-and-infographics/REAL-social-care-funding-gap

HM Government (2012) *Caring for Our Future: Reforming Care and Support*, Cm 8378, July, London: The Stationery Office.

HM Government (2021) Build back better: Our plan for health and social care, September 2021 https://www.gov.uk/government/publications/build-back-better-our-plan-for-health-and-social-care/build-back-better-our-plan-for-health-and-social-care

Holtham, G. (2018) Paying for care: An independent report. Welsh Government.

Hunter, D. J., Redgate, S., Hudson, B., and Peckham, S. (2020) Do policy implementation support programmes work? The case of the care act 2014. *Journal of Long-Term Care*, 2020, 196–207. http://doi.org/10.31389/jltc.42

Johnson, B. (2021) Prime Ministers statement at press conference on health and social care, September 2021 https://www.gov.uk/government/speeches/pm-statement-at-press-conference-on-health-and-social-care-7-september-2021

Johnson, P., Emmerson, C., Miller, H., Phillips, D., Stoye, G., Delestre, I., Stockton, I., Ogden, K., Joyce, R., Adam, S., Waters, T., Warner, M., and Zaranko, B. (2021) Am initial response to the Prime Minister's announcement on health, social care and national insurance. Institute of Fiscal Studies.

Jones, R. (2020) 1970–2020: A fifty-year history the personal social services and social work in England and across the United Kingdom. *Social Work & Social Sciences Review*, 21(3), 8–44.

King's Fund (2021) A short history of social care funding reform in England: 1997 to 2021. https://www.kingsfund.org.uk/audio-video/short-history-social-care-funding

Law Commission (2011) *Adult Social Care*, Report 326, HC Paper 941, 10 May, London: The Stationery Office.

Lewis, J., and West, A. (2014) Re-shaping social care services for older people in England: Policy development and the problem of achieving 'Good Care'. *Journal of Social Policy*, 431, 1–18. Cambridge University Press. https://doi.org/10.1017/S0047279413000561

Smith, R. C., Lloyd, L., Cameron, A. M., Johnson, E. K., and Willis, P. B. (2019) What is (Adult) social care in England? Its origins and meaning. *Research, Policy and Planning*, 33(2), 45–56. http://ssrg.org.uk/members/files/2018/02/1.-SMITH-et-al.pdf

Thane, P. (2009) History of social care in England: Memorandum submitted to the house of commons' health committee inquiry: Social care, October 2009. https://publications.parliament.uk/pa/cm200809/cmselect/cmhealth/1021/1021we49.htm

Thornicroft, G. (1994) The NHS and Community Care Act, 1990: Recent government policy and legislation. *Psychiatric Bulletin*, 18, 13–17.

UK Government (2021) Build back better: Our plan for health and social Care. https://www.gov.uk/government/publications/build-back-better-our-plan-for-health-and-social-care

Williams, K. (2021) Is Manchester greater: A new analysis of NHS integration. Centre for Policy Studies

9
EDUCATION

Terry Mackie

Introduction

This chapter is concerned with educational outcomes and standards under a future regional government arrangement for England, with fully devolved powers, on the same lines as the 'Celtic' devolutions of 1999, but going further with stronger powers in many areas including economic development and taxation powers.

Such a proposition is a radical one for English schools, as since 1988 the grip of the central state over every aspect of schooling has been ever tightening. This chapter is limited in its scope to pre-schools, schools and further education; higher education is dealt with elsewhere in the book.

Beneath the proposed regional government jurisdiction there would without doubt be a greater role for the more local governance of schools, though this is not going to be a reversion to the status of LEAs and schools pre-1988. Too much water has flown under the bridge of schools' locally devolved management of staff and resources under decades of legislation that has culminated in Academies, Free Schools, Studio Schools and what is now called 'self-directed schools'.

This chapter covers the following:

- The purposes of education
- What's wrong with education in the UK: Over-centralism
- Successful and unsuccessful education policies
- Key education issues for regional governments

The chapter makes scant reference to education in Northern Ireland for while it has many good schools, I do not think their system of national selection at age 11 and their deep religious sectarian differences being reflected in their schools,

DOI: 10.4324/9781003201892-12

together with the continuing instability of the devolved government, make for good comparisons with the rest of UK for the purposes of this book.

Purposes of education

To begin with, learner attainment and achievement as concepts need some unpacking as these relate to the first purposes of education. These extend further than employability based on measurable skills and qualifications. The 1944 Butler Act definition still remains the neatest encapsulation of the aims and purposes of education ('understanding and independence'). Academics and politicians have argued other definitions ever since then, as society, the economy and lifestyles (for example there are many, many more single parents and, best of all, parents have never cared more actively about their children's learning) have changed hugely in the intervening eight decades.

In Wales, the Welsh Government deserves some credit for the latest (2016) incarnation of the purposes of the curriculum (for which we may read 'education'): this is what the 2022 New Curriculum for Wales is predicated on:

- Ambitious, capable learners who are ready to learn throughout their lives
- Enterprising, creative contributors who are ready to play a full part in life and work
- Ethical, informed citizens who are ready to be citizens of Wales and the world
- Healthy, confident individuals who are ready to lead fulfilling lives as valued members of society

This broader set of meanings shows all the high energy of devolved new thinking (not without risk) but will suffice for my own definition of aims and objectives in this chapter. I am delighted by the intention to emphasise enterprise in the curriculum – even more so by the aspiration to school all learners in the creative arts, which I believe is essential to a rounded, more humane sense of education. New UK regional governments could do much worse than to aim and build for its future adult population as more aspirational, more enterprising, more civil in its original sense and more into health and well-being. Weaving these worthy intentions into how and what is taught is clearly a very tall order but it does give a broader feel to achievement as an aim and is refreshing compared to the narrowness imposed on many schools currently doing the bidding of the super-centralists of Whitehall, Ofsted and Estyn. UK regions will have unmatched advantages in pursuing new curricula and pedagogy that reflect rethinking about what level of educated citizenry they consciously plan to foster. That said, they should try to tread not too boldly. Lofty education visions do not make for easy implementation or cogent consensus.

Education also has an important role to play regarding the economy of a region. It is still a matter of debate among economists and educationalists if education is *the* key driver for economic prosperity and social well-being but nobody could reasonably argue against the premise that education is front and centre to achieving those objectives. Moreover, as the world, society and economies become more complex, through the ubiquity of technology, increasing longevity of life and the welcome spread of schooling, even in the poorer nations, learning has never been at such a premium. Against that cheering backdrop, we have to ask ourselves one very hard question: why is education, especially when we talk of public service schooling, considered in many so-called first-world countries to be in crisis? Learner outcomes, absolute or relative, are hardly considered acceptable or fair. Part of the problem is related to a general mistrust of remote government acting in a highly centralised modus operandi (plus very low esteem for politicians, all according to repeated surveys).

Another issue where education is relevant is that of social mobility. This concerns the movement of individuals, families or groups through a system of social hierarchy or stratification and the lack of social mobility in the UK is seen as a major problem. Improving social mobility would be seen as a good thing among people of most political persuasions and education is seen as a key issue in promoting social mobility but is not the complete answer. The historian Selina Todd has recently, and very sharply, drawn our attention to the need for deeper change to ignite social mobility: she wrote recently '*...that it was not the individual ambition or self-help, but state investment and strategy that determined a person's mobility or lack of it*' (Todd, 2021). Better and coherent strategy is what we need to construct with education as a keystone in the new UK regional edifice. We have to rethink, then plan with more optimism, but respecting 'context' far more and put a stop to treating teachers as inexhaustible workhorses, which is the depressingly rational conclusion to the failing 'school improvement/school effectiveness' philosophy. We need 'better hope'. As Robert Coe (2013) rather splendidly puts it:

> Even if hope is not rational or evidence-based, we need to hold on to it. Education is far too important to give up on.

The latest views of the Social Mobility Commission (2020) commenting on unshifting inequity in English education for the period 2013–2020 will suffice for the question of whether education has been a competent driver for social mobility. These views are that the attainment gap between the rich and the poor at 16 is not closing, despite efforts to improve teaching and change the curriculum.

Professor Robin Alexander, using a more rounded lens, cites the 2010 views of social scientists Richard Wilkinson and Kate Pickett to expound his firm belief that internal and technical changes are not nearly enough:

> If... a country wants higher average levels of educational achievement among its school children, it must address the underlying inequality which creates a steeper social gradient in educational achievement.
>
> *(Alexander, 2012)*

It cannot work the other way around, which is the erroneous premise of those who have led the dominant theory of 'school effectiveness' from the late 1980s. The inequality not only precedes and underlies whatever can be thrown at it internally in schools: it is too steep to surmount at its most important hurdles of statutory school entry, secondary school transfer and post-GCSE arrangements. 'The gravity of high odds' remains at work in our system. 'The steeper the social gradient', some would say precipice, requires change which is both deeper and wider. Without economic development being regionalised, without corresponding authentic reform in governance, education remains a ship without mooring in hostile waters. Without deep engagement in changes for the benefit of whole regions, without decisions being made at the regional level on equity-informed policy, taxation and investment, without a levelling-up of resources across regions that is federally led, schooling will achieve at best slow, barely incremental progress and inequality will persevere. The thin gruel of the sort served up in the Prime Minister's July 2021 speech on levelling up will not touch the sides. Even step change is not enough. Several regions need quantum leaps in standards and outcomes. Do we have any evidence so far that 'regionalisation' as we understand it can make *the* difference in education? I think we have half a good model at least. And it is no accident that it was tried in London itself. London-centricity tends to opt for itself as we will see later.

What is wrong with education in the UK: Over-centralism

Systemic trust cannot simply be regained in the present rocky relationship. When richer nations feel so unhappy about schooling we are not mistaken to conclude that we need new ways of making 'the big decisions' and carrying these out better. Things fall apart, yes... and also yes that the UK has a special way of mitigating creeping collapse. We can still reinforce our foundations, the supporting structures of public services and even the mindsets of our key public servants and consequently our communities of parents and families. Education cannot 'fix itself', let us be clear. We have tried and failed mostly to do that for the last 30 years. We call that historical approach 'school improvement/school effectiveness' (basically it focuses *within the school* only on pedagogical leadership and management and teaching and learning processes) and its category error has always been that it ignores very important policy bearing on schools, it says nothing about deep structures and it writes off the whole question of governance. We must now, not before time, reconnect schooling in particular with realpolitik. We must start with education's political and economic underpinnings, which show obvious signs of subsidence. This means looking at schooling in its full societal context and *re-examining with a view to deep change* governance, school structures and a few but critical curricular sine qua non which pre-determine equity. Right now, they bake in inequity. There's rather a lot at stake when we countenance the regionalisation of education. Thus, a five- to ten-year total redesign programme incorporating regionalisation for education makes strategic planning sense.

Earlier in this book we discussed the raging inequality of opportunity and performance in UK education, dependent on parental income and leading to huge national and regional variations which in turn harm our overall growth and productivity. As John Rawls and others have explained, equality of opportunity is not just desirable but essential for fostering stability in society. Waste of human potential on the current grand scale is terrible for economic productivity. Education should be accelerating our wealth for all strata of society of the UK, but it is not doing so. We should have a certain vibrancy of civil society, but we clearly don't. Indifference has lately given way to toxicity. In UK terms, we cannot go on as we are with such apathy and inequality; for one thing, it weakens the UK union itself. Centralism has an awful lot to answer for. Specifically, education mirrors all the shortcomings well-rehearsed in previous chapters on economic development and societal ills, such as doubtful productivity, gross inequality across the UK and poor governance, then throws in a few more particular deficits of its own. Not least built-in classism/academic snobbery, poor value for public money and a workforce which is not being respected, valued or supported sufficiently. If our armed forces were so low on morale as our teachers and other school staff, there would be a public enquiry underway. One in three teachers leaves the profession within five years. This churn is much worse in deprived areas. These are symptoms of serious morbidity in any system.

Since the 1988 Education Reform Act (ERA) centralisation has been rampant across schools and colleges. Top-down curricula; testing and inspecting learners and schools to distraction if not destruction; and the abolition of the biggest regional Education Authority in the UK, the Inner London Education Authority (ILEA), just to name its main elements, in the grab for central power. Later, local authorities and their LEAs themselves were undermined by academies, then Free Schools, with thousands of local institutions finding themselves answering directly to ministers – directed into fragmentation but many later corralled into Multi-Academy Trusts (MATs). These new structures, which in round terms do not make unreasonable sense, would all work better and more efficiently if regionalisation were put in place. Localism in our schooling, and regionalism as a concept, has been in retreat ever since.

The system across England is more fractured, divisive and less concerned with equality of rounded achievement than ever. The same applies to a lesser or greater extent for all countries of the UK. I have argued previously that Wales may be superficially less divided in its schools but centralism remains rife even under the devolved arrangement. The dangerous duality of centralism-as-devolution is now at the heart of the contradictory efforts of the Welsh Government to impose a new and more rigid national curriculum framework. Its purposes cited above may not be contentious but its curricular tenets and implementation planning are both muddled and the work of a coercive civil service.

The historical trend of education centralism has been insufficiently examined in the light of concerns about national standards across the UK. The chronic gap between wealth and learning is as bad in education as in health. Mainstream educational research has suffered a kind of cognitive dissonance in this respect. The floundering efforts of the devolved governments of Scotland and Wales to improve schools since 1999 caution that regionalism mimicking 1990s UK centralism will not work either. Scotland and Wales are operating not as dynamic regions, as this book envisages, but as nations aping 'Whitehall Central'. It would be certainly be a mistake to take those two as templates for English regionalisation. England itself has enormous variation across its regions; they range from powerhouses of frankly massive advantage to wastelands of embedded impoverishment and circular low aspirations.

The writer and former *Times* editor Simon Jenkins has long been a critic of first creeping, later endemic centralisation and has been a powerful advocate for what he terms 'localism'. Much of his 2004 work on this subject holds true 17 years later (even if he is undoubtedly a County Anglican traditionalist). 'All England is a suburb of London', as Henry James put it a century and more ago; Jenkins goes even further:

> This metropolitanism is hugely potent. It is the glue of centralism, of people who know one another, trust one another and do not trust those whom they do not know. This glue has seen British government through crisis after crisis, most of them self-generated.
>
> *(Jenkins, 2004, p. 124)*

The glue reference reminds us that we must 'replace the glue' that is still gumming up our constitutional and governance works. Care must be taken to not swap London-centric for Edinburgh- or Cardiff-centric, it needs reminding but new English regions would have an opportunity to make more of devolved power than the nations of 1999.

Simon Jenkins alludes in his 2004 critique to the blizzard of initiatives that howled down on schools under Tony Blair's Education Secretary, David Blunkett. In his first two years, Blunkett found himself issuing 315 consultation papers, 387 regulations and 437 items of guidance. Hansard reported that, in 2001 alone, schools received 3,840 pages of instructions from London, or 20 pages per school day (Jenkins, 2004, p. 58).

No central policy stone was left untouched by succeeding Labour or Conservative ministers at Westminster and similar ministerial franticness was constantly complained of under Scotland's and Wales's administrations from 2006 onwards. Targets, new policies, more testing, strategies and countless reviews bombarded the schools of the UK during this period: from uniforms to hairstyles and how to do mindfulness during collective worship. Myriad grants were the carrots for compliance. In England around this time 26 time-consuming grant streams were on offer for busy headteachers to navigate. While LEAs had limited staff to process grants in literacy and numeracy, local accountability was being supplanted by a huge demand for central data, be it from the ministries or their regulators (inspectors).

By 2004 England had transferred the Council responsibilities of school planning and development to the Secretary of State (and later to his new quango – extending the remoteness).

PISA is a three-year international standards survey undertaken globally by the OECD to assess comparisons of applied learning for 15-year-olds. In Wales by 2011 Local Education Authorities were being pilloried by its government for the 2010 PISA 'shock wave', following the abject findings of these tests of 2010. Six out of 22 authorities were deemed in 'special measures'. Education targets set by the centre in 2001/2002 were clearly in tatters after a decade of overpromise and under-delivery but the connection between centralism as the only show in town and local 'emasculation' was never admitted to by the Cardiff Bay leaders of some 12 years. This has sometimes been referred to as 'blithering incompetence' (Mackie, 2019).

How bad or good were and are UK standards, anyway, under unremitting centralism? Disappointing UK PISA results (of learners aged 15 years) every three years tended to grab the headlines but at the same time GCSE grades seemed to be heading ever north. Professor Robert Coe, a leading expert on school improvement, assessment and accountability, offered in 2013 the most credible answer to the key question: have educational standards really risen? No, broadly, standards have not risen; teaching has not improved (Coe, 2013). This research is still valid eight years on as centralism has only taken deeper root. By comparing evidence from three sources – international surveys like PISA; independent studies, including some of his own research; and data from national exams –Coe concludes that there is little compatibility between international comparisons going south and fast-rising GCSE grades between 1996 and 2012, to the extent that the rather vertical direction of in particular the English public exams of GCSE as outcomes are 'not believable'. That's a grave conclusion to reach. This period was also largely one of high investment in schools as well as central diktat writ large. We should add that Coe's work demonstrates that a large element of 'gaming' has been going on in schools and at other tiers to underscore centralism with putative success outcomes. Should we blame school's leaders for getting good at the bad game? No – we should blame the government who set the policies.

Successful and unsuccessful education policies

In this section I look at an example of education policy which will be seen as unsuccessful and another which is seen as successful. The differences between them are quite stark.

Progress 8

First, I look at one example of why re-engineering school structures from a command-and-control centre does not fundamentally improve outcomes on the grand scale in England. This, an example of attainment variation at Key Stage 4, is that using Progress 8 measure in English schools. This is a key school accountability metric aimed at measuring the progress of pupils across a selected set of eight subjects from the end of primary school to the end of secondary school. In 2019 the DfE statistics for Progress 8 for 102 (with nearly 90,000 pupils) Multi-Academy Trusts (MATs – defined as a minimum of three schools in the same trust) make relevant reading. In that year 35% MATs were above average or better across the whole of the national spread, including every type of school. Twenty-nine percent were below the national average, with 10% were well below national average. That's just another classic UK attainment spread that has been the same story for years. The year 2019 was not an exceptional outcomes year in any sense.

We can see by this level of variation that all the changes wrought over the years of centralism and structural change, during this century, including introducing academies and MATs, have done little to even out attainment levels to an acceptable standard. Unfettering these schools from local authorities has not made any appreciable difference. The problems are chronic and systematic improvement is not happening. These kinds of changes don't make much difference, except to the pay of Executive Heads. In spite of the new, rather freestyle governance arrangements and preferential funding for academies and the like, tangible upticks are just not there on any scale. Coe has done sterling work to evidence that real UK and English improvement judged on many global comparisons is doubtful. We can see from Progress 8 measures in 2019 that new school types and commercial structures bring insignificant system impact. Academies have now been around long enough to change the dial significantly. This new sector is not making the difference. If anything, these schools are subject to more directed centralism.

Coe's solution/antidote system-wise was that this concerning state of affairs needed a new approach from 2013. This should not involve more top-down testing, more teaching to the test or more central initiatives within the already crowded curriculum, but a school-based, locally evidenced implementation of a *toolkit* for better teaching and assessment, combined with smarter evaluation of what actual learning is; and, whether professional learning is genuinely effective; more accurate assessment about teaching quality then lastly; more robust impact assessments of improvement actions taken.

The toolkit itself has been widely employed by schools across England (and elsewhere) and its focus on pedagogy and classroom impact versus cost has been a partial success. Leaders and teachers are learning to get more value and productivity by reference to some highly readable research. That said, the toolkit is not devised for, or capable of, addressing fundamental issues of lack of investment (austerity was well under way by 2013), professional morale, governance stasis, community disengagement and regional inequality. The toolkit is only as good as it goes, which is not very far. Coe has come up with the best there is in 'school improvement' but as CLR James famously said: 'what do they know of cricket who only cricket know?' One does not need to be a Marxist like James to know that largely technical solutions are mechanistic and just too spotty. Schooling is too 'messy' and complex for such rational but overly reductionist solutions to work sustainably. We need to get into systems thinking mode.

London improvement and challenge

Let us now look at an example of education policies which can be seen to be successful. From 2000 to 2014 a concerted effort was put in by central government under both parties to improve London's schooling as a region. By that time London had its own version of devolved mayoralty so we can call this an attempt at regional educational planning and improvement. As a very useful review report by CfBT Education Trust (CfBT, 2014) makes clear London schools made dramatic improvement in that period, from a low base, benefitting from several key improvement interventions, including Teach First for recruitment and the London Challenge whose focus was on partnership and shared purpose between schools, as well as increased direct funding. The report also cites the academies programme as a key intervention; however, as we have seen from the DfE above, we know academies do not in or by themselves guarantee above-average improvement and they certainly do not appear to bridge the inequality gap per se. London academies did not gainsay that fact. There was no 'one silver bullet', as the report correctly concludes, for the exciting progress made across the region. What the report misses, however, is as important for our discussion of future English regionalisation as anything it says.

London is always a special case. It gets the lion's share of UK public funding in the first place. It is not a post-industrial wasteland, quite the opposite. It has a supra-local governance structure of sorts in place, with direct elections for the mayoralty. Education improvement was building on good contextual rock. The CfBT report was wrong to assert that 'the improvement cannot be explained in terms of the advantages that London has over the rest of England'. London was *the* ideal regional test bed for such a project. This whole concept showed more than anything that for education to flourish the economic conditions around it have to be underpinned by appropriate economic planning advantage (which the capital has in spades), appropriate governance and seriously felicitous investment, especially in respect of 'infrastructure'. Transport is hugely funded in the capital, jobs are plentiful and it is after all the seat of decision-making and influence, which makes for ease of contact between Whitehall and the London lower tiers of government.

I worked in London pre- and post-2000 and I have never seen such an upsurge in school buildings being developed or rebuilt in the first decade of this century. Even CfBT had to 'fess up' that London got 'substantial investment' from 2003 onwards and this in turn raised staff morale. There is also evidence that it got more than its fair share of the national cake for school building capital, mainly through the efforts of London MP, Stephen Twigg, who was appointed Minister for London Schools, in May 2002. It was unusual in the department for a minister to have a geographically-defined remit, but the role was created at the behest of the Prime Minister. This was one of Blair's first actions in the drive on secondary school underperformance in the capital.

The Rowntree/Institute for Government's view (2014) was correct that this was much more than regionally based. The line from No. 10 to this regional project was clear for all to see. But the reality is that if England had nine regions no PM could have such direct power as was the case in London education 2000–2014. Power has to be given away by the centre and the old ways of patronage and favour must go. London had many advantages to start with to boost its education mission. Nobody can dispute the success of the schools achieving their goals but they were playing on a downhill pitch with important star signings and a very wealthy board of directors.

As a footnote to this story of London, which as I intimated provides half a model for the future, is that a number of other 'City/Region Challenges' were initiated to improve school standards across many schools. The London venture encouraged the adoption of the City Challenge programme, in Manchester and the Black Country, from 2008 to 2011. Much later Wales introduced its own challenge (Schools Challenge Cymru), under the leadership of Mel Ainscow, hoping to borrow his expertise and experience from Manchester. These new Challenges were not up to the mark in making the kind and level of improvements London had manifested. Even a rather rosy official evaluation revealed that Manchester had failed to narrow the attainment gap (surely the main objective?) and, astonishing to note, the Black Country ended the period with more schools in Ofsted categories of concern than there were at the outset. The Welsh Challenge floundered from its later start in 2014. A third of those schools went back in attainments at GCSE in Year 1 of the project, in spite of substantial extra funding, training and advice (with all ten advisers directed from the ministry in Cardiff Bay). The project was chopped after two years and a term.

Those three challenges were just regionally incoherent 'school improvement type' initiatives with a fancier name. They did not bear on any wider or deeper changes outside school walls. London still provides the best model we have seen as far as regional education is concerned. But, like Scotland and Wales, what we witnessed in London cannot provide a mould or a template that can be transferred healthily, or even with impunity. That is unless one takes all the London advantages that there are and redistributes them across the country, then adds in a few more vital ingredients, like self-sustaining regional governance and new, area-based taxation powers, plus a hotline to the PM who famously pronounced education, education, education as his government priority.

We now know a little more about the failures of centralism and the potential for describing what can go part-right and part-wrong with regional developments in education. But what would it all look like for schools if England developed regional devolution 'good and proper'? Economic development set free has to be its bedrock. Governance must be devolved and realigned itself within regions (this is highly important for schools and LEAs, of which more later).

Local priorities get energy from local taxation and income. Top-down mandate lacks implementation engagement and sustainability. Countless studies by the Canadian educationalist Michael Fullan over 30 years have shone great light of this chronically poor practice in terms of schooling. UK social mobility is presently stalled at best. That's nothing to do with pandemics. What education shows in its yawning attainment gaps is that schooling is a good barometer of social mobility fossilisation in the UK. Schools are neither cause nor full solution. Teachers might dream the latter and parents may wish it to be the case. For three decades we have struggled with the day-to-day practice of this idealistic theory – and it is high time we had a serious change of heart and direction. Regionalisation provides a promising fresh start.

Key education issues for regional governments

In this final section I look at the potential advantages for education of operating under a regional government model, provided the new regional entities are built on reshaped governance and politics at local and regional levels. Constitutional changes, which must be widely consulted on and written down, taxation reforms and Council and LEA structural changes are the pre-conditions to the more 'virtuous forces' that will drive education forward within new regional systems.

This section addresses the following:

- Governance
- Admissions
- Reading
- Post-GCSE structures

Governance

At all tiers, institutional, local and regional government, governance has to be transformed in a planned and radical fashion. In my experience, the same shortcomings are being repeated over and over again over three decades. Too much bad politics and not enough good governance; the malign pressure bearing down on these levels in education has never ceased since 1988 to be from the same source, an overbearing centre based in Whitehall, Holyrood or Cardiff Bay. It's centralism writ large and weighing down the system like some eternal leaden sky. Teachers and learners bear the brunt: this workforce pressure is largely ineffective. We have thus arrived in the third decade of the 21st century at:

- Over-politicised but poorly governed schooling at all tiers
- Wanton short-termism marked out by projects and 'initiativitis'
- Relentless overload of accountability and monitoring

- A lack of true structural innovation away from the 19th century model for schools and colleges
- The onset of demoralisation of teachers and school leaders
- Democratic disengagement from major policy formation

Tellingly, nobody really delves much into educational governance in UK academia, education or social sciences. This is really unchartered territory. It's as if the professionals do not really think the 'amateurs' of local government boards or school bodies are worth the trouble. They just play out policy from above. And what can be done about the mighty centre(s) that directs and dictates all? Voters decide all that at elections. The larger context is hard and protean to grapple with for those experts who prefer narrow focuses like 'school improvement', 'teacher training' or 'special needs'. However, the great Canadian educationalist, Michael Fullan, recently teamed up with the former Executive Director of the California School Boards Association Davis Campbell to put educational governance under the microscope. They also confirm that 'there has been little attention paid to the study and improvement of school district {LEA} governance'. If our new English regions are going to get better at educational governance, the work of Campbell and Fullan is a good place to start. And the US system is sort of regional already.

The Governance Core (Campbell and Fullan, 2019) immediately distinguishes politics from governance:

- Politics is *holding* and *using* power.
- Governance is *exercising authority* on a daily basis.

Public education **success for all** requires good politics with good governance which is defined as:

- Politics dominating only during the election
- Building capacity relative to the core agenda
- Recognising that government is for all the people
- Having long-term as well as short-term perspective
- Practising the implementation versus adoption mindset

If all this comes together 'good democracy' in education is achievable. The depth of democratic disengagement at devolved and local government levels in the UK puts this intention into stark relief. The aim of all these above objectives is *continuous system improvement* at all levels of governance including the institutional tier, though that level does require major reconstruction in my view, of which more later.

'The Governance Core' is decaying for UK schools: actually, it has never had much of a core, just self-contained tiers and levels. It needs urgent surgery and modern therapies. For now, attention must be turned to what are to be the main contours of powers and responsibilities under a regional government model. We have to eschew an over-controlling central state then redraw the lines of strategy, policy, administration and 'the doing' for the three tiers at regional, local and institutional level. And in this description clarify and emphasise that regions will be 'free under the law' to diversify in strategy and policy. It is not rational to conceive of identical regions with cookie-cutter strategy and policy. That is centralism redux. What is pressing is to think of intelligent lines of demarcation between national, regional and local government roles and responsibilities.

However, it would be premature to rush into specifics of roles and responsibilities for each tier of governance for education, at this stage in our modelling. It's more useful to conceive of the future regional government structure mostly in terms of broad areas of accountability instead of functions. What we can state unequivocally is that there should be a huge shifting of powers (and political representatives plus civil servants) to the regional tier, which in its turn will be re-empowering local government (LEAs for education) and that tier will be consciously lightening the backbreaking burdens now seizing up the institutional machinery called school governing bodies. That's the direction of change I envisage as most likely to improve standards and narrow equity gaps.

Regional and local governance has to be recast for education. It can't be just Whitehall divided into a number of regions and their LEAs left simply to implement regional policy (with school governors being the ones 'getting their hands dirty', as those nearest to the chalk face). That would be more of the same centralism in fragments. Campbell and Fullan advocate a Governance Core at the heart of the system at all levels. Coherence is all important for any educational system to work best and it can't be bolted on. There must be from the bottom to the top:

1 Unity of purpose driven by a shared moral imperative (this is not another vague vision thing) in the governance system.
2 All children will achieve and there will not be an achievement gap.
3 All children will have quality teachers.
4 All children will be in a safe, healthy learning environment.

The ground-breaking work of Campbell and Fullan includes copious case studies of successful working at regional and local board levels. These are overwhelmingly the opposite in almost every respect (moral imperative, relationships and ways of working) to what has been failing for so long in our national, local and institutional governance bodies.

Last word from *The Governance Core*: at all levels, boards at LEA (and school level, in my experience) tend to fall into the trap of not focusing on children's issues but rather on administrative work. That's not true governance, it is displacement activity. There is not nearly enough debate or hard thinking about equity of attainment outcomes, about the quality of teaching, about important classroom-based implementation problem-solving. There is always too much about visioning of the latest policy to be finalised, or petty party point-scoring at school level but not nearly enough about the most the productive use of the budgets as opposed to its 'eternal inadequacy'. This has been the case for a very long time and Campbell and Fullan quote Michal Rosenberger, a governance consultant and trainer, who is not being too harsh for me when she says:

> The basic human need to overcome feelings of inadequacy encourages trustees/members/governors to grab hold of issues where they can display some expertise and avoid discussion they don't understand. As they fall into the habit of dealing with organisational, financial, and procedural matters they neglect their primary function of governing schools.
>
> *(Campbell and Fullan, 2019, p. 40)*

Regional governance

In line with practices in parts of the USA, I suggest each regional government creates a regional education board to lead the governance of the schools and colleges of a region of perhaps 3–6 million citizens. This is a huge responsibility. In line with the rest of this book, it is up to regional governments to decide what sort of education board they would wish to see – there is no national blueprint. Board members could be elected and/or appointed, and should be open to those representing political parties or unions and interested, experienced others. A body of a maximum of ten members, with four seats for non-political members (excluding serving teachers), would safeguard the need for high-level strategy and fiduciary integrity needed. The role of the board is governance after elections, not politics. Even more important still, the regional board members must be strategic thinkers (not strategic planners, that is for their officials) with unerring focus on governance issues not administration. Implementation questions should be limited to 'scheduled oversight reviews'. Energy and time must be reserved for decision-making based on 'quality information, evidence and data'. The role involves necessarily a lot of homework. It hardly needs underlining that a deep knowledge of the region, across both its private and public services, is a prerequisite for suitable potential candidates. That said, regions are not islands and national and international experience of governance and high-level leadership are required to make regional bodies capable of working productively with other regions. Regions, like LEAs, have to work laterally as well as vertically.

Local education authority (LEA) governance

Much of what is needed to be instituted and changed for the regional level applies to the local government level. But the landscape in which Councils and their LEAs will be operating in a regional system could not be more different than that of the world of rigid centralism of Whitehall and Council faux autonomy.

Leadership from the middle, that is local government, is the glue and cohesion X factor in the new system that Fullan and Campbell espouse. Taking what they call 'districts' in the USA, LEAs should be 'proactive consumers' of regional policy not graceless receptors. Inter-LEA regional working must be very active so that as 'system players' LEAs influence upwards and downwards both policy formation and its implementation processes. LEAs must also work vertically and laterally. No level should just be on the end of 'receiving policy from the higher-ups', as is the case with our Councils and governing bodies at present. The whole system has to become more organic and synergetic. LEAs will need to undergo root and branch reform of personnel, mindset and skills. No more leaving these things to chance. The emphasis has to switch from adversarial politics to good governance. Ask yourself this, do these bodies now possess any sort of genuine governance mindset, shared and strong moral imperative and unity of purpose based on sound principles and practices? Not in my experience. And neither do most governing bodies of schools. We will have to change how members of LEAs (plus their officials) and also governing bodies are elected/appointed, developed and assessed. They are all really just struggling along, heads just above the waters of centralisation, looking after their own for dear life (beholden to party lines or hobbyhorses) and lacking a real sense of any joined-up governance system. Nobody except at the omnipotent centre has trust or faith in the system. It is all on its last legs. How can anybody plan effectively for the closing of the achievement gap and more professional use of the public purse, let alone give a thought to the degrading conditions of work of teachers, when our elected and appointed custodians are always out on their feet, points-scoring, fire-fighting or toeing the party line?

School governors

Below the present tiers of regional and local governance of England and Wales, but not Scotland (which relies on having Parent Councils to maintain links with the school community), there is a basically parochial tier of institutional school governance. This is a throwback to the 19th century when the churches and similar community bodies founded state education. No such micro-system exists in the USA, for example. The onset of school-based financial management in the early 1990s (called Local Management of Schools) solidified and hugely expanded the roles and responsibilities of school governing bodies. But the same sort of people were and are in place and they lacked and still lack the *required skills and time* in general to stay afloat under the Niagara Falls of new responsibilities. And so, they go on being for the most part worthy but ineffective 'local trustees'.

I first joined a school governing body in 1982 in London and I am today still serving as a governor in Hertfordshire. In between I have been clerk to four governing bodies, been a Senior LEA officer serving hundreds of others in Wales as well as in England, acted as a troubleshooting consultant when such bodies sadly fall apart and also been a Vice-Chair of Governors for the primary school I attended as pupil. I have experience of the whole age range and types of schools, including many Special Schools and Pupil Referral Units as well as a Free School (which flew but did not quite stay airborne). Systemically and culturally, during this long period, school governorship has not evolved much, in my judgement. It is one of the main reasons why many of our better schools do not reach their potential. They are not governed well enough, that is to say they are not challenged or scrutinised enough. No school reached 'competent/satisfactory' just because of the excellence of their governors; too many goodish schools, though, are underachieving and unhappy because of the incapacity of their governing bodies. These tend to lack robust shared leadership; they have headteachers acting as proprietors; they veer towards coercive school leadership and they can have too often non-strategic budget setting and budget management. Their staffs are either martyrs or discontents. Good governing bodies do not permit this scenario. But they are in the small minority, succeeding in spite of the obsolete system in place.

None of the above critique is directed at individuals who are governors or in particular governing bodies. Some of the most giving of volunteers and most public-spirited of our society have been my pleasure to know as governors. The system we have is what is decaying and not fit for purpose. The culture around governance of schools is tired and very defensive. Decades of centralisation and overzealous high-stakes accountability have resulted in a mindset that says with a heavy feeling of sorrow: it is difficult to keep your eye on the horizon when you are always having to look over your shoulder. The centre commands, local government disposes and the school governing body is too often out of step because it is nearly always a squad of overloaded, underqualified and put upon 'infantry' who do not or don't feel able to ask enough difficult questions, of itself or the system. The legislators and inspectors tend to agree with me on this.

I have always believed these bodies need constant support from an experienced but independent professional educationalist on a paid basis, besides an efficient clerk. Nobody needs more than ten members on it and there must be a skills entry test on budgets. Their policy writing should be kept to a minimum. The current safeguarding training and administration obsession must be reformed (that actually makes people in power more complacent about key children's safety issues, breeding an admin mindset). LEAs should no longer appoint governors politically. Headteachers should not attend every hour of every meeting, as governors need their space. Governing bodies need this level of streamlining and repurposing. Lastly, more schools should combine into federations so that both leadership and governance can become smarter and much more productive of precious voluntary time and effort. Governors should be appraised every five years through agreed external mechanisms and could be rewarded with Council tax discounts for their years of valuable community service.

'A Competency Framework for Governance' produced in 2017 by the National Schools Commissioner for England is an elegant proposal that remains hopelessly administrative. To cite the seven Nolan principles to school governors is risible. Civil service HR-speak for unpaid volunteers is wrong-headed. Our unreconstructed system gets what it deserves. The system has to be reformed in order to attract those who are a better fit for the volunteer arm of this vital public service.

Ofsted has almost given up on governors and now hardly mentions their roles in inspection reports. Ofsted has nevertheless been a trenchant and unfair critic of governing bodies with so-called 'stuck schools'. It is the same story as with local government for them; if things are going badly, the tiers above school management and leadership 'cop it'. In Wales Estyn plays the same blame game without any notion expressed that the governor's system per se might be the problem. In 2017–2018 Estyn reported that a third of primary governing bodies *do not* have sound knowledge about their school's strengths and priorities for improvement.

The picture in Scotland is very different to England and Wales. It is almost back to pre-1988, with local authorities directing, hiring and firing, etc. There is no proper institutional tier of governance. Whatever the failings highlighted above in the school system that has fallen into disrepair south of Hadrian's Wall, it is little wonder that the Scottish central and local government tiers have been for some time in major conflict over the well-publicised shortcomings of their school system. There are no school governors to inculpate. The First Minister repeatedly promises education is the top priority for national improvement but there remains no sense that devolving powers to sub-regions or indeed institutions away from 1980s style centralism is on the cards. The 2021 OECD report on Scotland's 'bold' curriculum laid down this extraordinary critique of its remorseless centralism in its Curriculum for Excellence (CfE):

> Scotland's CfE exists within a busy policy landscape; the volume of documentation, policies and reviews is high and can sometimes be associated with policy overload. The OECD team was struck by the volume of guidance (and subsequent clarifications and additional guidance) that streamed from Education Scotland in particular. At one level, this is understandable given the extensive remit of Education Scotland. However, it may also be indicative of a system in constant reactive mode.

And that's just the curriculum! This sounds just like the Blair/Blunkett years of National Curriculum overload that Simon Jenkins illustrated graphically for us. But that was all 15 years back. Devolution to sub-regions and institutions are not on the Scottish government agenda, which is dominated politically by the almighty battle for national independence. Governance in education in Scotland is in a seriously bad way, even compared to the rest of UK nations.

How now to change governance in England? First, be honest about the importance in systems success of governance and its coherence demands at all tiers. Second, move steadily away from centralisation to 'pragmatic subsidiarity'. No responsibility devolved without decision-making power and associated funding. Third, competence frameworks, generally, are a good idea at all levels, including the centre of government (the new regions), local government and school governors. There must be standards, but to pretend school governors are the same as elected officials is stupidity. We need *a governance mindset* running through the whole system like a stick of rock. More professionalism for governance and less amateur politicking is what is needed. What is prescribed by Campbell and Fullan for the Americans is good also for a better English system. In a nutshell, systemic trust and integrity have waned dangerously; we need to co-construct a new system based on good governance with better politics.

While governance reform is a critical area for regionalisation to trump centralism, there remain three other key issues which I personally hold any newly formed and empowered region has to focus on without delay, to start tackling in earnest the equity divide besmirching nearly all our UK education system. It is high time our deep class obstacles and improvement risk factors are confronted. These are:

- School admissions must stop being a housing-related problem.
- The primacy of reading in all learning must be upheld as a professional and community issue.
- Post-GCSE education structures must be rigorously reviewed as a critical regional economic development set of issues.

Admissions

Class is a social construct and as such must stop being seen any longer as 'unfixable' in education. As the old song goes: *there's nothing surer, the rich get richer and the poor get children.* Aligning primary and secondary school catchments to a simple circle of local housing is to reinforce the biggest social advantage of the UK: where people live and how much they can afford to live there. We have ended up with, guess what, school intakes as the exact reflection of a poor, poorer, rich, richer housing stock. Catchments can readily be reconfigured to ensure more balanced intakes. That's what a comprehensive school should look like. It makes no sense at all that just because maybe 20%–40% of children are born into poverty and bad housing, they should be elbowed out by the middle classes for local school places in the most stable and higher-achieving schools. *Catchments have to be more planned for equity of entrance opportunity before children go to school.* All schools should have more balanced intakes, at the ages of 5 and 11. If all this incurs extra transport costs, bite that bullet. In the end, it would work out much better value for money than all the ineffective schemes and projects (mostly in early years, especially in Wales) that governments keep initiating to paper over the equity divide. Go to the source of the problem, once and for all. If the more advantaged classes put up a fierce fight about this fundamental reform, know that it is without doubt the correct thing to do. Parental choice for school places in the state sector is a myth (it is just parental preference) and should never be predicated on how much your house costs. Even our least advantaged families pay taxes and have a precious right (and greater need) to higher standards of fairness in admissions. That is how to get more adults and parents engaged in schooling; remove the deep sense of 'I'm giving up on a lousy, unfair system'.

Regions have an unmissable opportunity to turn around skewed admissions policy and practice within their first five years. Incidentally, regulators would also have much more accurate evaluations on 'school added value' under a fairer admissions system. That would also increase the likelihood of improving teacher quality.

Reading

The term 'reading' is used here as opposed to literacy because literacy is sometimes used to describe both reading and writing. The UK is among the six richest countries in the world. It has a long history of systematic state education, a free-at-the-point-of-service-for-all healthcare system and a sophisticated and benevolent welfare service dating back to 1945. So, why can't we still get reading instruction right with all these institutional, professional and societal things going for us? I don't know the answer but I do know it's really wrong and a dire waste of human potential. The important thing is how could regions do better, much better to achieve universal, functional reading proficiency for primary children. Many schools in England have improved their performance strongly since 2012 but there are still a few which do not adhere to the best practice tenets of proven methods of phonics and interventions that work best for those in greater need. We still have some primary teachers who have a 'Corinthian' attitude to the teaching of reading. In Wales and Scotland reading standards are reflective of a libertarian approach to teaching reading and their outcomes tell the sorry tale of early underachievement across the curriculum. If children cannot read fluently by the time they are progressing to secondary education, in 99% of non-disabled cases this is predominantly a professional failure. Illiteracy is actually educational suicide on the part of schools.

Reading is a taught skill that defines humanity. No child can read well without an expert and caring teacher (some parents can do this job, but many cannot). If any child is denied that entry capacity into our society and economy, that is an avoidable modern tragedy and a terrible waste of public resources. Regions can best attack structural class bias early on in schools by reforming admissions at key stages and being non-negotiable about great reading instruction in every classroom. I would stress that many institutions of teacher training are still backwaters as far as scientific reading instruction goes. Regions must act forcefully to ensure that they do not give credence to such local institutions.

Post-GCSE structures

Schools, like all public services, are there to serve the needs and aspirations of its citizens. There is a sense in which this has been completely inverted as an axiom in the case of school sixth forms. Learners are too often treated as the property of the school and an income stream. Larger colleges of FE are consequently underfunded compared with sixth forms. The UK governments have reinforced this, by the use of the public purse, the least free interests and choices of 16 plus learners, their parents and employers. Sixth forms militate by their lack of size and facilities against the best futures of our young people; this is one of the main reasons why the UK has such a sticky problem getting rid of structural and cultural bias against vocational education. Moreover, consortia arrangements organised across local secondary schools to give greater curricular choice are often very complex and can be unsustainable. Consortia cannot come near in effectiveness or equity to authentic tertiary colleges. They do not start from learner needs; sixth form colleges and colleges of FE work much better than school sixth forms, for learners across the 16 plus spectrum. They work more with business and employers; they can facilitate apprenticeships much easier than schools, whose staff have two other key stage age groups to manage. Tertiary colleges are *the* specialist places of learning for those who are considering the next steps options for work, training and university. They also have good records in Additional Needs and Disability provision, simply because they can cater for low incidence needs more economically. No one has put this complete argument better than the doyen of education journalism Peter Wilby in 2016:

> The traditional school sixth form has become a tribal totem for English education. It is an expensive, outdated and counter-productive luxury. Rarely big enough to sustain a wide range of subjects, it often neglects the creative arts, technical subjects and the less popular foreign languages, concentrating on a narrow range of academic offerings that appeal to (and will be of use to) only a minority of young people. It has prevented the emergence of a coherent vision for 14–19 education that could unify the vocational and academic strands of education and rid us of the pernicious belief that the academic strand is always superior.

Nothing much has changed since Wilby's cri de coeur. Regions would do well to grasp the unprecedented opportunity to build effective and equitable tertiary systems if they really do want to realise the dream of all educators who treasure the belief and purpose that 'all children will achieve and there will not be an achievement gap'. This will take time to achieve and resistance will be a brutal battle against united vested interests but tribal totems don't build economies or lead to diversity of prosperity. That has been a proven failure. If regional economic planning is to bear its natural fruit, it will need not just a better built school system but most urgently a tertiary approach that can align much more effectively with regional workforce skills and knowledge and signal an end to the academic/vocational divide that has for so long reinforced classism and negated aspiration in the UK.

The above are all equity considerations to 'address the underlying inequality which creates a steeper social gradient'. They are all a mixture of politics and education. They are all indeed hot potatoes for regional reform consideration. Whitehall has ignored or fudged them too long.

If too many kids are disbarred from entering proper comprehensive primary and secondary schools because they live in poorer housing, if they cannot get reading instruction good enough to access the curriculum, if school sixth forms continue to shoehorn successful learners into their inadequate, mainly academic provisions, then nothing much will change for the better for both the economy and society of a region. Nor for our teachers, who have suffered very badly under crushing centralism, antiquated governance, unnecessarily bad pupil behaviour and 50-hour weeks of overpreparation, relentless marking and Soviet-like data collection. Teachers are our main actors and agents for improving learner achievement and attainment. We must ensure that in all proposed regional reforms and changes their conditions of work start to improve and that does not equate to 'stay the same'. The reality is that unless we consciously improve teaching conditions, no matter what calibre of proposals turn into real plans for change, these will not properly take hold and flourish. Teachers have the ultimate 'make or break power', because they own the classrooms.

Conclusion

To sum up, the centre is not holding anymore but things are in time-honoured British fashion not exactly falling apart because this is an old and rich country that keeps 'buggering-on'. That said, the cracks in our heavily centralised education system are getting larger and more learners are dropping through them each year, with damaging economic and social consequences. Governance by the post-imperial centre is a broken wheel that cannot just be fixed. Throughout the UK, regions offer new and greater hope for all our learners, young and not so young. We must refocus on regenerating the structures, mindsets and cultures of governance at the three tiers, region, local government and institutions, once we break free of the centre's stranglehold. We ignore at our peril in this new regional world the paramountcy of equitable admissions, first-rate professional reading instruction for all and the setting up of fairer Post-16 opportunities by rationalising the monopoly providers, the secondary schools, to create at last good regional tertiary provision. If we cut though the Japanese knotweed of centralism gone rife we will then in consequence have a chance of giving our teachers better careers and better lives for the first time in over 30 years. Their healthier working conditions are key to better teaching standards across the piece. Regions must do more to relate to their local teachers, but make sure that is more than just a cosying-up to their unions. 'Reaching teachers' is one of other the great failures of centralism. Ninety-seven percent of teachers are in a union but they mostly treat membership as liability insurance. Teacher unions are not in any meaningful sense representative of the full spectrum of teachers. The remarkable unionisation level of teachers is a direct response to decades of uber-centralism, understandably, but regionalised governance should in time lead to a more inclusive voice for all teachers.

There's a lot to do but it really is all doable. Education reimagined in this way could actually become the powerful driver it was always meant to be for economic prosperity and social justice for all the citizens of the UK. The new regions of England could become engines of learning and fulfilment for all. At long last.

References

Alexander, R. (2012), *Visions of education: The global educational race and The Cambridge Primary Review,* http://cprtrust.org.uk/wp-content/uploads/2014/06/Alexander_Chile_GMU_lecture_1_121030.pdf

Campbell, D., and Fullan, M. (2019), *The governance core.* Thousand Oaks, CA: Corwin.

CfBT Education Trust (2014), *Lessons from London schools: Investigating the success,* https://www.centreforlondon.org/wp-content/uploads/2016/08/Lessons-from-London-Schools.pdf

Coe, R. (2013), *Improving education: A triumph of hope over experience,* Inaugural Lecture Durham university.

Jenkins, S. (2004), *Big Bang localism: A rescue plan for British democracy,* Policy Exchange.

Mackie, T. (2019), *Wales: The slow learning country; out of the dim into the light.* (self-published).

National Schools Commissioner for England (2017), *A competency framework for Gov,* DfE.

OECD (2021), *Scotland's curriculum for excellence: Into the future,* https://www.oecd.org/education/scotland-s-curriculum-for-excellence-bf624417-en.htm

Rowntree/Institute for Government (2014), *Implementing the London challenge,* https://www.instituteforgovernment.org.uk/sites/default/files/publications/Implementing%20the%20London%20Challenge%20-%20final_0.pdf

Social Mobility Commission (2020), Monitoring social mobility 2013–2020: Is the government delivering on our recommendations?

Todd, S. (2021), *Snakes and ladders: The Great British social mobility myth,* London: Penguin Books.

Wilby, P. (2016), School sixth forms: An outdated luxury. *The Guardian,* 29 March 2016.

10

HOUSING

Anna Birley

Introduction

Clearly housing policy is high on the public and political agenda. Close to 18% of the population identify housing as one of, if not the, most important issue facing Britain today, up from 6% a decade ago (Judge 2019). This isn't surprising. Housing is one of the basic tenets of our lives, and access to adequate housing has long been viewed as a basic human right.

It is more than simply having a roof over our heads. Our homes are critical to our well-being; they determine our health and life expectancy and enable access to services and employment. They're a space in which we grow up and bring up our children, and the quality of housing is a key factor in children's educational outcomes. Too often today, housing is seen as an investment asset which causes huge complications in the housing market. Housing is critical to the health of the economy too, and has a profound effect on equality, productivity and growth.

This chapter covers the following main issues:

- The meaning and purpose of housing policy
- An overview of past and current UK housing policies
- Devolving housing policy to UK regions
- Housing policy issues for UK regional governments

The meaning and purpose of housing policy

Housing has featured in manifestos and political promises for decades – but with no consensus on what the problems are or how to resolve them. Housing policy is shaped by ideology – market versus state provision, a shifting focus from supply to ownership.

DOI: 10.4324/9781003201892-13

The Conservative Manifesto 1955 specifically championed homeownership as an antithesis to Labour's post-war nationalisation (Keohane and Broughton 2013):

> We wish to develop in our country the idea of a property-owning democracy. That means that people should be owners as well as earners. Our theme is that property, power and responsibility alike must not become absorbed into the State machine, but be widely spread throughout the whole of the community. To this end, we shall encourage home ownership.

This divergence continues: the 2019 Labour and Conservative manifestos both included a commitment to increasing house building but the Conservatives sought to deliver this through planning liberalisation and investment to unlock sites for private development, while Labour envisaged the state itself re-emerging as a major player in house building rather than private providers (Judge 2019).

Despite this political focus, and regardless of ideological bent, the levers available to government to impact housing supply, quality, ownership and affordability remain limited. Unlike health and education, the state is not the main service provider. Rightly or wrongly, housing is a market and housing policy can be best described as attempts by the government to modify it in order to achieve its objectives (Lund 2017). These attempts at market modification manifest themselves in a number of ways, whether to address perceived market failures or to achieve other social objectives. The most interventionist is direct state provision in the form of government house building and ownership of homes for social rent. The government is the regulator of the housing market, with powers to determine minimum standards. The government decides the basis on which people have rights and obligations in their home – setting protections for renters and landlords for example. Through subsidies and taxation, the government can encourage or discourage housing investment and consumption. And through planning policy, the government has the power to release land and create or remove constraints on development.

However, there is a problem with housing markets. By most metrics, Britain has a housing affordability problem. Too many families struggle to afford a decent home with adequate space in the place that they wish to live and work. Over the past 30 years, the average proportion of income spent by families on housing costs has trebled – this proportion has increased generation to generation, meaning today's 30-year-olds pay far more of their income in housing costs than their parents, grandparents or great-grandparents did at 30 (Corlett and Judge 2017).

Headlines are filled with millennials unable to get on the property ladder, or the latest scandalous attempt by an estate agent to market a garden shed as a fashionable studio apartment. We hear about the housing shortage, escalating rents and the need to get Britain building. The coverage of the crisis is very London-centric – about how impossible it is for anyone on a normal salary to rent let alone buy in the capital.

What we don't hear about is the fact that in Northern Ireland, many homeowners remain stuck in negative equity after the credit crunch. That whole streets in some British towns and cities are so empty and undesirable that local councils are selling homes off for a pound to try and breathe new life into an area. Rather than demand outstripping supply uniformly across the country, many seaside towns experience an oversupply of poor-quality rental properties. Since 2016, the number of empty homes has begun rising again, with a disproportionate representation of empty homes in the lowest value areas (Action on Empty Homes 2019). So, the reassertion and acceptance of the cliché that Britain has a housing crisis is partly why we keep failing to fix it. The UK doesn't have a housing crisis at all: rather it has a whole series of different housing crises (Chakrabortty 2014). And how those crises are experienced, and by whom, varies hugely. When we define housing policy, we should in fact see housing not as one market but as many different markets, given the marked area variations in supply, demand, house prices, house building industries and economies (Lund 2017).

During the recovery from the 2008 crash, London house prices spiralled upwards, driven up by the city's international status. Stoke-on-Trent, however, saw a far slower return to upward housing prices (Barker 2014). Fast-forwarding to Britain today, there is very little that Grimsby and Greenwich or even Manchester and Wigan, just 17 miles apart, have in common. The short train ride from central Manchester to Wigan sees average house values drop by over £40,000. The balance between tenures changes; the type of housing, terraced versus flats, changes; quality and energy efficiency of homes changes; average income changes as does average age. But despite such large regional variations, housing policy has become increasingly centralised as will be discussed.

An overview of past and current housing policies

A number of housing policies which have been adopted by various UK governments over many decades are as follows.

The growth of centralisation of housing policy

Earlier chapters on other policy areas comment extensively on the extensive growth of central control and indeed the growth of centralisation within devolved governments. The same applies to housing policy. Until the 1970s, housing policy was broadly left to local authorities to lead. Legislation tended to be enabling so there were different tenure structures, policies and practices in different parts of England and Wales (Mullins and Murie 2006). However, Westminster took a centralising turn in the 1970s, thus reducing those differences. For example, the Housing Finance Acts removed local authority discretion in rent setting and granting rebates. It forced councils to raise rents in stages and link them to the "fair rents" that had been introduced in 1965 for private tenants under the Rent

Act. This decoupled council rents from the cost of provision and management of council homes, linking them instead to market rents. This was stalled by the incoming Labour Government in 1974 which introduced a rent freeze and re-established some principles of local control through the Housing Rents and Subsidies Act 1975 which allowed local authorities to fix reasonable rents. This was modified further with a housing policy review and taken up by the subsequent Conservative Government.

A major public policy driver in the 1970s was a reduction in public expenditure, in the context of high inflation and volatile interest rates. This resulted in central government spending limits being imposed on local authorities to replace targets for homebuilding. These changes started in 1972 with an ideological attempt to shift the role of social housing from part of the welfare state, to something which mirrored market conditions. Although Labour's housing legislation sought to undo this policy, they did not seek to re-establish a locally driven agenda in housing. Driven by the desire to limit public expenditure, the central government introduced cash limits to replace volume targets for local authorities. Councils were required under the 1974 Housing Act to prepare annual programmes of work covering the next four years. Capital would be allocated accordingly, and any spending above the cash limit would result in thorough central scrutiny. While the system was presented as an increase in local autonomy, in practice, it constituted an extension of central control and was used to bring about substantial cuts in investment (Mullins and Murie 2006, 35), and was subsequently expanded in scope in 1977–1978 Housing Investment Programmes.

This marked a fundamental shift in the balance of power. Rather than councils being empowered to take and enact decisions based on local conditions, costs and priorities, they needed permission via bids and allocations. The whole approach was presented as an increase in local autonomy when "in practice it constituted an extension of central control and was used to bring about substantial cuts in investment" (Mullins and Murie 2006, 35).

However, rather than creating a more uniform housing sector, decades of active centralisation and standardisation of policy have led among other things to far greater fragmentation in the housing experience. Gaps between tenures, between urban and rural places, and between generations have never been wider, and there has been a marked increase in regional inequalities. Furthermore, despite this centralising tendency, housing policy is impossible to pin down to one office in Whitehall. The Government Department formerly responsible for Housing, Communities and Local Government, now tasked with the more amorphous "levelling up", is also responsible for planning policy. The Department for Work and Pensions is the biggest public funder of the sector, through housing benefits and other individual subsidies. The Treasury creates the taxes and tax breaks to accelerate or slow down different aspects of the housing market. The Department for Business, Energy and Industrial Strategy creates the jobs and investments that stimulate housing demand in different parts of the country. This fragmented approach is part of the problem and centralisation has not led to greater co-ordination or better alignment of UK housing's priorities, problems and moving parts. Underpinning all of this confusion in the corridors of Whitehall (while there always has been, and should continue to be, some central role in housing policy), the scope today for local and regional leadership and intervention is limited.

Austerity and policy dumping

Devolution can be a blessing or a curse – depending on which policies are devolved, how it is designed and delivered, and whether the funds and powers match the responsibilities being decentralised.

In a scenario where the central government has run out of ideas, energy and the will or capacity to fund projects, the downward shift of responsibility to local government is best interpreted as policy dumping (MacLennan and O'Sullivan 2013). Whatever the formal division of powers, choices are either constrained or enabled by budgetary constraints or freedoms. Devolution of policy at a time of reductions in resources sees nominal autonomy rise and real autonomy fall – all that ends up devolved is the blame for policy failure and service reduction. This is not a problem restricted to the relationship between national and local governments. From Cameron's Big Society, to some iterations of local government community partnerships, this can be a problem locally too, when, under the guise of subsidiarity, social problems are passed onto local communities to fix without appropriate resources to do so (Flint 2006; McKee 2007).

Empowering a community to take on responsibility for developing a site as a community land trust, or handing over the keys to a youth club or park, achieves the opposite if the resources for that service are cut at the same time, or if the necessary powers and freedoms are not handed over too. In the context of an austerity agenda pursued for the past decade by a Westminster government, some ways that councils have sought to cope with less money is by dressing up policy dumping on their communities as a justification for doing more with less – claiming that this approach was based on empowerment and co-operation, with budget savings as a happy by-product. In reality, this approach results in less empowered communities, and if services fail as a result, there is a lack of clear accountability. And it also undermines confidence in the potential for co-operative models and community ownership.

Policy dumping to communities can also be a tool or at least an outcome of centralisation, whereby under the moniker of community empowerment existing structures are bypassed to give local actors nominal powers but only to secure the objectives shaped by central government (Bailey 2017). Some go so far as to describe the process of devolution unfolding in England as one of "elite co-option" that pays limited attention to the interests of citizens and does little to challenge the existing structure of power within the Westminster/Whitehall system. It is about the maintenance of power and central control in response to devolutionary pressures (Richards and Smith 2016). For an example outside of housing policy, we can look to the education system. Academisation and the replacement of local authority oversight with regional school commissioners have removed accountability from communities, bypassing local elected bodies to create an uninterrupted relationship between individual schools and central government.

In housing, the spectre of policy dumping appeared in different forms over the years which is why it is particularly relevant for inclusion in this chapter.

As referenced above, a centrally driven desire to cut public expenditure under the 1974 Labour Government was, in housing, reframed as an increase in local autonomy. Through the system of bids and allocations, local decision-making was limited by top-down scrutiny based on national policy wants rather than local priorities and needs. Overall, it was a means to impose top-down significant reductions in expenditure and investment.

Thatcherism emphasised choice, seeing people in their homes as consumers and using policy to bypass local authorities by growing the role of the market, with these housing consumers exercising their choice within it. The flagship "Right to Buy" shifted responsibility from the government at every level to the individual and market, and prioritised ownership. Cuts in expenditure limited local authorities' ability to either build or repair homes and when Labour came to power in 1997 there was an estimated £19 billion backlog in repairs (Lund 2017).

This period marked the end of meaningful municipal localism in housing (MacLennan and O'Sullivan 2013), and the trend towards central control continued and intensified under the subsequent New Labour Government, albeit with different aspirations and a softened stance towards social housing. Through this timeframe, the proportion of local government ownership within the non-market sector dropped. From 1981 to 1998, the share of local government-owned social housing within the non-market sector housing fell from 93% to 78%, and by 2009 local authorities owned less than half of all non-market sector housing (Wilcox and Pawson 2010/2011).

Under New Labour, central control was a key feature of the drive for service improvements, realised through increasingly intrusive social housing regulation (MacLennan and O'Sullivan 2013). Local authorities continued to shift from provider to enabler (Cowan and Marsh 2001) with very little change in overarching approach to the previous Conservative Government. The focus remained on quality, choice and ownership. The shift was where responsibility for these outcomes lay: Conservatives emphasised ownership and therefore individual responsibility of homeowners to maintain standards, while New Labour took a more interventionist approach.

The backlog or repairs which built up through the Tory administration's under-investment gave New Labour cause to mistrust local councils' ability to deliver better quality homes. Perhaps Conservative policy dumping was to blame for New Labour's centralisation and subsequent policy dumping too. Funding for housing repairs and stock improvements was conditional on centrally directed forms of governance, namely, the Arm's Length Management Organisation (ALMO) and large-scale stock transfers. Framed as an option for local councils, access to the borrowing and funding necessary to improve quality of social housing was entirely dependent on stock transfer to registered social landlords who could borrow outside of public sector constraints or creation of ALMOs to qualify for additional state resources (Lund 2017). ALMOs were not-for-profit organisations run by unpaid volunteer board members, including but not dominated by local councillors, as well as tenant and independent representatives. Ownership remained with councils but with day-to-day responsibility sitting with the ALMO.

Despite being couched in the language of choice, tenants at the time argued that the only "choice" left to them was between a decent home and remaining a council tenant (Sillett 2004). Options available to access funding were stock transfer to a housing association, creation of an ALMO or establishing a private finance initiative (PFI). No "fourth option" existed for stock to remain owned and managed directly by the council, regardless of whether tenants rejected the other options or whether the council's provision was to a good standard. Camden voted 77% against an ALMO, arguing that the council managed their homes well and that if the money was there for improvements, why couldn't the council do them?

As if to demonstrate the extent to which ALMOs were created purely to access funds rather than to achieve genuine local governance, most councils cited the completion of their Decent Homes programme as their reason for closing their ALMO and bringing housing management back in-house (Barker 2019). That isn't to say New Labour Government's policies didn't see a massive uptick in investment in social housing, and significant improvements in quality for millions of tenants. Instead, the point here is that the mechanism for doing so lauded greater tenant involvement, bypassing local structures. The greater investment was not because of the lack of local authority involvement, rather the access to investment was restricted to the point of removing all municipal policy autonomy.

Local decision-making and better outcomes

Another alternative governance model was the Tenant Management Organisation (TMO). The first TMOs were set up in the mid-1970s under a Labour Government, as Tenant Management Co-operatives' (TMC), spearheaded by Labour & Co-operative MP Reg Freeson as Minister for Housing. While earlier Conservative and Liberal support for tenant management co-operatives, in the first few years of the 1970s, technically supported decentralisation of housing policy, it did not translate into change in housing management, as local authorities would have lost government subsidy as soon as TMCs took over estates. However, Freeson's amendments to the 1975 Housing Rents and Subsidies Act allowed ownership co-operatives to gain access to generous grants and loans by being registered as housing associations, and allowed TMCs to take over estates with no loss of local subsidy (Birchall 1991).

Later, into the 1980s, many TMOs were established as estate management boards (EMBs) as new legislation in 1985 reinforced the policy allowing local authorities to transfer responsibility for housing management to willing tenants (Newton and Tunstall 2012). These were more top-down, formed predominantly in the more deprived areas of the country as part of a central government initiative.

While ostensibly another case, like ALMOs, of power bypassing local government, a TMO is actually very distinct in purpose and outcome. It begins life in a community hall rather than the corridors of Whitehall, with councils legally required to enable tenants to ballot estates and facilitate the development of legal agreements setting out roles and responsibilities. Through a TMO, residents take over a range of housing, and some non-housing, services including some or all of repairs, grounds maintenance, caretaking, cleaning, managing voids, community development, administering allocations and resident consultation.

The idea that tenants can choose their landlord had come and gone over time – for example, the Housing Act of 1988 gave council tenants the ability to choose a different landlord. There was, however, little evidence of private sector interest in taking over estates, as was possibly the intention of the legislation, and very few housing associations chose to damage their relationship with local councils to pursue ballots to takeover estates either.

Despite different governmental drivers for tenant management, a major difference between this area of housing policy and others like 'fair rents', ALMOs and Right to Buy is that there was significant lobbying for it from the bottom-up. The right to establish local community control over housing was one that activists and tenants demanded. Freeson was not creating policy to cut investment or increase central control when as Housing Minister he made amendments to legislation to support co-operative models – these practical changes came from personal involvement in setting up housing co-operatives on Willesden Council before his election to Parliament. Likewise, the rapid expansion of co-operative models of housing in Liverpool didn't come about because Westminster or Liverpool Council asked communities to do it or passed the buck on for slum clearance. In fact, quite the opposite – residents objected to the 'boss' politics of the council (Thompson 2020, 62) when they proposed decanting large numbers of inner-city residents to new overspill towns like Kirkby and Speke. Presented with a binary choice of city centre slum conditions versus new homes in overspill towns, Liverpudlian social housing residents chose neither. Instead, the period between 1960 and 1980s was marked by collective action and protest. For example, 3,000 tenants in Kirkby held a 14-month rent strike, led by women who later led campaigned for new housing co-operatives to replace their crumbling tenement blocks (Thompson 2020, 65).

The 'Right to Manage' was introduced in 1993, as part of the Leasehold Reform, Housing and Urban Development Act. It built on the previous decades' support for tenant-led housing management to enable tenants' groups to take over management and maintenance while the council remained the ultimate owner and landlord. This encompassed the earlier TMCs and EMBs, and by 2002 TMOs were responsible for over 84,000 homes in England (Mullins and Murie 2006).

The Grenfell tragedy re-sparked debate about TMOs. While officially being a TMO in name, the Kensington and Chelsea TMO (KCTMO) is an anomaly. Rather than being community-based and co-operatively run, KCTMO was set up to cover the entire borough, the entire housing department was TUPE'ed over with the Director of Housing becoming the CEO, and it took on all council housing management functions. It was more akin to an ALMO, and its legal structure formally changed to one in 2002 (Apps 2017). It was used by the council to reduce spend on housing repairs and maintenance as part of wider cost-cutting measures, and crucially, local tenants had no local control (Power 2017). Genuine TMOs, however, tend to result in service improvements. A government report in 2002 found that in most cases, TMOs were outperforming their host local authorities in terms of repairs, lettings and voids, rent collection and tenant satisfaction (Cairncross 2002).

Planning and land

Direct provision and governance of housing is not the only card in the government's deck. As mentioned at the start of the chapter, planning is a significant policy lever. Since 1960, the state has steadily withdrawn from housing supply, shifting the tenure balance firmly in favour of the market (Ryan-Collins, Lloyd and Macfarlane 2017). Increasing use of planning policy post-war has created a new means of subsidising or incentivising affordable housebuilding, as well as influencing land use, housing standards, design and regeneration.

In the post-war period of new towns, and local and national house building programmes, planning sought to curb private developers while accommodating local authority building programmes. The pre-war system whereby the Town and Country Planning Act 1932 required public bodies to compensate landowners for any lost development value should the local authority restrict their 'right' to develop. After the war, land remained in the same private hands but the 'right' to develop was effectively nationalised (Ryan-Collins, Lloyd and Macfarlane 2017). Thus, planning permission was born, equipping the state with a new tool to direct the market by facilitating or curbing private development.

As Thatcher focused on homeownership, new tensions emerged between central and local governments. Planning policy emphasis shifted from building homes for social rent to private developers building homes for private purchase. This came at the expense of land and resources for social housing, but the need for local authorities to find affordable housing for their residents remained pressing. Planning authorities sought ways to use the planning system to ensure private development was targeted at meeting local need (Mullins and Murie 2006). For example, this could include local planning conditions restricting new development to high-density construction or legal restrictions to force the sale of dwelling to local purchasers. These were generally not endorsed by central government, and any attempt to formalise them as policy risked veto by the Secretary of State. But, the 1990 Town and Country Planning Act did allow local authorities to enter into binding agreements with developers, with the developers having to deliver defined public benefits as part of an S106 Agreement. This can, in effect, constitute a direct subsidy for affordable housing (Ryan-Collins, Lloyd and Macfarlane 2017, 93). In 1992 local authorities were required to develop formal plans to deliver affordable housing but in their local plans and Unitary Development Plans (UDPs) not in structural plans (Mullins and Murie 2006).

While planning has become an increasingly important tool for promoting the construction of homes to meet local needs, it cannot and will not deliver the quantity and quality of new housing required. Often, the planning system is a barrier to delivering new homes. This is not simply an issue of a lack of council and affordable housing, but a supply-side failure in the private sector too (Stephens, whitehead and Munro 2005). Nonetheless, this use of planning powers by local authorities to impose local characteristics shows the want, need, inventiveness and ability of local leadership.

Tax and incentives

Taxation and subsidy are further tools at the disposal of government. These are targeted at developers or individuals and vary from taxes (e.g. stamp duty, second home taxes, capital gains on individuals, Community Infrastructure Levy, corporation tax on developers) to special financial products for first-time buyers or the recent stamp duty break offered post-pandemic by Chancellor Rishi Sunak.

In the sphere of social housing and low-income households, there has long been a recognition of the fact that without state intervention, some people will be left unable to adequately house themselves. As well as state intervention on the supply side of the market, through reducing the cost of housing at source, housing benefit is a demand-side intervention – or direct subsidy to low-income renters and their landlords.

This approach isn't new – the National Assistance Scheme established post-war in 1948 included some provision for housing costs. However, reforms introduced in 1982 marked a shift away from subsidising bricks and mortar, instead subsidising individuals and allowing for a greater role for market forces (Webb 2012) by means of testing and increasing council rents beyond the means of those in the lowest paid work. These changes also shifted administrative responsibility to local authorities.

As governments increasingly looked to markets to accommodate lower income households, housing benefits boosted rents paid to private landlords. In some ways, this constitutes an indirect state subsidy for landlords to expand their rental portfolio, rather than being reinvested in public housing stock (Webb 2012) or other means of increasing affordable housing supply. Whereas in 1975 more than 80% of housing subsidies were supply side, seeking to promote construction of homes at social rent, by 2000 over 85% of housing subsidies were demand side, focused on helping individuals afford rent payments (Stephens, Whitehead and Munro 2005).

Meanwhile, in an effort to drive growth in homeownership, tax and subsidies were increasingly focused on stimulating the market, incentivising certain demographics to buy and ensuring the financial products exist to further grow owner-occupation. Hence, housing became an investment rather than a home.

Home ownership has long been one of the most subsidised activities in Britain. Before the turn of the century, mortgage interest relief at source (MIRAS) was the largest housing subsidy. In the 1970s, MIRAS cost the government £5 billion a year (This is Money 1999). By 1990–1991 the bill was £7.7 billion (Jones 1999) – more than the just over £5 billion spent on housing benefit in the same period (Department for Work and Pensions 2020). MIRAS greatly distorted the housing market in favour of high-income owner occupiers, not only in its design (whereby those paying tax at the top rate received tax relief at that top rate too) but also because it was thought to have played a significant role in pushing up house prices, benefiting existing homeowners over new purchasers (Stephens, whitehead and Munro 2005). While MIRAS was finally phased out in 2000 for owner-occupiers, some relief still remains in place for buy-to-let landlords (Ryan-Collins, Lloyd and Macfarlane 2017).

Right to Buy also constituted a major public subsidy of home ownership with council tenants allowed to purchase their home at a significantly subsidised price. Over the first 25 years from its introduction in 1980, over 2 million formerly council homes were sold, many in the second wave of the scheme when discounts increased in 1984 and eligibility widened (Mullins and Murie 2006). The 1988 Housing Act created a scheme which offered cash incentives to social housing tenants who didn't wish to exercise their Right to Buy because their current property was not an attractive purchase but who wished to purchase a home in the private sector instead.

The phasing out or of MIRAS and the decline in support for Right to Buy did not mean that home ownership was no longer favoured by governments, which continue subsidising it in other ways. Help-to-Buy, introduced in 2013, seeks to stimulate housing demand among first-time buyers through equity loans, mortgage schemes, shared ownership and a "new buy" scheme allowing those buying new-build homes to do so with just a 5% mortgage.

With primary residence exempt from Capital Gains Tax and changes to inheritance taxes, the tax treatment of housing as opposed to other assets is further enhanced. The buy-to-let boom in the late 1990s fuelled by lenders creating new buy-to-let mortgages saw many, who had already accumulated wealth from home ownership, buying new houses (Ryan-Collins, Lloyd and Macfarlane 2017).

The only local tool for housing taxation is council tax, a regressive property tax paid by the occupier rather than the owner and based on out-of-date land and property valuations. Local councils are constrained in their ability to vary council tax levels, now requiring a referendum of their residents if they wish to increase it 2% or more in any given year.

Policy problems

When each of the above individual housing policies is judged on its own measures of success, many have been very successful. Right to Buy sought to enable and encourage council tenants to own their own homes and it certainly achieved that. Planning systems have sought to protect the countryside by limiting house building in certain areas that has likewise been a success. However, many of these policies have had unintended and often undesirable consequences. Right to Buy did raise the level of homeownership but it also depleted the stock of social housing and made it much harder to manage estate maintenance. Targeting housing subsidies at the poorest tenants resulted in disincentives for some to work, and helps landlords grow their own portfolio rather than increasing the supply of affordable homes. And more importantly, the sum of each of these policies' parts does not equal a coherent whole. With responsibility for different policy levers sitting across central government departments, we have a housing policy "bedevilled by initiatives rather than strategy" (Hull and Cooke 2012) characterised by constant tinkering around the edges all resulting in limited change. Housing policy epitomises the definition of insanity, rehashing the same policies under different guises, even when they failed to fix the problem previously. Variations on the status quo are unlikely to produce different outcomes.

Another part of the problem is the fact that any 'fix' for this crisis – or these crises – will result in perceived winners and perceived losers. The one group for whom the current housing system is working well enough is existing homeowners and investors in the property market. On the whole, this group benefits from long-term increases to house prices and a ballooning private rental market (Gallent 2019).

Market position determines our judgment as to whether something is good or bad, and so it is no surprise that the ratio of housing cost to income varies greatly by tenure type. Those who own outright, or who have mortgages, pay a below-average proportion of income on housing. Above average are local authority renters and housing association tenants, who pay an average of just under a third and just over a third respectively of their income on housing. Private renters pay well over a third of their income on housing (Corlett and Judge 2017).

The decline in social housing stock alongside a rising cost of home ownership and stagnant wages has caused the private rented sector to double in size over the last 20 years (Shelter 2021), further exacerbating both the affordability problem and the wealth inequality between generations. Younger generations consigned to the private rental sector are directly transferring wealth up as a significant proportion of their income is paid in rent monthly to landlords in their parents' or grandparents' generation. This distortion in favour of property ownership extends to the planning system too, which has resulted in the housing stock growing significantly less in local authorities with higher proportions of owner-occupiers among local households (Castro Coelho, Ratnoo and Dellepiane 2014).

Differences in regional housing markets, and how the solutions to these differences are perceived, are also a barrier to addressing Britain's housing crises. The concentration of economic activity in the South East contributes to growth in demand for housing while supply is limited by the green belt and other land use constraints. Housing demand in some other areas is forecast to fall. In the context of housing policy, the 'get on your bike' school of economics suggests that just as if no work is available locally someone should look further and further until they find a job. People struggling to find an affordable home in an area of high housing demand and low supply should simply move to places where housing is cheaper and more available. Taken literally, this leads some commentators to suggest that the supply shortage story is a "red herring" (Dmitracova 2019). Property pages declare that there is no housing shortage in the UK. But economics doesn't reflect real life, and the picture is far more complicated than that. People unable to afford to live within the urban areas they work in cannot up sticks to a cheaper small town far away – their equivalent job is unlikely to exist there, and the transport infrastructure, outside of London, required to commute to work likely doesn't exist either. The flipside is that taken to its logical conclusion, this argument would see London devoid of nurses and retail staff, Winchester without cleaners, and no care workers or street sweepers in Bath, Brighton or Oxford.

Instead, both from the very human perspective of not wanting to uproot households from their lives, families, friends and jobs for the sake of economic reorganisation, and from the very practical perspective of the need for vibrant mixed communities with the mix of professions every area needs, housing policy needs to account for people's preferences. On paper, policies do take this into account – homelessness guidance says residents should stay in their home neighbourhoods unless there are exceptional circumstances. In practice though, at least 55,000 Londoners were rehoused in temporary homes outside of their local area – Barnet and Bexley have sent people to Manchester; Barking and Dagenham to Bradford, both around 200 miles away from the capital (Barker 2021). Bradford has had to accommodate at least 290 households from 31 different boroughs, many in London, Kent and Essex, over the past two years. When London councils send residents to live in private accommodation in Kent and Essex, a domino effect is created. The leader of Basildon Council claims he is forced to house residents in northern counties because he is priced out of Basildon by London councils (Marsh 2020). And that only accounts for those who present as homeless to their local council. There is no protection for renters forced further and further away from their workplace or family networks, and little in place for those stuck in a low-income area where jobs are scarce. Their ability to get on their bike to find work is constrained by the increased cost of housing in those parts of the UK with stronger local jobs markets.

Where it does happen, this internal migration can have a role in increasing poverty concentration. Based on an evaluation of the previous Labour Government's New Deal for Communities area-based regeneration programme, "selective migration removes the more economically advantaged individuals to be replaced by relatively more disadvantaged individuals" (Jivraj 2012), accelerating housing demand in areas of low supply and exacerbating the downward spiral of poverty, low housing demand and moribund jobs markets in the places they leave behind.

Policies to address regional disparities in prosperity and economic growth, and the knock-on impact they have on housing demand, supply, affordability and tenure, are too often felt as pitting places against each other. Some of the post-pandemic 'levelling up' narrative implies that Darlington benefits at the expense of London, or that Sheffield and Bradford must compete for limited funding pots. Over a decade of austerity has created a scarcity mindset that assumes investment elsewhere results in less investment in your own neighbourhood, with per capita comparisons that frame uneven investment as unfairness rather than needs based.

Last of all, while historic housing policy focused on increasing supply of housing, especially through state provision, modern policy has centred on demand. In 1975, over 80% of policy was supply-side capital funding. This has entirely reversed, with 85% of spending routed through demand-side revenue funding via housing benefits. This is before we even explore demand-side policies in the form of discounts and incentives for homebuyers. The inevitable consequence is that housing costs have continued to rise, meaning the poorer have continued to need larger subsidies per household and more households will need subsidy – increasing the costs to the taxpayer. The only way to reduce cost without radically changing the way housing policy is developed and delivered is to be meaner – tighten the criteria for receipt of benefits or reduce the level of subsidy. Neither option fixes the housing market but both result in worse outcomes for the individual recipients and society as a whole.

Devolving housing policy to regions

Despite the range of housing policies described above, the reality is that the housing situation is a mess and an example of ongoing policy failure by all UK governments. Let us just recap the following situation today:

- High levels of homelessness – while there is debate about the definition of homelessness a figure of 200,000 is often quoted.
- 3.5% of all households in England are seen as being overcrowded.
- Difficulties in first-time buyers getting on the housing ladder.
- Rampant inflation in property prices especially in the South East.
- Governments of all parties set targets for housebuilding but repeatedly fail to meet them.
- The huge imbalances in the UK economy discussed in Chapter 6 and presided over by all governments mean that the imbalance between housing demand and housing supply is greatest in the South East of the UK. A rebalancing of the UK economy should ease this situation but this will take decades to achieve.

In the light of this, it is imperative to consider whether a move towards devolving housing policy to regional governments would be advantageous.

Impact of devolution on housing policy

Before exploring options for devolving housing policy beyond national government to regional and local government, it is worth looking at the impact of devolution in Scotland, Wales and Northern Ireland, which took place in 1999. While there is a valid argument that devolution in its current state has simply transferred top-down power from one distant institution to another, it still serves as a useful measure as to the impact of redistributing power, and whether the right powers have been devolved with the necessary financial and policy levers to make them impactful.

Before 1999, Scotland and Wales were constitutionally subject to the same housing regimes but with markedly different outcomes. Northern Ireland had much more autonomy until Stormont was suspended in 1972. The Barnett formula was based on historic spending and allocated according to relative population size – "giving some post-devolution administrations more scope than others to provide good services" (Lund 2016, 233).

In Wales, where there had not been a history of separate legislation, the tendency of the early devolved bodies like the Welsh Office was to follow English practices (Mullins and Murie 2006, 9). As a result, pre-devolution in Wales had similar housing policy to England. The housing stock was older, meaning a higher proportion of low-income households living in poorer-quality housing than England or Scotland (Smith, Stirling and Williams 2000).

More recently, Wales has begun to diverge. Stock transfers, for example, were encouraged by the Welsh Government as a way for councils to improve quality, but unlike in England this was much more community focused. A community model was put forward reflecting the Welsh Government's priorities of tenant empowerment (Birrell 2009, 96). The biggest and best example of this is Merthyr Valley Homes, a novel tenant and staff multi-stakeholder co-operative, in which residents and employees share ownership and control. This form of co-operative social housing management offers a model to other areas, as well as demonstrating how decentralised policy can result in different outcomes in the right circumstances.

The Welsh Government also used its powers to introduce secondary legislation to limit the scope and use of the Right to Buy in order to tackle a growing concern with homelessness. Instead they developed an approach tailored to Wales which reduced the maximum discount, and gave social landlords first refusal to buy back properties being resold within ten years and excluded certain rural areas where affordability was a particular concern. They have also been more hands on with the private rented sector too with the compulsory registration of private landlords and lettings agencies in the Housing (Wales) Act 2014.

Scottish housing policy had also been distinctive to the rest of the UK in the past (Sim 2004), but reducing in the 1960s as Whitehall exerted its own agenda.

Other than greater house building (25% more per capita than England), Scottish policy differences are therefore reduced, notwithstanding distinctive planning frameworks and subsidies which remained in place (Lund 2016). Nonetheless, some significant outliers exist. While stock transfers in Scotland were more limited than England, Glasgow City Council was the "highest profile example" of housing reform (Kintrea 2006), with 85,000 Glaswegian properties transferred in 2002. Presented to tenants as an opportunity for community ownership, it struck a very different tone to English transfers (Daly et al. 2005), creating a unique system of second-stage transfer from the original 60 local housing organisations to smaller RSLs (McKee 2007). While not a universal experience across Scotland – in Edinburgh stock transfer was rejected at the ballot box – community ownership and control have a long legacy in Scotland (Muir and KcKee 2015).

Northern Ireland meanwhile was home to the "worst housing conditions in Britain and amongst the worst in Europe" (Lund 2016). The existence of the Northern Ireland Housing Executive enabled a distinctly Northern Irish housing policy to emerge despite direct rule. However, this distinctiveness comes as much from social divisions and sectarianism as it does a wider desire to innovate. Instead, these "civic dynamics" have resulted in policy which reflects English policy in a Northern Irish context (Lund 2016, 255).

Broadly, the experience of devolution shows that approaches to housing policies remain fairly homogenised. Common drivers such as a cultural preference for home ownership, similar financial institutions and taxation systems, and similar or at least co-dependent economic environments (Birrell 2009, 95) may explain the limited divergence as well the incompleteness of powers devolved. However, a lack of imagination or political will could also be argued. However, the few examples of genuine divergence show that when devolved bodies are given genuine policy levers both the willingness and scope for innovation and local priority setting can shine through. The best examples, perhaps, are Glaswegian stock transfers and Welsh co-operative social housing models – both of these unique to their own jurisdiction.

Looking overseas, generally, greater devolution results in greater variation in housing policy. In Spain, housing is largely decentralised and policy is the responsibility of autonomous provinces. The national state's role is minimal – broad well-defined interventions and measures to protect renters such as preventing evictions. The Catalan government shows how regions can innovate and develop unique approaches. They have converted vacant public housing for sale into social housing for rent, created rights of first refusal and pre-emptive rights for properties that have been foreclosed and sold by a financial institution when located in an area of high housing demand. They maintain a registry of vacant dwellings and tax vacant dwellings, accompanied by measures to offer empty housing in the hands of private landlords at an affordable rent (Lambea Llop 2016). Switzerland is even more decentralised, with municipalities wielding powers over everything from income tax to public services. Cantons compete with one another to attract taxpayers through hitting the right balance between tax and public services. However, in practice, the minimum standards set by the federal government on public services remove the scope for significant variation (Hilber and Schöni 2016).

Why devolution can fix the UK housing problem

Successive UK governments have struggled to find the right balance between national, regional and local (Castro Coelho, Ratnoo and Dellepiane 2014) and nowhere more so than in housing. Decentralisation has been tarred by the spectre of policy dumping, leading to local actors unable to deliver policy, communities feeling disenfranchised because the lines of accountability for failed outcomes are unclear, and national government ever less inclined to share power.

Kate Barker, author of the Government's 2004 Housing Review, argues that housing policy has taken an even greater backwards step in terms of spatial policy and planning over the past decade. The end to regional planning brought on by the Coalition Government in 2010 made it "difficult to develop a coherent approach to regional spatial questions" (Barker 2014).

Thus, the case for devolution is strong – despite the complexity of housing policy:

- There is no uniform housing market, and therefore any uniform approach to interacting with it is doomed to failure. By acknowledging the UK's many housing markets and housing crises, we must acknowledge too that one policy cannot fit all. Regional policy which reflects regional conditions and priorities will be more effective in improving housing outcomes.
- Existing local powers are not accompanied by the levers and funds to make them meaningful. This policy dumping undermines trust in local institutions, prevents tangible progress on important areas of policy and damages accountability with everyone able to point a finger elsewhere.
- There is a tension between a central government focused on demand-side policies of housing benefit and incentives for first-time buyers, and a local government more focused on their housing waiting lists, the need to build more homes at social rent and the constraints of the planning system.
- Housing demand and supply is intrinsically linked with place – jobs available locally, average local income, transport infrastructure, access to green spaces and so on. When delivered at a regional and local level, these can be delivered in an integrated way that simply isn't possible to direct from Westminster.
- Housing policy has been defined by fragmentation resulting in many housing initiatives and very few comprehensive housing strategies.
- Devolution would enable regional government to bring together the levers of housing policy in a joined-up, strategic and long-term way.
- Devolved administrations have shown that when the necessary powers are devolved, variation to meet local priorities is possible. They also show the limitations of incomplete devolution.

However, devolution doesn't stop at the regional government or the town hall level. The case for continuing to decentralise certain aspects of housing directly to communities, with appropriate local checks and balances, is possibly even stronger. The evidence and experience of TMOs shows that tenant involvement can result in better housing outcomes in social housing.

When it comes to house building, community involvement can make or break a development and overcoming NIMBYism is easiest when local communities have not just a say but a stake in their neighbourhood. Community land trusts and co-operative housing models show the great appetite that exists for new development – so empowering communities to get building and engage in the housing market at a hyperlocal level is a positive natural next step.

While this chapter doesn't reach simplistic conclusions, it does question whether the current levels of government and their powers are having any success in creating a better functioning housing sector. Effective governance has to include proper top-down scrutiny and accountability, as well as genuine, empowered, bottom-up democratic structures which ensure priorities are locally driven and outcomes locally monitored, brought together by a clear framework to enable co-operation (Hetherington 2006). Thus, we suggest housing policy and strategy is better developed and delivered at a regional level, led by local actors and informed by the broad national priorities and context. In the longer term, this must include a significant level of fiscal devolution, giving regions the income needed to actually effect change and to avoid further policy dumping, as well as the ability to improve or better yet replace ineffective taxes like council tax or at the very least in the shorter term to have transparency on need and distribution of tax revenues. Greater variation of planning powers should be allowed, with those decisions made at a local and regional level, as well as the responsibility for future spatial planning.

Decentralising housing alone won't resolve many of the underlying factors that make housing particularly complicated. The other chapters in this book explore why and how other policy areas should be devolved too and for housing to be a success, regional economic development, transport and infrastructure investment should certainly be devolved. These are so co-dependent that it would be meaningless to devolve one without the other. Some devolution of benefits would be beneficial too and this could be administered nationally but with regional variations based on costs of housing and other costs of living as well as average wages and deprivation levels.

Combined, these tools would allow regions to develop holistic long-term regional plans encompassing everything from housing and jobs, to transport and infrastructure. These would need to be sufficiently flexible to accommodate any changes, opportunities and shocks while regular reviews with relevant community stakeholders will ensure the plan remains relevant and ensures policy makers are held to account for any failure to deliver.

Collaboration between regions is also important, and the central government can play a useful convening role, coordinating the extent of co-operation and partnership working between regions and ensuring regional decision-makers have access to all relevant information and upcoming decisions. The central government also has a role in redistribution, ensuring any national funding is reallocated according to need.

Region-proof national policy

As policies are developed, policy makers should always as a rule consider the impact of their policy on each region individually, taking into account particular regional characteristics – and adjust policy where appropriate to meet the needs and circumstances of that region.

However, given the diversity of housing markets and problems, and the multifaceted nature of housing policy, it is important that inadvertent levers aren't pulled at a national level which have knock on effects on regions' ability to drive their own housing plans. For example, in the pandemic, homeowners were offered a time-limited stamp duty break as part of the government's attempt to reignite the housing market. The relative impact of this in different regions may turn out to have been substantial – but there were no regional variations possible to the scheme.

Housing policy issues for UK regions

We have emphasised throughout this book and this chapter that there is no point in devolving policy, including housing policy, to UK regions if you are just going to create a series of mini-Whitehalls in Edinburgh, Cardiff, Birmingham, Manchester, etc. complete with hyper-centralisation and control freakery. Regional governments need to be radically different and this section looks at some of the major policy issues that should be considered by regional governments throughout the UK.

Empower local authorities

Councils have historically proven themselves effective housebuilders. Their lack of success in building new homes for social rent does not come from a lack of willingness, but a lack of access to land, finance and powers. Councils should be able to borrow against the value of their existing housing assets and rental incomes to invest in building new homes. Grant funding to increase affordable housing supply from the central government, along with an end to Right to Buy stock depletion, is a more impactful investment in the long-term than housing benefits.

The house building sector is heavily reliant on a small number of big developers, resulting in a sector driven by commercial self-interest with little incentive to build new homes any faster. More than half of all new homes are built by the country's eight largest housebuilders. Councils should be empowered not simply to be more interventionist in house building, but also in the markets for building, construction and maintenance. A mixed economy of municipal, co-operative, community-owned and SME companies is better placed to design, build, maintain and repair housing than large multinationals.

Councils' compulsory purchase powers should also be strengthened, so that local authorities can buy at existing use value plus 'reasonable' compensation for the landowner, rather than prices inflated by any 'hope value' associated with the likelihood for future development. Land assembly, and fragmented land ownership, is often a barrier to residential development. The ability to assemble land was critical for the creation of Garden Cities, and in other countries stronger compulsory purchase powers allow local authorities a far greater role in land assembly.

There should be new partnership models for land assembly so that landowners of sections of a wider development site, as defined by the local authority, can be given the option to enter into an equity partnership with other landowners and the local authority as an alternative to compulsory purchase. They would be able to exchange their land for shares in the partnership and will earn a fair profit when the value of the new development is realised. A similar approach is followed in Germany where, in order to redevelop areas with fragmented ownership, the municipality assembles the land so that the increase in value is shared proportionately among existing landowners.

These partnerships could create new Development Corporations like those that created the Garden Cities. The New Towns Act 1981 should be updated to enable these partnerships, and to specify that Development Corporations be organised co-operatively, so that landowners, the local authority and the local community all have a voice in any development and all benefit from its success (Birley 2017).

Councils should also have the ability to design relevant local taxes – privately held undeveloped brownfield land could be taxed in places where land banking is an issue. Paid to local government to finance other land acquisition or house building, this could encourage land to be brought forwards for residential or other appropriate use.

Put tenants in charge

In social housing, TMOs have demonstrated that better housing outcomes can be achieved when the community who live somewhere decide how it is run. Having control over your own life and where you live is empowering – we should want that for social housing residents.

Too many local councils are reluctant to cede control, and sometimes the desire to remain in charge overrides any objective assessment of what model of management will result in better outcomes. Barriers are put up for tenants looking to exercise their right to manage their estate (Rowlands 2009). Large housing management contracts make it difficult for tenants to use new powers should they be successful. In addition, the housing repairs and maintenance market is broken, dominated by large contractors who take advantage of large council-wide contracts, making it harder for smaller TMOs to find appropriately sized contractors.

TMOs should be promoted, using models closer to the original tenant management co-operatives created in the 1970s whereby each tenant is a member and each member a tenant, managing the property collectively through an elected board – as opposed to the watered-down estate management board model where the board includes some tenants elected from the estate as well as local council and other representatives. The law surrounding TMOs should be strengthened. This should include protections against councils creating 'fake' TMOs as happened in Kensington and Chelsea. There should be new provisions for street properties which currently struggle to organise as they are more dispersed, and 'right to manage' powers for housing association tenants as well as council tenants.

Furthermore, so long as the local authority remains the ultimate owner, the threat of local politics will always remain. Stock transfer with community empowerment at its heart is one way to neutralise this uncertainty, but better protections against a municipal power grab should also be put in place for TMOs. Taking an estate out of the hands of the community and back into municipal control should be a last resort for a failing service, with the right checks and balances in place to ensure it is in the best interest of tenants and the wider community. Support for TMOs should be improved too – as they provide a model for what local people in socially excluded communities can achieve where training and support is available (Rowlands 2009). Adequate resourcing, succession planning and improved networking between TMOs is critical to their success, and the improvement in outcomes outweighs the cost of providing this.

Let communities lead

Around 10% of Europeans live in housing co-operatives – compared to 0.6% in the UK (Birley 2017). There is clearly an appetite for an alternative to the binary choice of private renting or homeownership – which too often isn't even a choice to people priced out of the first rung on the housing ladder.

Co-operative forms of ownership and community-led housing create an efficient and affordable alternative whereby local communities retain control and can reinvest their own rents in more housing or in improving their current stock. It is as long term and secure as social housing or homeownership but without the personal debt or long waiting list. Housing co-operatives are generally robust and financially stable and perform, on all measures, better than other types of affordable housing providers (Co-operative Housing International 2020). In order for co-operative housing to be more easily defended and promoted, as well as to reduce unintended consequences, a new legal definition of 'Community-led Housing' must be established. Recognition in law would ensure the house building industry, professionals and financial services are better placed to facilitate and promote co-operative and community-led housebuilding. New co-operative housing tenure would enable more straightforward legal navigation by new schemes and improved legal understanding.

Regions in England need to follow the Welsh best practice, where the Welsh Government lifted the ban on fully mutual co-operatives granting assured tenancies and gave greater powers to lenders to fully mutual co-operatives in the Housing (Wales) Act 2014. This has created a better environment for housing co-operatives to exist and allows them to develop more robustly and independently, while creating certainty, assurance, protection and security for tenants. Most importantly, it has resulted in new homes actually being built.

Access to finance is often a challenge for new co-operative housing. Government should underwrite a guaranteed buyback scheme of last resort on mortgage products for homes that are co-operatively owned or include the community land trust principle of 'affordability in perpetuity', and banks should be asked to develop a standard mortgage form for mortgage products that include a 'perpetuity' arrangement to encourage lender participation. As the Building Societies Association recommends, this could be funded using NS&I Pensioner Bonds. The importance of secondary co-operatives like CDS and Co-op Homes (Rowlands 2009) is clear in the development and continuation of the existing housing co-operative sector. Support for secondary co-operatives at a regional level would help would-be co-operatives build or refurbish homes faster and more sustainably.

Reform planning and land use

Much of the framework of the planning system rests on the principle of reducing barriers to developers and much of the analysis of the planning system has focused on how planning stifles a 'free market' in development (Ryan-Collins, Lloyd and Macfarlane 2017). Instead, planning, at a regional level, should be reimagined as an explicit and proactive tool that communities and public bodies can use to democratically decide how land should be used, what kinds of homes should be built and how the uplift in land value after development should be reinvested.

Other supply-side factors

The failures to build enough houses in the UK are often put down to local government reluctance to give planning permission to developers. While there is some truth in this, it is not the whole story and there are other supply-side issues which will also need to be addressed by regional governments.

- **Land banking** – often private developers obtain planning permission to build houses on land they own but don't actually get around to building those houses. There are business reasons behind this but regional governments may need to introduce sanctions and or incentives to use that land to build more houses.
- **Building materials** – at the time of writing there are difficulties obtaining the raw materials, such as timber needed for house construction. Much of

the reason for this is the fact that, over a period of years, the UK has moved towards acquiring these raw materials from overseas rather than developing them in-country. This is also the case for items such as food and energy. There seems to be no practical solution to this problem in the short term but it is something regional governments may wish to consider for the longer term.

- **Labour force** – once again there are shortages of skilled labour in the building industry and this has been exacerbated by Brexit and access to overseas labour. In Chapters 9 and 12, the importance of regional governments getting to grips with the vocational education and training system as a means of meeting the labour needs of the regional economy cannot be overemphasised. This is especially true in relation to the construction industry.
- **Modern construction methods** - these involve off-site construction techniques, such as mass production and factory assembly, as alternatives to traditional building. These approaches have been described as a way to produce more, better quality homes in less time but there is often resistance from several quarters. Regional governments need to consider these methods in the light of housing needs.

Private rented sector reform

In the short and medium term, the private rented sector will continue to play a significant role in providing housing. In this context, the sector needs far tougher regulation in terms of quality, fairness and affordability. Mechanisms should be introduced to link rents to median local incomes and for tenants to be able to challenge unduly high rents, alongside restrictions on the pace and extent of rent increases, longer rental periods and greater consumer protections in place for tenants.

The balance of power needs to shift between tenant and landlord. Rather than the onus being on the tenant to raise issues of poor quality or disrepair, the responsibility to ensure homes meet minimum standards should sit with the landlord. Local councils are best placed to regulate the private rented sector and should have wider powers to design landlord licensing schemes, in order to secure better quality and more affordable homes for their residents. A responsibility that might be retained at the national level is defining what a decent home looks like and ensuring that the proper rights to redress and consumer protection exist.

Conclusion

This book considers UK policy in a wide range of public policy areas. In its various chapters, the reader will have observed many examples of ongoing policy failure in each of the areas discussed which is in line with the comments in Chapter 2 about public policy failure being endemic in the UK.

This is also the case with regard to housing. My co-authors may disagree but I would like to suggest that having read this chapter the reader might conclude that the situation in regard to UK housing policy is the worst of the lot. It is a mess and probably getting worse. Over many years, we see examples of over-centralisation, buck passing, incompetence, etc. from UK governments at a level difficult to believe.

Throughout its history, there were two things which were the primary needs for humans to survive – food and shelter. We often talk about the "Man from Mars" syndrome – what if a man came down from Mars and looked at the UK housing system – what would he think? In the fifth largest economy in the world where many cannot get this basic need of shelter, is it not reasonable to assume that he would conclude that humanity was deluded, stupid, incompetent, etc.?

Centralised UK housing policy has repeatedly failed and needs to be replaced with a regional approach.

References

Action on Empty Homes, 2019. *Empty homes in England 2019,* London: s.n.

Apps, P., 2017. *Once upon a time in the west: the history of KCTMO.* [Online] Available at: https://www.insidehousing.co.uk/insight/insight/once-upon-a-time-in-the-west-the-history-of-kctmo-52300 [Accessed August 2021].

Bailey, D., 2017. Economic renewal through devolution? Tax reform. *Competition & Change,* 21(1), pp. 10–26.

Barker, K., 2014. *Housing: where's the plan?* s.l.: London Publishing Partnership.

Barker, N., 2019. *ALMO closures: how are they affecting services?* [Online] Available at: https://www.insidehousing.co.uk/insight/insight/almo-closures-how-are-they-affecting-services-60071 [Accessed August 2021].

Barker, N., 2021. London councils place homeless households more than 200 miles away. *Inside Housing,* 4 June.

Birchall, J., 1991. *The hidden history of co-operative housing in Britain,* s.l.: s.n.

Birley, A., 2017. *Bricks, mortar & co-operation,* London: The Co-operative Party.

Birrell, D., 2009. *The impact of devolution on social policy.* Bristol: The Policy Press.

Cairncross, L., 2002. *Tenants managing: an evaluation of tenant management organisations in England,* s.l.: Office of the Deputy Prime Minister.

Castro Coelho, M., Ratnoo, V. & Dellepiane, S., 2014. *Housing that works for all,* London: Institute for Government.

Chakrabortty, A., 2014. New Era estate scandal: families at the mercy of international speculators. *The Guardian,* 19 November.

Co-operative Housing International, 2020. *About United Kingdom.* [Online] Available at: https://www.housinginternational.coop/co-ops/united-kingdom/ [Accessed August 2021].

Corlett, A. & Judge, L., 2017. *Home affront: Housing across the generations,* London: The Resolution Foundation.

Cowan, D. & Marsh, A., 2001. New labour, same old story housing policy? *The Modern Law Review,* 64(2), pp. 260–279.

Daly, G., Mooney, G., Poole, L. & Davis, H., 2005. Housing stock transfer in Birmingham and Glasgow: the contrasting experiences of two UK cities. *European Journal of Housing Policy,* 5(3), pp. 327–341.

Department for Work and Pensions, 2020. *Outturn and forecast: Autumn Budget 2020.* [Online] Available at: https://www.gov.uk/government/publications/benefit-expenditure-and-caseload-tables-2020 [Accessed August 2021].

Dmitracova, O., 2019. Building more homes won't solve UK housing crisis, new report argues. *The Independent*, 21 August.

Flint, J., 2006. Maintaining an arm's length? Housing, community governance and the management of 'problematic' populations. *Housing Studies*, 21(2), pp. 171–186.

Gallent, N., 2019. *Whose housing crisis? Assets and homes in a changing economy.* Bristol: Policy Press.

Hetherington, P., 2006. *Connecting England: A framework for regional development,* Oldham: The Town and Country Planning Association.

Hilber, C. A. L. & Schöni, O., 2016. *Housing policies in the United Kingdom, Switzerland, and the United States: lessons learned,* Tokyo: Asian Development Bank Institute.

Hull, A. & Cooke, G., 2012. *Together at home: a new strategy for housing,* London: IPPR.

Jivraj, S., 2012. Modelling socioeconomic neighbourhood change due to internal migration in England. *Urban Studies: An International Journal of Research in Urban Studies,* 49(16), pp. 3565–3578.

Jones, R., 1999. *'Time is right' for mortgage relief to end.* [Online] Available at: https://www.theguardian.com/uk/1999/mar/10/budget1999.budget3 [Accessed August 2021].

Judge, L., 2019. *Streets apart: an analysis of manifesto commitments on housing,* s.l.: Resolution Foundation.

Keohane, N. & Broughton, N., 2013. *The politics of housing,* s.l.: The National Housing Federation and the Social Market Foundation.

Kintrea, K., 2006. Having it all? Housing reform under devolution. *Housing Studies,* 21(2), pp. 187–207.

Lambea Llop, N., 2016. Social housing management models in Spain. *Revista catalana de dret públic,* June, 52, pp. 115–128.

Lund, B., 2016. *Housing politics in the United Kingdom.* 1st ed. Bristol: Policy Press.

Lund, B., 2017. *Understanding housing policy.* 3rd ed. Bristol: Policy Press.

MacLennan, D. & O'Sullivan, A., 2013. Localism, devolution and housing policies. *Housing Studies,* 28(4), pp. 599–615.

Marsh, S., 2020. English councils breaking law in 'secretly' relocating homeless people. *The Guardian,* 1 July.

McKee, K., 2007. Community ownership in Glasgow: the devolution of ownership and control, or a centralising process?. *European Journal of Housing Policy,* 7(3), pp. 319–336.

Muir, J. & KcKee, K., 2015. *Briefing 3: devolution, localism and housing policy,* St Andrews: ESRC.

Mullins, D. & Murie, A., 2006. *Housing policy in the UK.* Basingstoke: Palgrave Macmillan.

Newton, R. & Tunstall, R., 2012. *Lesson for localism: tenant self-management,* s.l.: Urban Forum.

Power, A., 2017. *How Tenant Management Organisations have wrongly been associated with Grenfell.* [Online] Available at: https://blogs.lse.ac.uk/politicsandpolicy/the-truth-about-tmos/ [Accessed August 2021].

Richards, D. & Smith, M., 2016. Devolution in England, the British political tradition and the absence of consultation, consensus and consideration. *Representation,* 51(4), pp. 385–401.

Rowlands, R., 2009. *Forging mutual futures - Co-operative, mutual and community based housing in practice: history & potential,* Birmingham: Centre for Urban and Regional Studies.

Ryan-Collins, J., Lloyd, T. & Macfarlane, L., 2017. *Rethinking the economics of land and housing.* London: Zed Books.

Shelter, 2021. *Denied the right to a safe home,* London: Shelter.

Sillett, J., 2004. *A level playing field.* [Online] Available at: https://www.theguardian.com/society/2004/sep/28/localgovernment.labour2004 [Accessed August 2021].

Sim, D., 2004. *Housing and public policy in post-devolution Scotland.* Coventry: Chartered Institute of Housing.

Smith, R., Stirling, T. & Williams, P., 2000. *Housing in Wales: the policy agenda in an era of devolution.* Coventry: Chartered Institute of Housing.

Stephens, M., whitehead, C. & Munro, M., 2005. *Lessons from the past, challenges for the future. An evaluation of English housing policy 1975–2000,* London: Office of the Deputy Prime Minister.

This is Money, 1999. *Farewell then to Miras, the kindest cut of all.* [Online] Available at: https://www.thisismoney.co.uk/money/news/article-1582689/Farewell-then-to-Miras-the-kindest-cut-of-all.html [Accessed August 2021].

Thompson, M., 2020. *Reconstructing public housing: Liverpool's hidden history of collective alternatives.* 1st ed. s.l.:Liverpool University Press.

Webb, K., 2012. *Bricks of benefits? Rebalancing housing investment,* s.l.: Shelter.

Wilcox, S. & Pawson, H., 2010/2011. *UK housing review,* s.l.: s.n.

11

OTHER REGIONAL PUBLIC SERVICES

Peter Murphy, Nick Howe and Malcolm J. Prowle

Introduction

The previous five chapters have discussed, in some detail, the key aspects of public policy formulation and public service delivery that would be the responsibility of UK regional governments under a federal structure. These areas of policy and public services will probably consume, in expenditure terms, around three quarters of regional budgets but there will, of course, be many other areas of policy and public service delivery that will or could be the responsibility of regional governments. It is beyond the scope of this book to discuss, in detail, the public policy and public service aspects of these services and so this chapter tries to provide a brief overview of these issues in relation to the following services:

- Policing
- Fire and rescue
- Higher education
- Social welfare

Policing

Policing services in the UK currently comprise 45 territorial police forces and three functional police forces.

The functional police forces are given as follows:

- British Transport Police: responsible for policing the rail network in Great Britain

DOI: 10.4324/9781003201892-14

- Civil Nuclear Constabulary: responsible for non-military nuclear installations and non-military nuclear material in transit
- Ministry of Defence Police: responsible for MOD property, personnel, other defence interests, UK nuclear weapons and special nuclear materials

In addition, there is the National Crime Agency which is not a police force but an agency responsible to a Secretary of State.

It is suggested that these organisations should remain the province of national government subject to appropriate consultation and liaison arrangements with regional governments.

Turning to territorial police forces, these can be considered as follows:

- **Scotland** – one police force (Police Scotland) which is accountable to the Scottish Parliament
- **Northern Ireland** – one police force (Police Service of Northern Ireland) which is accountable to the Northern Ireland Assembly
- **England and Wales** – 43 police forces all accountable to the UK Home Office

In the light of the above, there seems no reason why police services in England and Wales should not follow the example of Scotland and Northern Ireland and have police forces accountable to UK regional governments rather than the UK Home Office. It is insulting to suggest (as some do) that regional governments would somehow "not be up to the job" or cannot be trusted with having responsibility for regional policing and that this should not be devolved to regions. As already noted, policing in Scotland is already devolved and indeed, it is often suggested that Welsh police forces are already de facto accountable (at least in part) to the Welsh Government as well as the Home Office. Similarly, policing in Germany follows a regional model, where German state governments are responsible for the bulk of Germany's police forces. The regionalisation issue, with regard to UK policing, was fully discussed in a 2005 report by HMIC (O'Connor 2005).

A first action for regional governments would be to consider the appropriate structure of police forces in their region. There is already considerable variation here with Wales having four police forces and East Midlands having five police forces compared to just one in Scotland. However, in line with what was suggested earlier in this book, we see these decisions as being something that should be left to regional governments and not the UK Home Office to decide.

The next issue for regional governments concerns the role of Police and Crime Commissioners. These were introduced in England and Wales (but not in Scotland and Northern Ireland) in 2012 as a means of having some form of local democratic accountability for police forces. However, the transfer of police forces to democratic regional governments would seem to make the PCC role redundant and they should be abolished and brought in line with practice in Scotland and NI.

In relation to funding, police forces in England and Wales are currently funded via a combination of Home Office government grants to PCCs, local precepts and national priorities monies, e.g. terrorism. Under regional government arrangements, Home Office grants will cease, and funding will be derived from national, regional and local sources. Consideration will need to be given to how this should operate.

Under these arrangements, policing policy in a region will become the responsibility of regional governments while operating within the constraints of policing legislation and the criminal law. There may still need to be some form of national coordination of the policing mandate concerning concepts such as recruitment standards, pay, terms and conditions, public order policy, firearms, training, IT procurement, communications and intelligence systems to ensure regional interoperability when forces might need to support each other on a national basis. Not all of this is currently covered by policing legislation. Thus, regional governments will need to work with chief constables to establish policies and working practices for policing activities in the region. These policies will be tailored to the specific circumstances of the region and will not be blanket policies laid down at national level as at present. Such policies could include the following:

- Crime prevention focus
- Neighbourhood policing
- Partnership working with other public services
- Stop and search
- Use of tasers
- Use of PCSOs
- Recruitment, retention, etc.

Regional governments will also need to consider the extent to which they should collaborate with police forces in other regions, particularly those which are adjacent. Some degree of collaboration will be essential in terms of dealing with emergency situations like terrorism or other major incidents where high volumes of policing are needed at short notice. However, regions will need to explore ongoing approaches to collaboration with one another, in particular, in specialist areas of policing where an individual region may find it difficult or uneconomic to conduct its own activities.

Her Majesty's Inspectorate of Constabulary and Fire & Rescue Services (HMICFRS) independently assesses the effectiveness and efficiency of police forces (and fire and rescue services (FRS)) in England and Wales to provide information about the quality and efficiency of policing services. However, Scotland has its own inspectorate body. If all regions in the UK adopted a similar approach then we would be left with 12 regional regulatory bodies for the UK which may sound excessive. Hence, this issue of inspection and regulation is one which would need to be addressed.

Finally, we turn to the issue of the Metropolitan Police which is the territorial police force responsible for law enforcement in the Metropolitan Police District, consisting of the 32 London boroughs. However, this does not include the "square mile" of the City of London, which is policed by the much smaller City of London Police. The force, by officer numbers, is the largest in the UK by a significant margin, and one of the largest police forces in the world. In addition to its territorial policing, the Metropolitan Police has significant national responsibilities, such as coordinating and leading on UK-wide national counter-terrorism. However, the Metropolitan Police is frequently subject to many criticisms of many types and from many quarters. It is often referred to as a dysfunctional organisation. Whatever the truth of these statements, it would seem that a major reorganisation of UK policing services based on regionalisation would provide a good opportunity for reviewing the longer-term future of the Metropolitan Police.

Fire and rescue services

FRS in the UK are delivered by fire and rescue authorities. Currently, in the UK, there are a total of 54 FRS authorities as shown in Table 11.1.

There are a number of aspects to the FRS agenda that have strong resonances with a potential regional agenda or a debate about empowering regional governments. When you look at a regional agenda you need to consider if there are national or widescale issues that either could be tackled with the help of regional structures/entities or could be better done altogether at a regional scale (i.e. following the principle of subsidiarity which holds that social and political issues

TABLE 11.1 Fire and rescue services

Region	*No. of fire and rescue authorities*	*Regional population (millions)*	*Area (sq. miles)*
North East	4	2.7	3,312
North West	7	7.4	5,447
Yorkshire and Humber	4	5.5	5,948
East Midlands	5	4.9	6,033
West Midlands	5	6.0	5,019
East of England	6	6.3	7,381
London	1	9.0	607
South East	8	9.2	7,364
South West	8	5.7	9,203
Wales	4	3.2	8,005
Scotland	1	5.5	30,080
Northern Ireland	1	1.9	5,455

Sources: https://www.statista.com/statistics/294729/uk-population-by-region/, https://www.nationalfirechiefs.org.uk/Fire-and-Rescue-Services

should be dealt with at the most immediate (or local) level that is consistent with their resolution). You also need to consider what is currently being done at a local level that could be done more economically, efficiently and/or effectively at a greater geographical scale for example through the capture of economies of scale.

The configuration and delivery of FRS provides a surprisingly illuminating lens through which to evaluate the potential contribution to and from a regional government in England and Wales.

Prior to devolution, all parts of the UK had the same legislative basis for FRS which were "modernised" during the New Labour Government of Tony Blair. The 2004 FRS Act provided the basis for strategic and operational activity during regular periods of activity while the 2004 Civil Contingencies Act, as its name implies, makes provision for periods of widespread emergencies or civil disasters when much wider co-ordinated responses are needed from the core first-category responders – which of course includes the three blue light emergency services.

Policy delivery and assurance at the local level

Fire and rescue is a particularly useful "lens" for a discussion on regionalisation when you realise that since devolution the direction of policy, delivery and public assurance in the emergency services and particularly FRS has been quite different in Scotland and Northern Ireland (and to a lesser extent in Wales), than in England. The geographical scale (in terms of areas and population served) of Scotland, Wales and Northern Ireland is of course roughly akin to the nine standard geographical regions of England. In addition, since devolution the structure and governance of FRS in Scotland and Northern Ireland contrast strikingly with England's.

The policy agenda in England since the Conservative-led coalition government of 2010–2015 has been to bring the local Police and FRS under a governance model based upon single directly elected officials (Police and Crime Commissioner and later Police, Fire and Crime Commissioners). This is based on the North American model rather than the European model of directly elected individuals. In Scotland, Northern Ireland and, to a lesser extent, Wales the devolved administrations have sought service improvements and financial savings through service amalgamations producing larger organisations to achieve economies of scale and functional subsidiarity from the devolved administrations.

In 2012, the Police and Fire Reform (Scotland) Act 2012 created both a single Police Service for Scotland and the Scottish FRS, to replace the previous eight local police forces and eight FRS in Scotland. An evaluation of the performance of the FRS in Scotland in comparison with England over the period 2011–2018 clearly favoured the Scottish experience (Murphy et al. 2019) where service improvement, improved value for money and greater accountability were achieved in contrast to the deterioration of all three in England.

In Northern Ireland there is a single police force, a single FRS, a single health service and a single ambulance service. As in Scotland these single services are geographically coterminous but with separate governance and management structures. In England there is a long-term trend for local FRS to enlarge through a series of voluntary mergers (the latest being Hampshire and the Isle of Wight in 2021). There are therefore currently 44 FRS which, with the exception of London, are local services albeit with a variety of governance arrangements. The London Fire Brigade has been a single service since 1865 and could be considered a regional or at the very least a sub-regional fire service.

The Civil Contingencies Act created national, regional and local resilience forums and risk registers to plan for and co-ordinate responses to significant emergencies. The regional forums in England were based in the Government Offices for the Regions which kept the regional risk registers, organised the forums and provided strategic co-ordination to the emergency response. They were coterminous with the standard geographical regions, and they supported and co-ordinated local resilience forums and provided data and intelligence to central government. The closure of the regional offices in 2011 broke an important central-local link as regional level resilience was weakened in England (Murphy 2014), at a time when local emergency planning expenditure by local authorities and emergency services fell by 35% in real terms between 2009/2010 and 2018/2019. The consequences of this reduction in funding and fragmentation of infrastructure are unfortunately seen in the asymmetric response to the COVID-19 pandemic (Davies et al. 2020, Ogden and Phillips 2020) as well as previous widespread emergencies such as the regional and national flooding emergencies which have been increasing in number and intensity since the turn of the century (Mizutori and Guhar-Sapir 2021).

Policy issues for regional governments to consider

While all regions and fire and rescue authorities will face, broadly, the same challenges, the extent of these challenges will vary from place to place. Hence, the details of the individual responses should also vary from place to place. The following are some of the most relevant issues.

Organisation

As with local authorities and police authorities, the first task for a regional government would be to establish the optimum pattern for fire and rescue authorities in their region. At the same time, regional governments may wish to consider the other emergency services such as police and ambulance and consider the extent to which there might be shared services and joint working between the three services. Prior to devolution, Scotland had eight fire authorities, but these were amalgamated into one authority between 2012 and 2013 after the devolution of fire services to the Scottish Parliament. As fire and rescue was not a service delegated to the Welsh Government, no changes to the organisation of services were made.

Funding

Under a regional government arrangement, we see a merging of public expenditure into a single regional "pot" to be distributed at a regional level in line with what has happened in the devolved governments. It is then up to regions to decide the distribution of these funds between services.

Data and intelligence

Improved accountability, resilience, legitimacy and scrutiny all rely on adequate data and intelligence. While piecemeal improvements have been made (by the National Fire Chiefs Council (NFCC) and HMICFRS), the three recent reports investigating the FRS contribution during the pandemic highlight the continuing inadequacy of the data and intelligence for national, regional and local decision making (Levin 2020, HMICFRS, 2021, Hill 2021).

Evaluation of risk

Integrated risk management planning is the basis of fire service deployment and the configuration of its resources. The NFCC therefore has risk assessment and evaluation as its key priority in its community risk programme. Risk assessment underpins service and contingency planning at local, regional and national levels. All three are in need of strengthening none more so than at the regional level.

Deployment of staff

Recent years have seen a substantial decline in the numbers of fires addressed by fire service teams. The number of fires attended by fire services has been on a steady downward trend, falling from a peak of around 473,000 in 2003/2004 to around 151,000 in 2020/2021, a decline of 68%. There are many reasons for these reductions including reductions in smoking, better public awareness, improved fire safety and fire resistant materials. The reality is that the FRS is an emergency service and fire incidents cannot be predicted. Hence, they need to have sufficient staff on duty to deal with any fire incidents even though the numbers of such incidents have declined sharply. One outcome of it is that fire service staff have more time available to devote to preventative measures such as building inspections, fire alarm testing, education, and training. Some fire authorities have gone further and have collaborated with health and social care services to undertake tasks such as checking on the status of vulnerable individuals and groups, providing additional services, and (during the pandemic) driving ambulances and assisting with the vaccination programme. These are areas of collaboration which regional governments and all three emergency services may wish to investigate and enhance.

Collaboration

Collaboration between public services is something that is discussed in some length in Chapter 13. The lesson from this chapter is that greater and successful collaboration is not something which cannot be proscribed and insisted upon by governments, in a top-down manner, but is something which has to be bottom up based upon reciprocity, mutual trust and respect. By enabling local initiatives to determine what drives the reasons for collaborating and the form it should take, this will result in the collaborative experience being richer and more sustainable.

Collaboration in FRS can take two forms. First, there is collaboration between neighbouring fire and rescue authorities regarding the joint provision of specialist services and the provision of support with regard to major incidents. This has always taken place and will continue under regional governments. Second, there is collaboration between FRS and other public services, most notably police and ambulance services. There have sometimes been problems in this area but the fact that all three emergency services will fall under the remit of the same regional government should help to facilitate this further.

Reforms

In 2017, the Home Office issued a document concerning a programme of reform for FRS. This programme was based on three pillars which are illustrated in Table 11.2.

Overall, this seems a comprehensive (but very challenging) programme for reform of FRS but is not dissimilar to the experience of Scotland and Northern Ireland. At the outset, given the establishment of new FRS in the region, it would seem appropriate for regional governments to adopt this framework for reform and to pursue it, vigorously in the context of the specific circumstances of the individual region.

Higher education

In Chapter 9, we discussed the topic of regional education policy in relation to schools and colleges. The other main education topic is that of higher education but whereas schools and college can easily be seen as a truly regional and local public service, higher education is far more complex and difficult to consider in the context of regional government.

The higher education system in the UK is complex and often difficult to define and describe in a comprehensible manner developing as it has "like Topsy" grown substantially and haphazardly over a period of decades. While the UK

TABLE 11.2 Fire and rescue services: programme for reform

Efficiency and collaboration	*Accountability and transparency*	*Workforce reform*
• Obtain efficiency and effectiveness through collaboration • Promote value-for-money procurement	• Strengthen governance • Establish independent inspectorate • Revise peer review process • Obtain accessible performance information	• Establish professional standards-setting body • Undertake leadership development • Improve flexibility deployment of front-line staff • Improve diversity and equality of opportunity • Reform of the national negotiating bodies and modernise conditions of services

Source: Local Government Association, 2017.

higher education system is often described as a "national" system the reality is that the UK devolved administrations already have certain aspects of HE under their control. A few examples of this are:

- **HE policy** – while HE policy in England is the responsibility of the Department for Education, policy in the devolved areas is the responsibility of local parliaments and assemblies.
- **HE funding** – there are separate HE funding organisations for England, Wales, Scotland and Northern Ireland.
- **Student finance** – there are separate organisations administrating student loans and grants for England, Wales, Scotland and Northern Ireland.

However, some aspects of HE such as the Research Excellence Framework (REF), the Teaching Excellence Framework (TEF) and relationships with research councils operate on a national UK basis.

Universities, themselves, vary enormously in size, configuration and perspective. At one end the older and more prestigious organisations such as Oxbridge and some London universities see themselves as major players in an international HE market and don't necessarily see themselves as public service providers at all but as independent private organisations. At the other end, there are the newer universities which are largely seen as regional providers of education, training, research, etc. and which do see themselves as public service providers. In between, there are many well-established universities which probably see themselves as falling somewhere in the middle of these two extremes. However, in line with the comments made in Chapter 2, it should be noted that while there are excellent universities in all parts of the UK, the older and most affluent and influential HE institutions tend to be congregated in London and the South.

In addition to the issue about where UK universities are seen to position themselves along the regional-national-international axis, the other issue is what they see as their roles. The issue with universities is that there are widely different views as to what their roles should be (Collini 2012). These roles can often be considered in two groups – traditional roles and modern, more marketised roles. Some examples of the roles universities might be seen to pursue are shown in Table 11.3.

Again, different universities will have different views as to where they sit in relation to these two models.

Given that Wales, Scotland and Northern Ireland already control their HE systems, it seems likely that English regions will, quite reasonably, want to do the same. Why should the North West Region of England (7.4 million population and with 15 HE institutions) not control its HE system when Northern Ireland (1.9 million population and five HE institutions) does control its HE system.

As far as regions are concerned, universities are very important to a region and should be key players regarding the provision of education and training and the conduct of research and consultancy for local businesses, government organisations, etc. However, there are potential tensions here since some universities in a region might see themselves as national (or international) players rather than regional players and will want to operate on a national or international basis. Similarly, some universities might be keener to participate in "leading-edge" research which has a global impact rather than research which is of direct relevance to the region itself.

TABLE 11.3 Purposes of universities

Traditional views about the purposes of a university	*Modern (marketised) views about the purposes of a university*
• Scholars engaged in acquiring, communicating and advancing human knowledge • To pursue balanced knowledge about virtually everything • To be concerned with the "whole" community of scholars and students engaged in a common search for truth • To be concerned with the teaching of universal knowledge	• Awarding academic degrees in various academic disciplines • Meeting the learning needs and aspirations of individuals and local communities • Meeting the manpower needs of public and private sector employers in the region • Providers of research and consultancy support to local businesses, public service organisations, etc. • Providing innovation that can be translated into advantage in a fast-changing global economic environment

Source: Collini (2012).

The reality with the HE sector is that many believe the sector is probably "not fit for purpose" and in need of urgent and radical reform but this seems an almost impossible task for any government. The HE system has strong supporters in the most influential parts of UK society including the aristocracy, politics, the media, the professions and the City and the sector will fiercely defend its privileges. Even Margaret Thatcher, who, for better or worse, tried to reform most public services, shied away from reforming the HE sector. Some would suggest it is easier to reform the monarchy than the universities.

Overall, there seems no simple or obvious solution to how universities should fit into a system of UK regional government but a more "regionally sensitive" approach will need to be formulated.

Social welfare

In 2020/2021 government spending on pensions and social welfare was as shown in Table 11.4.

The total amount represents 28% of total public spending and is easily the largest component of public expenditure followed by healthcare at 24% of public expenditure.

Prior to devolution to Scotland, Wales and Northern Ireland, in 1999 (and for several years thereafter), the management and funding of pensions and benefits across the UK was the responsibility of the UK government. Following the passing of the Scotland Act 2016 certain powers relating to social security, including responsibility over certain benefits, were passed to the Scottish Government which then became responsible for setting the rules for eligibility and receipt of these benefits. The situation is as shown in Table 11.5.

The value of benefits transferred is a relatively small part of the total UK welfare bill but does include some important areas of financial support.

In Wales and Northern Ireland none of these social welfare benefits have been devolved to the devolved governments. In Wales there have been calls, from

TABLE 11.4 Spending on pensions and social welfare

Heading	*£billion*
Pensions	111
Incapacity, disability and injury benefits	44
Unemployment benefit	2
Housing benefits	25
Family benefits, income support and tax credits	46
Personal social services and other benefits	35
Total	263

Source: ONS (2016) https://www.ons.gov.uk/economy/governmentpublicsectorandtaxes/publicsectorfinance/articles/howisthewelfarebudgetspent/2016-03-16

TABLE 11.5 Location of benefits

Benefits transferred to Scotland	*Benefits which stay in the UK system*
• Payments for children and young people • Benefits for carers • Funeral support payments • Disability allowance • Universal credit Scottish Choices • Winter Heating Assistance • Council Tax reduction • Help with paying the rent • Scottish Welfare Fund	• Bereavement benefits • Child benefit • Employment and support allowance • Guardian's allowance • Housing benefit • Income support • Jobseeker's allowance • Maternity allowance • Pension credit • State pension • Statutory payments such as statutory sick pay and statutory maternity pay • Tax credits • Universal credit

Source: Scottish Government.

some quarters, for certain benefits to be devolved to the Welsh Government but this move has not been supported by the Welsh Government itself.

Under a regional government arrangement for the UK, it seems likely that, for the foreseeable future, the bulk of pensions and welfare benefits will remain the responsibility of the federal UK government but there could be some moves to transfer the payment of certain benefits to regional governments if there were good reasons for doing so. One important aspect of this concerns the impact of welfare payments on incentives to work. The OECD (2005) has stated that "*Ensuring that the provision of welfare benefits is consistent with work incentives has become a major policy priority in many OECD countries*". Having incentives to work may be key to the economic development strategy of regional governments and, thus, they may feel the need to have some influence over the administration of benefit payments in their region should this be seen to be inhibiting economic objectives.

References

Collini, S. (2012), *What are universities for?* London: Penguin Books.

Davies, D., Atkins, G., Benoit, G. and Sodhi, S. (2020), *How fit were public services for Coronovirus?* London: Institute of Government.

Hill, R. (2020), "C19 National Foresight Group: Report - rationale to extend the flu vaccine", C19 National Foresight Group, available at: https://www.ntu.ac.uk/about-us/nottingham-civic-exchange/c19-national-foresight-group/c19-national-foresight-group-outputs (accessed 19 September 2021).

HMICFRS (2020), "State of fire and rescue – The annual assessment of fire and rescue services in England 2019", HMICFRS, London.

HMICFRS (2021), "State of fire and rescue – The annual assessment of fire and rescue services in England 2020", HMICFRS, London.

Levin, C., Owen, J. and Waring, S. (2020), "Fire and rescue service response to COVID-19 Reports for the NFCC COVID-19 Committee", available at: https://www.nationalfirechiefs.org.uk/write/MediaUploads/COVID-19/NFCC_Covid-19_FINAL_December_2020.pdf (accessed 19 September 2021).

Local Government Association (2017), Fire and rescue services in England: A guide for police and crime panel members.

Mizutori, M. and Guhar-Sapir, D. (2021), *Human cost of disasters: An overview of the last 29 years 2000–2019.* New York Centre for Research on the Epidemiology of Disasters (CRED)/United Nations Office for Disaster Risk Reduction.

Murphy, P. (2014), "Flood response hit by regional austerity cuts", *The Conversation.*

Murphy, P., Lakoma, K., Greenhalgh, K. and Taylor, L. (2019), "A comparative appraisal of recent and proposed changes to the fire and rescue services in England and Scotland", In: P. Wankhade, L. McCann and P. Murphy, eds., *Critical perspectives on the management and organization of emergency services.* Routledge critical studies in public management. Abingdon: Routledge.

O'Connor, D. (2005), *Closing the gap: A review of the 'fitness for purpose' of the current structure of policing in England & Wales.* Her Majesty's Inspectorate of Constabulary.

OECD (2005), "Increasing financial incentives to work: The role of in-work benefits", available at: https://www.oecd.org/els/emp/36780865.pdf

Ogden, K. and Phillips, D. (2020), *The financial risk and resilience of English local authorities in the coronavirus crises.* London: Institute of Fiscal Studies.

PART D
Cross-cutting themes

12

RESOURCE TRENDS AND RESOURCE PLANNING IN REGIONAL PUBLIC SERVICES

Malcolm J. Prowle

Introduction

Part D of this book comprises three chapters which are not specific to any one public service but are seen as having over-arching relevance to many or all of the public services discussed in Part C. These three chapters discuss themes which are exceedingly important and would need to be taken on board by regional governments at a very early stage of their existence.

This chapter is focused on the resources needed to deliver public services, the future trends in the use of these resources and the need for effective resource planning, by regional governments, to ensure that the resources needed to deliver public services, within a region, are available when required. In using the term "resources" we are not just talking about money. Money is important but it is the resources needed to deliver public services acquired through money that are important. Examples of such "real" resources are human resources, buildings, equipment, etc.

Unfortunately, many examples have been seen, over a period of years, where certain types of resources (mainly human resources) were insufficient to meet the needs for certain public services and shortages occurred. Examples here concern shortages of nurses in the NHS, shortages of classroom teachers and shortages of social care workers. Quite often these shortages in human resources were filled by recruitment from overseas but such an approach may be seen as dubious on moral grounds, because it deprives the exporting country of key public servants. It is an approach also fraught with uncertainty – just consider the impact Brexit has had on the ability of UK public services to recruit and retain staff from Eastern Europe on whom they had become reliant. Something is wrong here and regional governments need better and more effective approaches to resource planning than has been seen in the past.

DOI: 10.4324/9781003201892-16

This book is about regional government in the UK, and hence it is important to discuss the issues of resources and resource planning for public services in the context of regional government. The chapter covers the following issues:

- Types of resources required to deliver public services
- Trends in public service resources
- Key aspects of resource planning
- Resource planning in relation to regional public services
- Potential for collaboration
- Conclusions

Types of resources required to deliver public services

Clearly public service organisations utilise a myriad of different types of resources in order to deliver services to clients. However, in order to discuss this matter more fully we need to classify those resources into a finite number of groups of which the main ones are:

- Human resources
- Buildings (and other fixed assets)
- Equipment, vehicles, etc.
- Digital resources
- External services
- Consumables

It will be noted that the one thing not included in the above list is that of finance or money. Now there are clearly some public services where money is of direct importance to the delivery of public services such as things like benefits payments and grants to businesses. However, it is more usually the case that money is used to acquire what might be termed "real" resources like human resources and equipment which are used directly to deliver public services.

Human resources

Human resources are a key element in the delivery of most public services. In 2018/2019, the costs of human resources amounted to some 30% of total public spending (HM Treasury 2020), although the proportion of expenditure taken up by human resource costs will vary enormously between different public services.

Some public services will have already adopted high degrees of automation and the use of technology while others still rely very heavily on the use of human resources, although the picture varies from service to service and between different parts of the country.

Public services utilise a wide range of different human resources spanning a spectrum from unskilled or semi-skilled employees to highly skilled professionals such as doctors, managers, teachers and engineers. However, whatever the skill level all of these employees they have a vital role to play in public service delivery.

Buildings (and other fixed assets)

Public services utilise a wide range of fixed assets which might encompass, buildings, roads, bridges, etc. Examples of buildings would include hospitals, schools, fire and rescue stations, offices, etc. Fixed assets involve an initial construction cost and then on-going costs each year concerning maintenance, cleaning and security. Basically, as the name suggests, these fixed assets are fixed and cannot easily be moved from one location to another so once a decision is made as to where they should be located, this cannot easily be changed. Hence, the planning of new fixed assets for public services is one that has to be addressed with great care for once the fixed asset is constructed, there may be little that can be done to remedy any errors made in size, location, design, etc.

However, it should also be noted that not all fixed assets used for public service delivery necessarily require the public service organisation to acquire ownership of the fixed asset. The key is to have use of the fixed asset and in undertaking resource planning the options of renting, leasing or some form of public-private partnership may also be available.

Equipment

Public service organisations use a wide range of different equipment some of which is relatively mundane in character but others are very complex and extraordinarily expensive to purchase and operate. Moreover, on-going technological developments mean that a piece of equipment can often become outmoded very quickly and needs to be replaced even though it may still have a useful working life. Some examples of public services equipment include the following examples:

- Specialist medical equipment for diagnosis and treatment of medical conditions
- Learning technologies for use in schools and colleges
- Vehicles for use by emergency services
- Scientific equipment
- Equipment associated with heating of buildings.

Digital resources

This is a wide ranging and imprecise term which concerns the convergence of digital technologies with public services, service users and society to enhance the efficiency and effectiveness of public service delivery. It uses information and communication technologies to facilitate better understanding of the problems and challenges faced by people requiring services and to deliver those services. Digital technologies include both hardware and software solutions and services, including online communications, wearable devices, augmented reality and virtual reality. Generally, digital technologies aim to improve the use of computational technologies, smart devices, computational analysis techniques and communication media to aid service professionals and their clients in resolving problems and issues.

External services

Although public service organisations directly employ many different kinds of people, there are some situations where it is not practical or efficient to employ someone to conduct specific tasks. In these situations, they will frequently buy-in services from an external organisation which may be another public body or, more likely, a private sector company. Examples of such services might be the repair and maintenance of specialist equipment, the acquisition of legal advice, the use of external consultants, etc.

Consumables

Public services utilise an extremely wide range of consumable items in the delivery of many public services. Just a few examples would be:

- Drugs and other items in hospitals
- Learning materials in schools and universities
- Catering consumables in many public service organisations
- Fuel costs for heating, lighting, transportation
- Clothing including uniforms and protective equipment
- Road salt for local authority maintained roads in winter

Trends in public services resource use

In any walk of life, planning, at strategic or operational levels, always has some focus on looking ahead to the future whether that be short term or longer term. This applies, very much, to resource planning for public services.

Planning often involves extrapolating existing trends into the future and much public service planning tends to focus on this. On its own, such an approach can be dangerous. What has gone on in the past may not be a good predictor of what will happen in the future. This is especially the case in relation to regional government. While some resource trends may be broadly similar in all parts of the UK, for other trends there may be significant variations between regions for a number of reasons such as different service needs, different service models and availability of specialist resources locally.

Predicting what will happen in the future is difficult and the degree of difficulty gets worse the further ahead one is predicting. The future is always uncertain and there are many things which are unknown and uncertain. These unknowns and uncertainties are often set out as discussed below.

Risk and uncertainty have often been classified according to what is sometimes termed knowns and unknowns. The well-known statement by former US defence secretary, Donald Rumsfeld, brought much fame and public attention to the concepts of known knowns, known unknowns and unknown unknowns, but this approach has long used an analysis technique referred to as the Johari window (Luft and Ingham 1955). These are described as follows:

- **Known knowns** – these are things we definitely know about (or should know about) with a fair degree of certainty. An example might be likely increases in employee pay rates for the year ahead.
- **Known unknowns** – these are things that although we know of them or have awareness of their existence we have no details about them or the likelihood of occurrence. An example here might be the impacts of climate change which are certain to happen but about which we have only a limited idea of the magnitude.
- **Unknown unknowns** – these are things we don't even know that we don't know about. In other words, we have no idea about their existence or the probability of occurrence. Some might argue that Covid-19 was an example of something which fell into this category as it just could not be predicted. However, others will argue that this is not true and that warnings about the inevitability of a global pandemic were there for everyone to see for many years prior to the pandemic.

In undertaking resource planning in public services, consideration needs to be given to all of the above.

If we consider the different types of resources in public services there are a number of factors we can discern which would need to be borne in mind when undertaking resource planning. These factors may affect both the supply and/or demand for those resources. A few examples are discussed below.

Human resources

Human resources are, and have always been, a key resource for many, if not most, public services and they constitute a large proportion of public services expenditure. We can also be certain that for the foreseeable future, human resources will still constitute a major resource for public services but both the magnitude and mix of the human resources required will inevitable change over time.

For example, history has shown that technological change means that certain jobs will inevitably become redundant or will change. Local authorities no longer employ people to go around lighting gas powered street lamps as the

TABLE 12.1 Factors influencing the regional planning of human resources

Factors affecting the need/demand for public service staff in a region	*Factors affecting the availability of public service staff in a region*
• New services coming online • Profiles of staff retirement • Levels of automation • Changes in job requirements • Changing regulations	• Output of regional training establishments • Competing employers in the region • Immigration constraints • Pay rates • Workload pressures

gas lamp technology is redundant. The role of nurses in our hospitals has also changed enormously in recent decades and such changes will probably continue.

It is inevitable that the public services will be faced with opportunities to introduce new technologies into various aspects of their activities and that such technologies may have implications for their future human resource requirements. Examples here concern new medical technologies in hospitals, new learning technologies in education, new communications technologies in many public services, etc.

Planning for human resources in public services involves looking at factors that might influence both the need or demand for public service staff and the factors that will affect the availability of specific groups of public service staff. Some aspects of this are shown in Table 12.1.

Buildings

Public service organisations utilise a wide range of buildings, examples of which include:

- **Health** – hospitals, GP surgeries
- **Education** – schools, colleges, universities
- **Emergency services** – police, fire and ambulance stations
- **Social care** – day centres, residential homes

In addition, public service organisations will make varied use of office accommodation.

If we look ahead, buildings will continue to be important for public services but consideration should be given to possible trends which will impact on future buildings requirements of public services. These include:

- Shifts in some patient care provision from hospital based to clinics and patient's homes, coupled to digital health methods, might have implications for future hospital designs.

- The Covid pandemic accelerated a trend that was already taking place, that being home-based working. This has implications for staff accommodation requirements.
- The need for social distancing, following the pandemic, might herald a need for bigger buildings where large groups of people can meet safely. Examples here might be schools, libraries and leisure centres.
- The need for buildings with greater energy efficiency consequent on climate change.
- Changes to family structures, and other factors, will impact the future needs for social housing.

Digital resources

There can be no doubt that digital resources will play an increasing role in the delivery of many public services in the years ahead. This is especially the case in the English NHS where, in spite of a poor historic track record of managing IT projects, there are very ambitious targets for increasing the scope and depth of the use of digital resources for the delivery of health and social care.

Many technologies are already available and it almost seems that new technologies of relevance to public services are being launched on a daily basis. It does seem that there is considerable scope for applying these new technologies in areas such as health, social care, education and emergency services but the key issue is the rate of technological take-up among public service organisations. Digital transformation has become a something of a rallying cry for public bodies. Yet all too often, organisations limit themselves to what they know, and don't truly explore new technologies or entirely different business models. Developing a systematic approach for identifying and harnessing opportunities from technology is an essential first step in making digital transformation concrete and achievable.

However, there are a number of barriers to the take-up of digital resources in public services which include:

- Lack of knowledge about the potential of digital approaches
- Lack of skills to utilise digital adequately
- Lack of confidence about "new" approaches to service provision
- Lack of financial resources to implement digital
- Organisational resistance to the proposed changes.

Consequently, because of these, and other, barriers, it appears that the take-up of digital developments might not be as great as expected. Thus, in terms of resource planning it will be necessary to make some realistic judgements or estimates about the potential take-up of digital approaches in the region and the likely implications involved.

Consumables

As already noted, public services utilise a wide range of consumable items often in high volumes. Although there may sometimes be shortages of some items due to transportation problems, border difficulties, etc., the general assumption would be that these items can be purchased from suppliers in the open market.

However, procurement arrangements, supply chains, storage requirements, etc. need to be established and in order to do this, forecasts need to be made, for several years ahead, about possible changes in the range and volumes of various consumable items that are needed. As well as extrapolating from the past, consideration will also need to be given to potential changes in requirements for certain consumables based on changes in the operating environment.

Regional resource planning approaches

Regional governments in the UK would constitute major providers of a range of public services and thus will require a range of different resources in order to deliver those services. However, as noted in Chapter 6 when discussing regional economic development, regional governments will also have a key role in ensuring that the resources needed by the regional economy and private businesses in the region will also be met if the objectives of regional economic development plans are to be achieved. Thus, regions will need to ensure that these resources are available to deliver the public services and to meet the needs of the private sector economy. Thus, regions must develop and apply robust planning methods to ensure these resources are available.

These planning roles and tasks must be undertaken initially at a regional level. There are too many examples of failures of national UK resource planning for regions to leave this important task to the federal government. Regional needs for resources will often vary considerably and planning needs to recognise this reality. This does not preclude the possibility of several regions collaborating together and/or collaborating with federal government but this must be done on the basis of equality and not top-down control of the planning tasks.

In this section we look at just two of the most important planning processes that are needed by regions:

- Regional human resource planning
- Regional land use planning

Regional human resource planning

As already noted, in a regional government this task will have to cover the HR needs of both public service organisations and the private sector economy. In saying this, it must be recognised that while some classes of employee are largely

TABLE 12.2 Human resource utilisation

Largely public	*Largely private*	*Both*
• Doctor • Nurses • Teachers • Police officers	• Personal care workers • Retail assistants	• Engineers • Builders • Scientists

private sector, others will be largely public sector and others will be both. This is illustrated in Table 12.2.

The planning approach should be as follows

- Develop a framework for analysing regional manpower requirements
- Estimate/forecast likely requirements for each type of staff for several years ahead
- Identify likely numbers of new staff who will become available from regional education institutions
- Identify gaps in likely manpower requirements
- Identify and implement gap reduction strategies

The gap reduction strategies could involve additional training and educational programmes in the region, recruitment from other parts of the UK or overseas, offering incentives for people to stay in the region, etc.

Regional land-use planning

In every country the volume of land is finite but in a heavily populated country like the UK the availability of land will be more restricted than in a large country like Russia, China or the USA.

Land-use planning basically involves the regulation of the use of available land by a central authority, in this case the regional government. Usually, this is done in an effort to promote more desirable social and environmental outcomes as well as a more efficient use of land resources. The goals of modern land-use planning may also include matters such as environmental conservation, restraint of urban sprawl, minimisation of transport costs and a reduction in exposure to pollutants.

Land-use planning seeks to order and regulate land use in an efficient, ethical and equitable manner. Governments use land-use planning to manage the development of land within their jurisdictions, taking account of the competing uses for land in relation to housing, public services, business, leisure, etc. Also, in doing this, the government can plan for the needs of the community while safeguarding natural resources. To this end, it is the systematic assessment of land potential, alternatives for land use, and economic and social conditions in order to select and adopt the best land use options. Often one element of a comprehensive plan, a land-use plan provides a vision for the future possibilities of development in neighbourhoods, districts, cities or any defined planning area.

Land-use planning must be a responsibility of regions and not national government and is a key task for regional governments. As such it will link to other regional policies on economic development, housing and public services. When we look at the UK, closely, we will realise that the nature, need and scarcity of land will vary hugely between different regions and within regions, and between urban and rural environments. Thus, it is inevitable that land-use planning will be very different in some UK regions than others. To this end, regional governments must be free to develop and apply their own planning laws and regulations and to develop appropriate planning procedures. This is more appropriate than a "one size fits all" national approach.

Potential for collaboration

As we have described in this book, a system of regional government in the UK would involve the establishment of a series of regional governments which are substantial in size and comparable to many independent nation states in the world. Just in Europe alone, the North West Region of the UK would be larger in population than Denmark, Finland or Norway.

Given the size of these UK regions, they are quite capable of, independently, developing effective and efficient ways of planning and procuring the public resources they require. Moreover, some regions may wish to focus on regionally focused procurements in order to contribute to regional economic development.

However, there is always a temptation in these situations to believe that such arrangements could be made better if they were based on bigger and bigger units and that national UK approaches to resource planning and procurement would be better. This assumption is based on the "economies of scale" argument that the bigger the unit the better the outcome. Unfortunately, this is often not the case as such approaches often get bogged down in bureaucracy, delay, inappropriateness, etc. The history of the procurement of the National Program for IT (Taghreed 2017) which ended in failure at huge cost to the public purse is a prime example of this.

Nevertheless, there may be situations where a regional government may see benefit in planning and procuring public service resources in collaboration with other regions. This could involve collaboration between two or more geographically neighbouring and compatible regions. A few possible examples are mentioned below.

- **Procurement of consumables** – there are many types of consumables which are widely where the region is of such a size that it would have the purchasing power to extract good deals from suppliers. This is all about having an effective procurement function focused on getting VFM for public funds. However, there may be other types of consumables where the level of usage is low and where it may be worth two or more regions collaborating on a joint procurement exercise to get more advantageous prices.

- **Digital service development** – some digital service initiatives may involve the development of bespoke applications which may be highly complex and expensive to undertake by one regional government. Hence, there may be merit in collaborating with another region to undertake such a development and share the costs and the risks. However, it is probably best if the collaborating regions are proximate to one another and have broadly similar profiles and outlooks. This would minimise the chances of conflict over the design and avoid the possibility of compromise which resulted in a development which satisfied nobody.
- **Highly specialised human resources** – there may be examples, possibility in the medical, scientific or technological fields, where regions have a need for some very specialised human resource but only in small quantities. In these circumstances, there may be merit in collaborating with another region to share the use of such scarce resources.

Caution should be expressed about potential national UK collaborations for the simple reason that procuring public service resources for a country as large and diverse as the UK may lead to a situation where the national arrangement fails to meet the requirements of individual regions. There is also a danger of such large organisations fall into the trap of becoming a bureaucracy and losing sight of their purpose of getting the right resources, at the right time and at the right price for regional public services.

Conclusions

This book is about the importance of developing a system of elected regional government across the UK with regional governments having total responsibility for the planning and provision of most public services for their citizens, including ensuring the availability of key resources. Furthermore, as has been discussed in Chapter 6, we see regional governments as having major responsibilities for economic development in their region and this will require them to ensure that regional economies can get hold of the resources they need to achieve regional economic objectives.

The federal government would have the role of resource planning for those public services for which they are responsible, the armed forces being the most obvious example. Similarly, there may be circumstances where resource planning for certain specialist resources might be best undertaken at a national UK level on behalf of the regions. This would be the exception rather than the rule.

However, it is absolutely vital that regional governments in the UK, from the outset, establish robust and comprehensive approaches of resource planning for their region. This is not something that can be left to national government because, under these arrangements it is regional governments which are responsible to their electorate (and others) for the delivery of public services and for creating successful regional economies. It is absurd to suggest that UK regions are incapable of undertaking the resource planning required to support the regional economy and regional public services when many countries much smaller than UK regions undertake these tasks perfectly adequately. Moreover, a regional focus in resource planning is more likely, than a national approach, to ensure that regional needs are met. In the light of the above, it is clear that effective resource planning is a key role for regional governments and one which needs to be developed extremely quickly. Suitable approaches to HR, land use and other aspects need to be adopted and suitably resourced. Also, where deemed appropriate, collaborative approaches with other regions also need consideration early on.

References

HM Treasury (2020), Whole of government accounts: Year ended, 31 March 2019, https://www.gov.uk/government/publications/whole-of-government-accounts-2018-2019

Luft, J. and Ingham, H. (1955), The Johari window, a graphic model of interpersonal awareness. *Proceedings of the Western Training Laboratory in Group Development*. Los Angeles: University of California, Los Angeles.

Taghreed, J. (2017), The UK's National Programme for IT: Why was it dismantled? *Health Services Management Research*, 30(1), 2–9.

13

COORDINATION, COLLABORATION AND INTEGRATION IN PUBLIC SERVICES

Tony Garthwaite and Terry Mackie

Introduction

Getting public service agencies to consistently work effectively together for the public good has eluded public policy makers for decades. Despite numerous efforts by government to create more meaningful collaborative working, some enshrined in statute, frustration in the inability to join up policy formulation and the delivery of services persists.

The principles of collaborative working apply to both private and public sectors and at national, regional and local levels. It is, therefore, one of the key components of effective service delivery. In this chapter we examine why, despite a plethora of collaborative initiatives, endemic, sustained collaboration remains elusive and a continuing target of government policy. We argue that it is necessary to gain a better understanding of the theories underpinning collaborative working to demonstrate their relevance to achieving the fundamental changes needed in approaches to public policy and practice that are proposed in this book. Only with this enhanced understanding of the intricacies of working together will we be able to implement best practice and achieve a different default position for public sector agencies and their partners in a devolved governmental context. By deliberately referring to literature that is not new, we emphasise the longevity of collaboration theory which raises further questions about why it is still not routine practice. Finally, we examine how collaborative working is being applied in the specific cases of health and social care and in education.

Definitions of terms

It is important to start with an exploration of the terminology. Widely used terms in this arena of study are collaboration, co-operation, coordination, joint

DOI: 10.4324/9781003201892-17

working, partnership working, multi-agency working and multi-disciplinary working. In particular service areas, descriptors such as integration, partnerships and consortia are commonly found. The fact that these terms are often used interchangeably can be confusing and ignore the differences and nuances between them (Vangen, Hayes and Cornforth, 2015). Regrettably, these differences can also lead to somewhat esoteric debates about meaning at the expense of action. In some cases, they have erroneously been interpreted as being part of a continuum where one is implied to be more ambitious than another. Although it is acknowledged that dictionary definitions may apply accurately on occasions, mature conversations amongst policy makers and implementers should obviate any temptation to hide behind any confusion about definitions in order to avoid getting on with the job in hand of ensuring citizens receive services that are products of agencies with common goals and purpose.

For the sake of clarity, we are satisfied that the concept of "collaborative advantage" (Huxham, 1993, 1996) is a more than adequate basis on which to understand what we are discussing in this chapter. This is defined as occurring when "something unusually creative is produced – perhaps an objective is met – that no organisation could have produced on its own and when each organisation, through the collaboration, is able to achieve its own objectives better than it could alone" (Huxham, 1993). Importantly in the context of discussions about public services, Huxham argues that "in some cases, it should also be possible to achieve some higher-level objectives for society as a whole rather than just for the participating organisations" (Huxham, 1993). Some might suggest that this sets the bar too high, particularly in terms of expectations of private sector organisations working together, but we would argue that this level of ambition ought to be the norm, certainly in a public policy context.

However, we also acknowledge the need to be aware, when discussing collaboration, that individuals may have different points of reference and different understandings. For example, collaboration may be considered as a process, i.e. a way of working with others (Sullivan and Skelcher, 2002), or simply a joint activity (Bardach, 1998) or even the creation of a new type of organisation (Finn, 1996). These differences can affect the enthusiasm for collaboration, particularly when an ambition of two agencies to simply work informally together develops into the possibility of formal organisational merger as a means of achieving the overall objective, thereby increasing the anxiety of staff about jobs and careers. Perversely, such threats can also lead to tokenistic collaborative efforts in order to preserve autonomy, thereby missing opportunities for more ambitious initiatives. For example, the 22 local authorities in Wales have been accused by some of being willing to engage in a plethora of different partnerships as much to avoid further formal local government reorganisation as embracing the need to collaborate. Collaboration is not synonymous with any particular outcome of collaborative form and, for example, should only lead to organisational merger if that is the appropriate objective for the participants involved.

Rationale and objectives of collaboration

Let's begin with understanding the rationale for agencies to collaborate. Most explanations in the literature are predisposed to positivity about collaborative working despite there not always being hard evidence to justify the collaboration in outcome terms. This positivity is perhaps not surprising given that alliances were responsible for winning two world wars! An early contribution to understanding collaboration was made by Levine and White's (1962) exchange theory which is founded in organisational behaviour, the argument being that organisations will volunteer to exchange relations on more than an ad hoc basis where they identify it leading to system-wide goals. A more pessimistic view is that collaboration is based on self-interest, taking place in order to preserve or enhance power or make individual organisational gains. This resonates with some of the fears local authorities may have about the motivation behind their social services functions being absorbed formally into a much more powerful NHS.

In simple terms, the various rationales for collaborating can be summarised alongside the following theories shown in Table 13.1:

All of these theories are often in play in public services and knowing, and mutually accepting, which of these is in play during a collaborative initiative is bound to impact on its success, not least because of their relevance to the development of mutual trust (more of which later). The rationale for collaborating is likely to be driven by at least one of these theories and more than one in some instances. For example, the central government may be mandating specific forms of collaboration to promote a particular public policy but in doing so it may be inviting local agencies to see the benefits inherent in a number of the other rationales. Some collaborations may be motivated by the pursuit of economic, cost-saving benefits whilst others centre on improvements in outcomes for citizens and customers. At first sight, some will appear to be more relevant to

TABLE 13.1 Theories of collaboration

Theory	*Core meaning*
Exchange theory	*If we give each other something we will both be stronger*
Resource dependency theory	*We both have something that the other needs*
Rational choice theory	*It's obvious that working together will make us better off*
Self-interest theory	*I can't survive without you!*
Rational-altruistic theory	*We need to work together for the greater good of our customers or the public*
Hierarchical/mandated theory	*The Government or Board told us we had to*

private sector collaborations but this is a false dichotomy as both private and public sector organisations have multiple ambitions and goals.

Brexit and the Covid-19 pandemic have provided students of collaboration with some rich research material. In the case of Brexit, leaving aside the hard-line views of those at each end of the remain/leave spectrum, most people, including the Prime Minister apparently, accepted the need for a positive ongoing relationship with our European partners after the UK left the EU. It was the increasing federalism of a new European state that worried many leavers prior to the referendum and for Remainers, it was the notion that sovereignty could lead to isolation, with false dreams of a return to our imperial past, that largely exercised their minds. We see in practice here not only those theories outlined above but concerns about the form a collaboration might take, the confidence in leadership to produce a meaningful outcome and the degree of mutual trust that is needed amongst those negotiating the deal. All of these are major factors in enabling successful collaborations.

Similarly, in the case of the Covid-19 pandemic, we learned new expressions like "vaccine nationalism" as countries sought to protect the interests of their own citizens whilst simultaneously acknowledging that the pandemic could not end until and unless the whole world was protected. We also saw the four UK nations apply their discretionary powers to determine strategies for controlling the spread of the virus. The relationship between the NHS and social care was tested to the extreme as people infected with Covid-19 were discharged from hospitals into care homes without appropriate consultation and preparation. The tiered system of determining lockdowns led to arguments between local and national political leaders about issues of equity, financial support and who was best placed to assess risk. Debates about the role and organisation of social care and public health returned to the top table.

In recent years we have seen collaboration played out on the global stage. President Trump's isolationist policies saw him withdraw the USA from the Paris climate agreement and the Iran nuclear deal. He also threatened the very existence of NATO when he claimed America was unfairly subsidising other countries. Here, he was not only applying his view of economic and fiscal logic but also invoking resource dependency theory, knowing that there was an imbalance of dependency between Europe and America in terms of military might. The alternative case for global collaboration was put strongly by Vice President (then Senator) Kamala Harris who stated; "There are real limits to what we can do alone and we must work in partnership with our allies" and "Only together can we reverse the trends of climate change and prevent some of its more terrifying outcomes" (Harris, 2019).

Motivation for collaboration

The theories also provide an indication of the source of motivation for collaboration and whether this is bottom-up or top-down, both being important criteria in the context of public policy if one accepts the proposition that public policy can be created at national, regional and local levels. It is understandable that some may argue that it is inconsistent for a book that argues for greater devolution of power to nations and regions should simultaneously espouse the merits of greater collaboration amongst those involved. This, however, belies a stronger argument that service delivery will benefit from smaller units of government seeing and embracing the necessity of working collaboratively much more than any prescribed mandate to do so by a centralised government. We are not talking here about "ever closer union" between agencies but a mutually beneficial means of gaining improvements and benefits for people. Of course, there are always likely to be politically motivated rationales for collaboration, such as it providing an alternative to competition as the foundation for public services. This was exemplified by the proclamation by the then First Minister in Wales, Rhodri Morgan, that he wanted to create "clear red water" between Wales and England (Davies and Williams, 2009) in terms of the use of market forces as an approach to public service reform.

In acknowledging the political motivation evident in this example, we need to remember that there are always likely to be competitive elements in any collaboration, such as the battle for limited resources between a local authority and an NHS organisation, and the fact that public sector agencies cannot manage in a way that is exclusively detached from the market. For example, outsourcing to private and not-for-profit agencies has become the norm for many public services and has worked most effectively when commissioners and providers have worked in partnership instead of relying solely on a contractual relationship. It could also be argued that consumers of public services are not able to exercise the option of exiting a service delivered by a single provider in the same way as they can, say, with utilities or insurance although it should be noted that the risks to the public are much greater when the businesses of inefficient or unviable service providers, appointed via competitive tendering processes, collapse. It is more appropriate, therefore, to see competition, and for that matter conflict, as being an integral part of collaborations that need to be managed well, rather than as alternative policy choices. Politicising collaboration is often unhelpful, whether it be motivated by right-wing thinking when the Thatcher government created the commissioner/provider split in the NHS, or left leaning arguments in the case of the Welsh Government's response cited above. Collaboration in this context should be viewed as a means of achieving better outcomes for people, not a political end.

Delivering good public services, especially those that require attention to the specific needs of individuals, is complex and it is right that government should expect agencies to co-ordinate their approaches so that delivery is as seamless as possible. The notion that these services can be delivered without crossing organisational boundaries does not stand up to scrutiny. Collaboration is also likely to occur as a logical and necessary response to turbulent conditions (Gray, 1996, Bryson, Crosby and Stone, 2006) where predictability and regularity are at a premium. There is no greater example of such turbulence than the Covid-19 pandemic and it is unsurprising that ministers should have reacted by promoting greater integration of health and social care in England in their most recent White Paper.

Forms of collaboration

Collaborations can take many forms ranging from very informal networks and ad hoc meetings through to organisational mergers. A commissioner/provider contract can be regarded as much of a collaboration if used constructively as a formal partnership. Some argue that collaboration is inherently spatial (Gerber and Loh, 2014) whilst others believe collaborations can be virtual without any geographical constraint. The emergence of the digital age has exemplified this.

Collaborations display the practical implementation of elements of organisational, institutional, network and agency theories and are frequently inextricably considered as instruments of governance. Networked systems used by local government, for example, historically adopt a form of shared governance (Abels, 2012) where actors are able to develop interdependent relationships. Governance has also been viewed as a concept to achieve the increased networking required by joined-up government following the decline of the New Public Management movement in the 1980s (Acevedo and Common, 2006) and a shift from the 1990s in political management from government to governance (Rhodes, 1996, Derzken, Franklin and Bock, 2008). It is important to recognise collaborative governance as a concept in making the definition of collaborative advantage provided earlier a practical reality. A range of collaborative governance models are available, e.g. self-governing, lead organisation or joint committees, that can influence collaborative effectiveness. These models are sometimes inappropriately used to describe the collaboration itself.

A wide range of factors impact on the chances of collaborations succeeding. These change as they move through a life cycle of different phases from pre-partnership collaboration, through consolidation and delivery, and possible termination (Lowndes and Skelcher, 1998). Collaborative working can occur vertically and horizontally in an intra-, inter- and cross-sector context reflecting both hierarchical and market forces as means of implementing public policy. Therefore, collaboration can take place at the operational, management and strategic/governance levels at different times and in different ways and each can play an effective role in achieving shared goals.

The debate between the respective merits of hierarchical, mandated and voluntary collaboration persists. The early history in community care integration is considered by some to have not been one of prescribing organisational structural change through integration but encouraging collaboration across boundaries (Johnson et al., 2003). Some scholars have recognised that informal agreements about the collaboration's composition, mission and process can work, but more formal agreements have the advantage of supporting accountability (Bryson, Crosby and Middleton Stone, 2006). Others have suggested that removing central direction as to the form of collaborations could result in local impetus being orientated towards the development of more flexible, fluid and open collaborative structures (Lindsey, 2014).

These are critically important issues to understand in the context of more devolved public policy. Voluntary collaborations are less likely to emerge if agencies feel threatened by the prospect of lost autonomy through organisational change such as a merger, but the alternative represented by a totally hierarchical, mandated approach, whereby government prescribes the routes to be followed, seems equally unattractive because it belies the complexity inherent in the subject matter. Within collaborative activity there are strong socially interactive forces at play, such as power and trust, illustrating a dependence on certain behaviours to fulfil the collaborative objectives.

Characteristics of collaborations

It is helpful to think of successful collaborations as being dependent on getting two sides of an equation right. On one side are all those structural issues that need attention such as establishing the rationale for collaborating, the form of collaboration preferred, the governance model, and the legal and financial arrangements. Some of these are underpinned by the theories we have explored in this chapter. On the other are the people factors, such as the skills of participants, the leadership, the politics and, perhaps most importantly, the ability to engender trust and manage power. Each of these sides needs to be applied in the context of being clear about definitions, rationales and policy contexts. These are referred to here as foundation themes. See Figure 13.1.

These characteristics of collaborations are invaluable in adding to knowledge and furthering our understanding of collaborations and collaborative behaviour but do not readily lead to a straightforward typology of collaborations. For example, we know that mutually beneficial motives can disguise residual elements of conflict and competition. Similarly, the pursuit of a neat organisational design for the collaborative form has to take account of numerous informal networking aspects, some of which are not immediately evident. Because the issue of governance can become inextricably linked with the collaborative initiative, it is often difficult to precisely identify the shared objective of a strategy.

Fundamentally, collaborations are dependent on the contribution of people networking and operating as reticulists, boundary spanners, leaders and stakeholders who need to display a wide range of skills and competencies. One of the outcomes of social networks is increased opportunity to collaborate (Gazley, 2010) and networks can be regarded as form of collaboration and offer public value benefits to managers and agencies such as learning opportunities, access to information and technology, and delivering concrete results (Agranoff, 2006). Effective networks often have a lead agency, acting as a system controller or facilitator, which helps to reduce the complexity of self-governance and enhance the legitimacy of the network (McGuire, 2006).

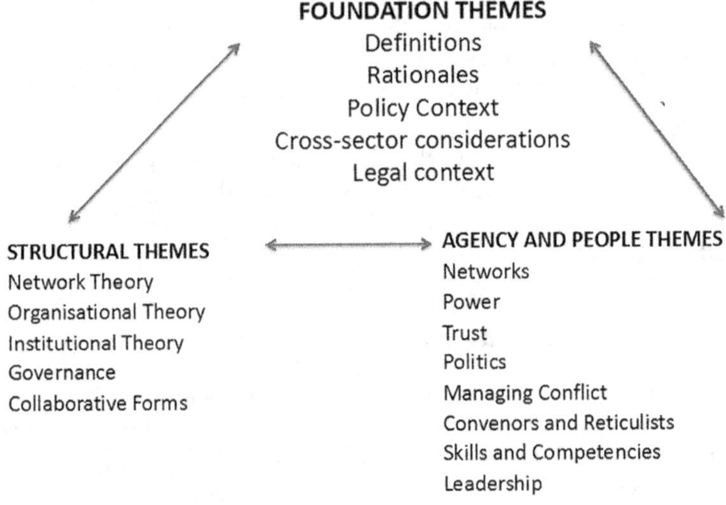

FIGURE 13.1 Understanding collaboration

A useful typology for understanding where networks fit with collaborations emerged from research into 14 networks involving federal, state and local government managers working with non-governmental organisations in the USA (Agranoff, 2006). This suggested four types of networks ranging from simple "informational" networks wherein partners came together almost exclusively to exchange policies, programmes, technologies and potential solutions, to "action" networks wherein partnerships led to interagency adjustments, formally adopting collaborative courses of action, and delivering services. This research also detected as many as six distinct pre-decision strategies and the predominant outcome related rather modestly to learning. The relatively minor reference to concrete outcome-based action chimes with government's frustration that local partnerships are too often concerned with process, and rely too heavily on some form of brokered consensus, rather than a dynamic action-centred drive for change. This again raises further questions about the need for mandated collaboration to accelerate the pace and scale of local efforts.

If, as we suggest, people factors are critically important in making collaborations work effectively, it follows that those people will need a range of high-level relevant skills and competencies, particularly leadership skills. The skills needed by modern public service managers relate to building sustainable relationships, influencing and negotiating, and managing complex issues involving many interdependencies. They need to be able to innovate, communicate, resolve conflicts, empower people and build trust. These represent a challenging personal skills portfolio and the absence of leaders and managers to display them consistently is arguable one of the main contributors to what Huxham (1996) describes as "collaborative inertia".

Conditions for effective collaboration

Research evidence (Prowle 2006) and practical experience suggest that for collaboration, in public services, to be effective, there are three "mutuality" conditions that need to be fulfilled:

- **Mutual understanding** – many of the individuals and groups asked to collaborate in the delivery of public services often come from different experiences, different training and different perspectives. Very often they do not understand the roles and objectives of those they are being asked to collaborate with.
- **Mutual gain** – different groups and agencies will often have different service objectives. For collaboration to be effective there must be some degree of shared objectives resulting in a mutual gain for all parties.
- **Mutual trust** – this is discussed in more detail below but basically mutual trust between the parties is an essential need to foster collaboration.

This is not to say that no collaboration will be achieved in the absence of these conditions but that its effectiveness will be heavily constrained.

The role of power in collaboration

Power is an interesting and (no pun intended) powerful concept in the context of collaboration. It has been argued that inter-organisational capacity is unlikely to flourish in organisational structures that are based on hierarchical control and power and that new capacities are needed to manage conflict, inter-personal behaviour and fragmented and contested power relations (Williams, 2002). Power imbalances and disparities amongst collaborating partners can be a source of mistrust and therefore a threat to effective collaboration. Power imbalances become most significant when partners fail to agree on a shared purpose and are affected by numerous events over time.

The shift in power relations as partnerships develop and change can result in managers no longer maintaining full control of services, losing their power as their organisations stretch out with boundaries becoming more fluid (Brandsen and van Hout, 2006). This can lead to an increasing need to operate through incentives and persuasion rather than hierarchy. Power is also relevant to explaining differences between exchange theory and resource dependency theory. Whereas both recognise the mutual dependency of resources, in the former, mutually beneficial collaboration is likely to result, where in the latter each party attempts to control or influence the other's activities, suggesting that power resides implicitly in the other's dependency.

Power is associated with authority and sovereignty and public sector agencies rightly point to their individual statutory responsibilities as the basis for their public accountability. It is important, therefore, not to lose sight of collaboration as being both a form and a function of joint working. It is both an outcome and a process which requires organisational flexibilities in the construction of joint agendas, joint resourcing and joint working. This means the surrender of some definitional power as well as resource control. We must recognise that autonomous, publicly accountable bodies will be naturally hesitant to share sovereignty and risk without inbuilt control mechanisms which protect them against failure. They will not wish to see fulfilling their statutory responsibilities compromised by third parties and will be concerned to know whether the scarce resources they are investing in developing partnerships will produce a return on that investment. This highlights the importance of collaborations being underpinned by a shared purpose and a shared vision. Agencies will also have different starting points in respect of the need for exchange and the degree of resource dependency so whilst these organisational factors are relevant to the public sector, they need to be supplemented by a greater need to collaborate relating to achieving public good, i.e. collaborations based on the rational/altruistic theory. This means accepting the notion of seeking a net gain for people from the collaborative effort over and above individual gains for each partner agency.

Paradoxically, partnerships can also be seen as an instrument to exercise power through incorporating others within close reach. Modes of power such as authority, inducement, coercion, seduction, manipulation, persuasion and negotiation are as important as domination and command, and can be viewed as positive forces of power in the collaborative context (Derzken, Franklin and Bock, 2008). So, if inducement and authority are perceived as "power over", or forms of control, then negotiation and persuasion can be seen as "power to" as a form of mutual gain. Both concepts can work in the absence of force as the basis of some sort of voluntary arrangement as can "power for" which involves the transfer of power to others (Huxham and Vangen, 2005), thereby, for example, giving another party the capacity to set priorities and control resources.

The presence of underlying forces related to power is often underestimated in collaborative ventures and terminology relating to sharing responsibilities, values and visions is sometimes used as a euphemism for what is more accurately a conscious attempt to share power or perhaps duplicitously to gain it. This suggests that the positive aspects of understanding different modes of power may be lost to more negative connotations connected with the traditional hierarchical concepts of control, such as takeover, found in organisational theory. This in turn leads to a conclusion that opportunities to overcome perceived barriers to working together, or even translate them into enablers, are being lost.

The vital importance of trust in collaboration

Closely linked to power as an enabler or barrier is trust. Scholars of collaboration theory have referred to the need to address the gap between the common wisdom that trust is necessary for collaboration to be successful and the common practice which suggests that trust is frequently weak or lacking altogether, and suspicion is rife (Huxham and Vangen, 2005). There does not appear to be general agreement about what a manager can do to build trust as an important component of public management. Encouraging trust clearly helps to reduce conflict in respect of those exchanges referred to earlier but excessive trust can militate against the positive effects of collaboration if it leads to complacency within the relationship to find the best solutions possible. Unconditional co-operation in this respect is not necessarily as attractive as it first appears.

In thinking about implementing public policy, one has to be conscious of whether partnerships are creating high trust relationships and reducing negative conflict. If they are not, sustainability in the longer term may be at greater risk. Community strategies in Wales in the early 2000s were developed as policy instruments because the government felt they would provide a voluntary framework for local co-operation, recognising the operational autonomy of partners, as this was the only way to develop trust (Sullivan and Williams, 2009). However, the relevance of applying hierarchical theory was highlighted in this example by some agencies questioning whether a voluntary arrangement was sufficient to secure the necessary commitment from their partners.

Trust is undoubtedly a complex concept requiring analysis beyond the scope of this book and has links with issues such as faith, goodwill, values, respect and compatibility as well as more rational calculated norms such as risks and benefits. Prior, embedded relationships are clearly relevant and trusting relationships can be ironically both the lubricant and the glue in collaborations, simultaneously facilitating their work and holding them together (Bryson, Crosby and Middleton Stone, 2006). There is a need to invest in trust to develop and sustain it in a collaboration. Trust must be real and not subject to hollow rhetoric, nor a veil to disguise manipulation. Once lost, trust is difficult to recover. Considering trust, therefore, as a one-dimensional positive aspect of collaborative relationships is a flawed approach. The benefits of trust as a positive force must be consciously harnessed by partners as they are always vulnerable to the powerful forces of mistrust. This suggests a need for trust to be better understood as an enabler of collaboration with renewed strategies to embed it as an antidote to negative conflict.

Summary of collaboration issues

To sum up, collaboration is a complex subject where it is possible to identify many theories and characteristics but not as easy to convert them into a neat comprehensive typology. However, these theories and characteristics can help identify the common features necessary to improve the chances of collaborative success in a brave new world of greater devolved government where the degree of mandated, hierarchical approach felt necessary to date would not be needed. New principles of governance would be needed whereby any lack of conformity in collaborations should be celebrated, and criticism of the diversity of approach to collaboration across the UK seen to date resisted. Instead, new bottom-up initiatives could herald a refreshed, healthier approach to effective public policy. There are already many local and regional collaborative ventures and partnerships on which to build a different future. By enabling local individual initiatives to determine what drives the reasons for collaborating and the form it should take, it could be argued that this will result in the collaborative experience being richer and more sustainable and relatively free from state control. To a large extent, this has been the approach taken to date in the devolved nations, within a framework of devolved government policy favouring collaboration.

Implicitly, this conclusion assumes that the merits of working collaboratively will be embraced by devolved regional governments and there is little or no evidence to suggest that this would not be the case. However, the principle of devolved government is to allow discretion in policy making and should the tide of popular opinion turn against collaborative working, a change of policy direction would be a matter for local accountability. In any case, it is worth noting that individual and organisation actions at a local level are always likely to be guided and constrained by the institutional logics of which they are a member. The notion of there being a "parent department" (Rigg and O'Mahoney, 2013) – in this case the new regional government – is therefore likely to remain in any governance structure. What will be important in this model is that the parents understand the need to work constructively with the children!

Examples of public service collaboration

Before drawing our thinking to a conclusion, we briefly examine some examples of how collaboration applies in different ways to some major public services. The examples concern:

- Health and social care
- Collaboration in education

Health and social care

Earlier chapters included reference to the development of health and care services and how they have culminated in renewed efforts, most recently in England, to embed integration as the preferred way of working.

An in-depth study of integration can now be accessed via research bodies like the King's Fund and the Social Care Institute for Excellence (SCIE) without recourse to textbooks. Accessing these organisations' websites for further learning is highly recommended. At the international level, the *International Journal of Integrated Care* is an online, open-access, peer-reviewed scientific journal that publishes original articles in the field of integrated care on a continuous basis. In this chapter we confine ourselves to a brief examination of some of the features of integration in the context of putting the theories of collaboration discussed earlier into practice and understanding their relevance to a system of devolved government.

The term "integration" has sometimes inappropriately been used interchangeably with "collaboration" whereas here it is discussed as a form of collaboration. Its progress has suffered from attempts to arrive at a universally accepted specific definition which has arguably led to too many debates about meaning and too little concentration on implementation. One interpretation that has gained popularity, and is sufficient for our purposes here, emerged from work commissioned by NHS England on behalf of the National Collaboration for Integrated Care and Support and co-developed with the health and system by National Voices, a grouping of 130 health and social care charities. It suggests that people should be able to plan their care with people who work together to understand them, their family and carer(s), giving them control, and bringing together services to achieve the outcomes important to them. In essence, integration can be easily understood as being the opposite of fragmentation in terms of how services are planned and delivered.

Integration can occur on a large number of fronts including strategic approaches, information, advice and support, public consultation and engagement mechanisms, career paths for the health and social care workforce, devising new models of health and social care, organisation accountability and governance, reporting arrangements and infrastructure, systems and resources. Discussions on integration often refer to the need to harmonise services or make them seamless. True integration involves not solely the joining up of statutory health and social care services but also harnessing the work of other public services such as housing, the third and independent sectors and ideally, through processes of co-production, fully involving users and recipients of service in the planning and delivery of their care and support. It should have no limits on the ages of those it applies to nor to those involved in working to achieve it. Integration does not, however, mean ignoring the distinct features and differences of health services and social care outlined in earlier chapters.

When integration occurs at an organisational level, this usually results in new formal partnership bodies being created. At the coal face, it can simply mean people from different agencies interacting to ensure the best outcome for an individual. It can, therefore, be effective at strategic and operational levels and at the macro-, meso- and micro-levels. Occasionally, attempts at integration have resulted in confusion of means and ends where actions taken to enhance integrated working become proxies for having achieved the goal of people experiencing care and support that is seamless (Llewellyn et al., 2018). So, means and methods such as co-located teams, pooled budgets and joint appointments – all useful initiatives in themselves – falsely assume the mantle of being integrated outcomes for people.

- A significant contribution to our understanding of integration was produced by the King's Fund in 2013 which outlined a 16-point plan for increasing the scale and pace of integrated care, whilst recognising that changes to national policy and to the regulatory and financial frameworks were needed for local leaders to fully realise a vision of integration. A toolkit prepared by the Social Services Improvement Agency in Wales in 2016 to support the production of population needs assessments drew on this work and other literature on integrated care to produce a checklist of some of the features one would expect to see in a fully integrated approach where:
- partners work together on a common cause and are prepared to share sovereignty;
- integration is commonly understood and leadership to deliver integrated solutions is shared;
- integrated care is built from the bottom up as well as top down;
- professionals are tolerant of each other's business pressures and the complexities of the challenges therein;
- resources are pooled, teams are co-located, and commissioning undertaken jointly;
- the workforce is used flexibly and effectively and is open to innovations in skills mix and staff substitution;
- information is shared widely and openly;
- there is shared governance and shared accountability;
- assessments of need and care pathways are developed jointly with the aim of maximising joint working for the benefit of the individual.

The need to acknowledge the structural and people factors referred to in the earlier discussion on collaboration is evident here too. The factors needed to achieve successful collaboration are essentially no different from those needed to achieve integration of health and care services. In this sense, integration can be regarded as a form of collaboration. What differs, however, is the context, the actors and the degree of interest in considering integrated care as a specific public policy goal. This has led central governments across the UK to promote integration in different ways.

In England, the most recent 2021 White Paper proposes Integrated Care System (ICS) being put on a statutory footing. In Wales, the Social Services and Well-being (Wales) Act 2014 requires local authorities to co-operate with their relevant partners. Northern Ireland has had a structurally integrated system of health and social care since 1973 and now organises integrated care via 17 collaborative networks of service providers, referred to as Integrated Care Partnerships. Scotland legislated in 2016 to bring together health and social care into a single integrated system through the creation of 31 integration authorities which are responsible for services previously managed separately by NHS Boards and local authorities. The Scottish Government has described this change as the most significant change to health and social care services in Scotland since the creation of the NHS in 1948. Integration is clearly, therefore, a central plank of health and social care policy throughout the UK that is likely to be around for the foreseeable future. In the case of the English White Paper, there is some interesting insight into central government thinking about some aspects of regionalism relevant to this book in that it is recommended that the "system" dimension of the new ICS proposals, in which the whole area's health and social care partners in different sectors come together to set strategic direction and develop economies of scale, be based on population sizes of 1–3 million.

Despite all these initiatives, health and social care services have not been perceived as being integrated during the Covid-19 pandemic. Social care was barely mentioned as a priority area for attention prior to the revelation of the number of people in care homes who had died from the disease, many of whom had allegedly been discharged prematurely from hospitals whilst still infected. Even then, media coverage concentrated on the work of the NHS, largely ignoring, for example, the contribution of relatively low paid domiciliary care workers to maintaining older people's safety and well-being in their own homes. The experience of the pandemic and the divergence of approaches across the UK lead to two conclusions: first, that the integration of health social care is still work in progress and second, that regional governments are (rightly) likely to adopt different methods of achieving integrated care to reflect regional differences.

Achieving the progress needed to make integration of health and social care an unambiguous reality will require the removal of all those barriers that hinder any collaborative effort – mistrust, imbalance of power and clinging onto self-autonomy being amongst the most difficult to overcome. It will require strong leadership at political and executive levels, renewed commitment from managers and frontline staff and an inversion of the pyramid that places patients, service users and unpaid carers at the bottom. There are undoubtedly major complexities in achieving true integration but tackling these is a fundamental responsibility of leaders and managers.

Collaboration in education

Collaboration is often seen as the Holy Grail, an ideal of ways of working in public services that borders on the meta-social, maybe the spiritual. "Working together" has been used in many social policies as an objective in its own right rather than a means to an end (i.e. better public services). However, in education circles it is often viewed pejoratively with, terms like collusion, appeasement and the like are not unheard of in describing collaboration. Hargreaves and Dawe (1990) warned of the wastefulness of "contrived collegiality", where leadership mandate determines that professionals or groups will enter into joint working per se. And this is just joint working between groups of educators. The stakes are far higher across public services.

Collaboration, in both theory and practice, is much easier said than done in public services operations. Collaborative advantage, the working out why and how the whole is likely to be greater than the sum of parts, is not simply a matter of rationality. This is complex, to say the least and instances of collaboration resulting in poorer service delivery are not uncommon in the education sector. As already noted, evidence suggests that effective collaboration requires three conditions:

- A good knowledge of what the other partners actually do and their objectives
- Some shared objectives which provide for mutual gain through collaboration
- Mutual trust between the collaborating partners

In relation to education, we have considered collaboration from three standpoints:

- Collaboration within schools
- Collaboration between schools
- Collaboration between schools and other public services

Collaboration within schools

Collaboration within schools, across subject areas and departments and whole school, has gathered good momentum in the past 20 years. Teacher individualism, though by no means extinct, is now considered poor professional practice. Large-scale studies have shown strong links between teacher effectiveness and professional collaboration. This is surprising, for why would teachers not share expertise or see the advantages of teamworking? Part of the traditional answer to this query lies in the physical isolation of classrooms. Attempts to tackle that inhibitor in the 1980s and 1990s by designing school spaces without walls proved disastrous. A class is a group of learners under the specific direction of a trained teacher, walls or not. Where progress was rapidly made was in looking at curriculum and pedagogy as shared experiences, to be planned, delivered and assessed under common methodology. Technology has helped a lot and social media is a treasure trove for sharing great ideas and links.

Collaboration between schools

Collaboration often takes place between individual schools in a number of different areas, including:

- Sharing of certain administrative or learning support functions between schools
- Joint training of staff

- Sharing of specialised physical space such as laboratories or sports locations
- Shared teaching resource in specialist subject areas

In some situations, collaboration can lead to full merger but this may not be inevitable or even desirable

Collaboration between schools and other public services

Fullan (1991) was right when he said that "educational change depends on what teachers do and think - it's as simple and complex as that". And nearly always teachers are not even considering any change effort if educational improvement is not part of the package. Fullan has summarised a body of solid research about the main criteria teachers use pertaining to the balance of rewards and costs for proposed change, which adds up simply put to "Why should I put my efforts into this particular change?"

But the collaboration problem posed is not just based on what the teachers do and think. Fullan is clear: "Equally important is what those around them in other public services do. This is not simply about mandate, alignment or planning coherence as a guarantee of "collaborative advantage". At the beginning of New Labour and of Scottish devolution a huge reform programme started across Scotland to create 150 *New Community Schools* (NCS). Taking up the New Labour key policy priority thrust as early as 1998 to integrate public services, the Scottish Government moved quickly to develop *Integrated Children's Services* (ICS). This was a major plank in this reform. The rational, correctly, was that more joined-up services for schools, health and social, emotional support would tackle more effectively educational outcomes and life chances with a more holistic approach. By 2004 the Scottish Education Inspectors were proposing that this vision be refocused. They found leadership and commitment to integrated working to be inconsistent and reported that in many instances it was being seen as just an "add-on" to the mainstream school business. The Inspectorate agreed that the reform lacked "strategic vision and support". This major reform programme is no more. Collaboration on a very ambitious scale centred on schools had failed even though it was being developed in the years of New Labour economic feast.

This example took place during the New Labour command and control era where targets and objectives would be set from London or Edinburgh and it was assumed that people on the ground would follow instructions to collaborate. In practice, people easily find ways not to do what they are told to do. Teachers care passionately about safeguarding, disability support and intergenerational underachievement. But they take huge convincing that genuine collaborative advantage is on offer with most multi-agency endeavours. They have had their fingers burned in the past. They mostly opt for the small gains their professional effort can secure rather than the oversold advocacy of external schemes and projects (especially those that are generated by overweening national governments, whose theoretical and practical knowledge and experience of collaboration can be gravely inchoate). In doing this, teachers may know the odds better than some would give them credit for in estimating collaborative advantage. They see that in their work on the ground and in one's own professional competence, not in more multi-agency protocols, training manuals and procedures, that best practice can save lives.

Changing this mindset amongst teachers is difficult but not impossible. One example is locating social workers in school. This fulfils the three "mutualities" referred to above. Teachers get to understand what social workers do, they come to trust them and they see additional resources in the school.

To summarise, collaboration between schools and others will not be achieved by central diktat. It requires time, patience and resources to convince teachers of the benefits of such collaborations.

Conclusions

In this chapter we have identified some of the theories, barriers and enablers which surround the subject of collaboration and it is only by fully understanding how these impact on practice can collaborative efforts become more consistent and sustained. It appears that working collaboratively across public services is accepted in principle yet still requires a mandate from central governments to enable collaborative practice to flourish to its full potential. Ironically, therefore, by politicising the subject, the government has inhibited its progress as well as facilitating it.

The prospect of a devolution of power from Whitehall to English regions and possibly further devolution to the other three home nations reinforces the importance of collaboration as a means of both creating public policy and providing public services. The appetite for more purposeful collaboration will arguably increase as smaller units of government recognise their greater levels of interdependence and the benefits of moving away from Whitehall control. Future opportunities presented by further devolution must not, however, be wasted by establishing regional arrangements which do not enable cross-boundary working. Critics of the current devolved governments point to an unnecessary apparent insistence on "home-made" policies that are motivated as much by a desire to demonstrate autonomy as to reflect local circumstances. It is understandable that the government could claim currently that a blend of prescription and enablement is the right approach but this is a complex objective with mixed results and requires a new formula in the light of the complexities identified. For example, the divergence of approach across the four nations suggests there is no one right way and that decisions should relate to more local assessments of need and culture free from central determination. Where regional and devolved governments can help is by creating the right climate through supporting greater understanding of the benefits, promoting best practice and formulating guidance.

In the case of health and social care, the change needed does not necessitate blind, unconditional commitment to integration but a predisposition to collaboration as the expected norm unless justified otherwise through evidence-based arguments. The same argument applies to the education sector. Strong and clear leadership at all levels will be key to overcoming barriers caused by systems, culture and history. In other words, not collaborating and not integrating need to be embedded as the exception not the rule and levers, incentives and, if necessary, sanctions should be put in place which are geared towards ensuring this in practice. The chosen level of government will determine where authority to issue those sanctions rests.

References

Abels, M. (2012) Managing through Collaborative Networks: A Twenty-First Century Mandate for Local Government. *State and Local Government Review*, Vol. 44, No. 1_suppl, pp. 29S–43S.

Acevedo, B. and Common, R. (2006) Governance and the Management of Networks in the Public Sector: Drugs Policy in the United Kingdom and the Case of Cannabis Reclassification. *Public Management Review*, Vol. 8, No. 3, pp. 395–414.

Agranoff, R. (2006) Inside Collaborative Networks: Ten Lessons for Public Managers. *Public Administration Review*, Vol. 66, Special Issue, December 2006, pp. 56–65.

Bardach, E. (1998) *Getting Agencies to Work Together: The Practice and Theory of Managerial Craftsmanship*. Washington, DC: Brookings.

Brandsen, T. and van Hout, E. (2006) Co-management in Public Service Networks: The Organisational Effects. *Public Management Review*, Vol. 8, No. 4, pp. 537–549.

Bryson, J.M., Crosby, B.C. and Middleton Stone, M. (2006) The Design and Implementation of Cross-Sector Collaborations: Propositions from the Literature. *Public Administration Review*, Vol. 66, December 2006, Special Issue, pp. 44–55.

Davies, N. and Williams D. (2009) *Clear Red Water: Welsh Devolution and Socialist Politics*. London: Francis Boutle.

Derkzen, P., Franklin, A. and Bock, B. (2008) Examining Power Struggles as a Signifier of Successful Partnership Working: A Case Study of Partnership Dynamics. *Journal of Rural Studies*, Vol. 24, pp. 458–466.

Finn, C.B. (1996) Utilising Stakeholder Strategies for Positive Collaborative Outcomes. In Huxham, C. (Ed.) *Creating Collaborative Advantage*. London: Sage.

Fullan, M. (1991) *The New Meaning of Educational Change*. London: Cassell.

Gazley, B. (2010) Why *Not* Partner With Local Government? Nonprofit Managerial Perceptions of Collaborative Disadvantage. *Nonprofit and Voluntary Sector Quarterly*, Vol. 39, No.1, pp. 51–76.

Gerber, E.R. and Loh, C.G. (2014) Spatial Dynamics of Vertical and Horizontal Intergovernmental Collaboration. *Journal of Urban Affairs*, Vol.37, No.3, pp. 270–288.

Gray, B. (1996) Cross-Sectoral Partners: Collaborative Alliances among Business, Government and Communities. In Huxham, C. (Ed.) *Creating Collaborative Advantage*. London: Sage.

Hargreaves, A. and Dawe, R. (1990) Paths of Professional Development: Contrived Collegiality, Collaborative Culture, and the Case for Peer Coaching. *Teaching and Teacher Education*, Vol. 6, No. 3, pp. 227–241.

Harris, K. (2019) *The Truths We Hold: An American Journey*. London: The Bodley Head (e-book edition).

Huxham, C. (1993) Pursuing Collaborative Advantage. *Journal of the Operational Research Society*, Vol. 44, No. 6, pp. 599–611

Huxham, C. (1996) *Creating Collaborative Advantage*. London: Sage.

Huxham, C. and Vangen, S. (2005) *Managing to Collaborate: The Theory and Practice of Collaborative Advantage*. Abingdon: Routledge.

Johnson, P., Wistow, G., Schulz, R. and Hardy, B. (2003) Interagency and Interprofessional Collaboration in Community Care: The Interdependence of Structures and Values. *Journal of Interprofessional Care*, Vol. 17, No.1, pp. 69–83.

Levine, S. and White, P.E. (1962) Exchange as a Conceptual Framework for the Study of Interorganisational Relationships. *Administrative Science Quarterly*, Vol. 5, pp. 583–601.

Lindsey, I (2014) Prospects for Local Collaboration into an Uncertain Future: Learning from Practice within Labour's Partnership Paradigm. *Local Government Studies*, Vol. 20, No. 2, pp. 312–330.

Llewellyn, M., Garthwaite, T., Blackmore, H. and McDonald, M. (2018) Working for a Shared Common Purpose: Experiences of Health and Social Care Integration in Wales. Welsh Institute for Health and Social Care, University of South Wales.

Lowndes, V. and Slelcher, C. (1998) The Dynamics of Multi-organisational Partnerships: An Analysis of Changing Modes of Governance. *Public Administration*, Vol. 76, pp. 313–333.

McGuire, M. (2006) Collaborative Public Management: Assessing What We Know and How We Know It. *Public Administration Review*, Vol. 66, December 2006, Special Issue, pp. 33–43.

Prowle, M.J. (2006) *Effective Partnership Working in Local Government: Towards a Framework of Leadership and Management Competencies*, unpublished paper presented at the Public Administration Conference, Durham University.

Rhodes, R.A.W. (1996) The New Governance: Governing Without Government. *Political Studies*, Vol. XLIV, pp. 652–667.

Rigg, C. and O'Mahony, N (2013) Frustrations in Collaborative Working: Insights from institutional theory. *Public Management Review*, Vol. 15, No. 1, pp. 83–106.

Sullivan, H. and Skelcher, C. (2002) *Working Across Boundaries: Collaboration in Public Services*. Hampshire: Palgrave Macmillan.

Sullivan, H. and Williams, P. (2009) The Limits of Co-ordination: Community Strategies as Multi-purpose Vehicles in Wales. *Local Government Studies*, Vol. 35, No. 2, pp. 161–180.

Vangen, S., Hayes, J.P. and Cornforth, C. (2015) Governing Cross-Sector, Inter-Organizational Collaborations. *Public Management Review*, Vol. 17, No. 9, pp. 1237–1260.

Williams, P. (2002) The Competent Boundary Spanner. *Public Administration*, Vol. 80, No. 1, pp. 103–124.

14

COMMUNITY DEVELOPMENT AND THE ROLE OF THE THIRD SECTOR IN PUBLIC SERVICE DELIVERY

Graham Lister

Introduction

This is the last chapter of this book but, in many ways, it could be seen as the most important chapter given that it provides an essential blueprint for the future sustainability of public services.

The chapter discusses the role and concepts of community development which are of fundamental importance to public services, both in theory and in practice. Also, it considers the related topics of well-being, social capital, equity and the role they can play in community development. Finally, it also considers the roles of the statutory sector and the third sector in community development.

The development of policies to improve well-being through community development, and to measure progress, is described together with evidence of current outcomes. This evidence indicates the need for further steps to engage communities in the policies and plans that guide public services and in the delivery of services with co-production at local levels.

Notwithstanding the limited progress achieved, to date, in recognising and responding to the inequality between regions, there is much still to be done. The thrust of this book is the development of regional governments in England (and the existing devolved administrations) but with wide ranging powers over economic and public policy. Regional governments for England could then play a similar role to those of the existing devolved governments in determining policies and plans for an integrated action by public services organisations and community support organisations in the third sector.

However, it is apparent that the introduction of English regional governments coupled with greater delegation to existing devolved governments must be underwritten by an amended UK constitution that establishes the roles and powers of statutory authorities at every level and transforms the way decisions are

DOI: 10.4324/9781003201892-18

made from top-down instructions to support for community development and whole society engagement.

The chapter is structured as follows:

- The importance of public engagement with public services
- The meaning and purpose of community development
- Community development, social capital, well-being and equity
- Community development in public services provision
- The roles of statutory agencies in community development
- The roles of the third sector in community development

The importance of public engagement with public services

The current understanding of the role of public services in enabling well-being draws on Capability theory, developed by the Nobel prize-winning economist and philosopher Amartya Sen in his 1979 book *Equality of What*, his editing of "Quality of Life" in 1992 with Martha Nussbaum and his 2009 book "The Idea of Justice". Capability theory defines the role of government as enabling individuals and groups to overcome the obstacles they face to enhance their well-being in ways that they choose as communities and individuals.

The 2009 Stiglitz, Sen and Fitoussi "Commission on the Measurement of Economic Performance and Social Progress", set up by French President Nicholas Sarközy, proposed measures of well-being at individual and community level to evaluate the performance of public services in enabling communities to achieve progress and equity in terms of:

- Material living standards
- Health
- Education
- Personal activities including work
- Political voice and governance
- Social connections and relationships
- Environment (present and future)
- Security of an economic and physical nature

This recognises that well-being is not simply a product of wealth and health but requires a full range of public services and the active engagement of communities in local and national decision making and action.

Capability theory acknowledges that public services such as health, social care education, housing, policing and support for economic development can only enable people to achieve their goals if they work with individuals and communities to co-produce well-being outcomes. Personalised and community-targeted public services should enable each person to define their own goals for well-being according to their choices and the obstacles they face, in a sustainable and equitable way. This approach underlies current policies for well-being, at international and national levels, including the UN Sustainable Development Goals and the policies of the UK Home Countries.

The "Putting People First protocol" launched by Prime Minister Gordon Brown (HM Government 2007) used the term "co-production" to refer to the engagement and empowerment of individuals and communities as a key to the "personalisation and transformation" of health and social care services. This was reflected in the Cabinet Office paper of the same year "Building on Progress", which described co-production as to "empower citizens to shape their own lives and the services they receive".

Co-production is not a simple task for most public services staff, it requires them to develop trust and understanding with community organisations and to transform the way they approach their duties. It is equally difficult for community organisations to learn to trust and work with "officials". This is made more difficult if the public service is seen as remotely controlled from Westminster or some authority which does not reflect the way people perceive their local communities. The public need clear lines of communication with their services, and clear points of contact that gives them a voice in key decisions: this could be a local authority or a regional government.

The meaning and purpose of community development

The United Nations defines community development as "*a process whereby community members come together to take collective action and generate solutions to common problems*" (Lau Wai Kei Rosamond). Communities are self-defining groups sharing a locality, ethnicity, religion or other mutual interest that provides a focus for their shared goals. The development of community action has been described by Shelley Arnstein (1969) as a step-by-step process: starting by improving information, building better consultation processes, involving community organisations in decision making, developing joint action programmes and supporting independent community organisation actions.

This process both builds on and depends upon community social capital, which is the framework of values and norms that fosters bonds within community groups, bridges between groups and links with formal and informal organisations. A well-functioning society requires a balance between these elements; a community that defines itself solely by bonds within closed groups may lack essential bridges and links to other elements of society, and conversely a community only defined by formal links may lack social cohesion. The lack of bridges between groups and links to community leaders was exemplified by a series of riots and disturbances in Bradford, Harehills and Oldham in 2001. These revealed the extent of rifts in local communities between ethnic groups and between these groups and the police and other authorities. This was described as a lack of community cohesion.

Community development, social capital, well-being and equity/equality

In this section, three themes are discussed which are inextricably linked to community development. These are:

- Social capital
- Well-being
- Equity and equality

Social capital

Social capital is defined as a set of shared values that allows individuals to work together in a group, to effectively achieve a common purpose. Social capital refers to a positive product of human interaction and the outcome may be tangible or intangible and may include such things as useful information, innovative ideas and future opportunities. Thus, social capital can be seen as a key driver for community development.

The Office of National Statistics Annual Survey (ONS 2016) of 300,000 people is used to measure social capital using indicators in four categories: personal relationships, social network support, civic engagement, and trust and cooperative norms. The results of the analysis of the 2014 survey showed:

- Northern Ireland, Scotland and Wales had the highest proportion of people feeling that they belong to their neighbourhood (73%, 69% and 67% respectively) and that others around their local area are willing to help their neighbours (80%, 75% and 75% respectively).
- London and the East Midlands had the lowest proportion of people feeling that they belong to their neighbourhood (59% and 61%) and that others around their local area are willing to help their neighbours (65% and 67%).
- Around seven in ten of those living in Northern Ireland (73%), Scotland (70%) and the South East (68%) reported that most people in their neighbourhood can be trusted, compared with only 56% of those living in London, 61% in the North East and 62% of those living in West Midlands or in East Midlands.

Community development and the social capital it builds are essential to well-being and equity because most community goals and behaviour are determined by community norms and equity is defined by community beliefs. Social capital can be said to define "who we are" and "how we behave". Lack of social capital results in greater loneliness, poor health and poor mental well-being. It has also been shown that higher levels of social capital are reflected in better health outcomes, lower rates of crime and anti-social behaviour, better education outcomes, greater satisfaction in housing and the environment and better economic prospects.

Well-being

Well-being is identified as a human right in Article 25 of the 1948 UN Universal Declaration of Human Rights, which states:

> Everyone has the right to a standard of living adequate for the health and well-being of himself and of his family, including food, clothing, housing and medical care and necessary social services, and the right to security in the event of unemployment, sickness, disability, widowhood, old age or other lack of livelihood in circumstances beyond his control.

Well-being must be considered as an important aspect of public policy but many people involved in public services see well-being as somewhat "wishy-washy", but it could be argued that, perhaps, the over-arching objective of public services is to improve population well-being. However, it is a difficult concept to work with because of difficulties in its definition and its relationship with other factors such as life satisfaction, mental health, comfort, quality of life (QoL) and happiness. There is no universally agreed definition of well-being, it is a subjective response to our quality of life, which varies depending upon local and personal circumstances. Studies by researchers such as Richard Layard (Layard 2011) suggest proxies such as wealth and income are not good proxies for well-being and so other factors must be at play.

Two broad perspectives exist on well-being (Vanhoutte 2015):

- ***Hedonic perspective*** – this states that increasing an individual's pleasurable experiences, and decreasing painful ones, maximises well-being. The hedonic approach takes a "subjectivist" view, in that the individual is perceived to be in the best position to determine their own level of well-being.
- ***Eudemonic perspective*** – this approach to well-being takes an "objectivist" view, as well-being is considered from an outside perspective, where others (e.g. governments) are able to ascertain if an individual is living a "virtuous" life.

To take an example, as noted below, the Welsh Government has developed a framework for assessing well-being and it is probably fair to describe this approach as being based on a eudemonic perspective. However, it is only fair to point out that this framework of measures wasn't just imposed by the Welsh Government but built up via an extensive process of consultation throughout Welsh society. Although we have no evidence on this matter, we would suspect that similar approaches to developing well-being frameworks would be applied in other countries.

Factors that may improve perceptions of well-being include a political system that is seen as fair and representative, physical and financial security, education, family and social support, community engagement, housing, a pleasing and protected environment, employment, music, art, culture and health and social care. The benefits of investment in services which improve these outcomes are personal and social judgements about the quality of life, which determine how well-being goals are defined for an individual and a community.

Another key difficulty with well-being is the lack of available data and the inability to use that data if these were available. It is to be hoped that the digital age with the capability for mass collection of data, coupled with the use of artificial intelligence (AI), will enable the analysis of that data resulting in improvements in this area.

Equity and equality

Equity is achieved by providing public services and other forms of support to ensure that people deprived of opportunities for well-being, as a result of personal disabilities and local disadvantage, have opportunities to achieve their well-being goals. All UK Home Countries include reducing inequity and improving equality as a key target for public services and an ethical imperative. Inequity also leads to productivity losses to industry of between £31 and £33 billion each year. Lost taxes and higher welfare payments resulting from health inequalities cost in English regions of £28–32 billion, as identified for the Marmot Review (Frontier Economics 2010).

Unaddressed deprivation can be regarded as the converse of equity. Deprivation in England is measured by the Index of Multiple Deprivation (IMD). This combines a weighted score of 39 indicators, reflecting household income levels, unemployment, poor health and disability, lower levels of education, skills and training, lack of housing and support services, levels of crime and low environmental standards.

The index is calculated for "Lower Super Output Areas" which are areas of about 1,500 people. The distribution of deprivation by English local authority areas and regions in 2015 is shown in Figure 14.1 (DCLG 2015a), with areas of greater deprivation shown in darker shades. In Figure 14.2 (DCLG 2015b), levels of deprivation can be compared with the spending power of local authorities per dwelling (higher spending power shown darker) to show if needs and resources are (or are not) matched.

It is notable that while many areas show a mismatch between relative needs and expenditure as indicated by these measures, all London authorities show relatively high levels of expenditure, perhaps reflecting, in part, the higher cost of London services (and the London weighting applied to public sector salaries) but also, possibly, higher levels of resources.

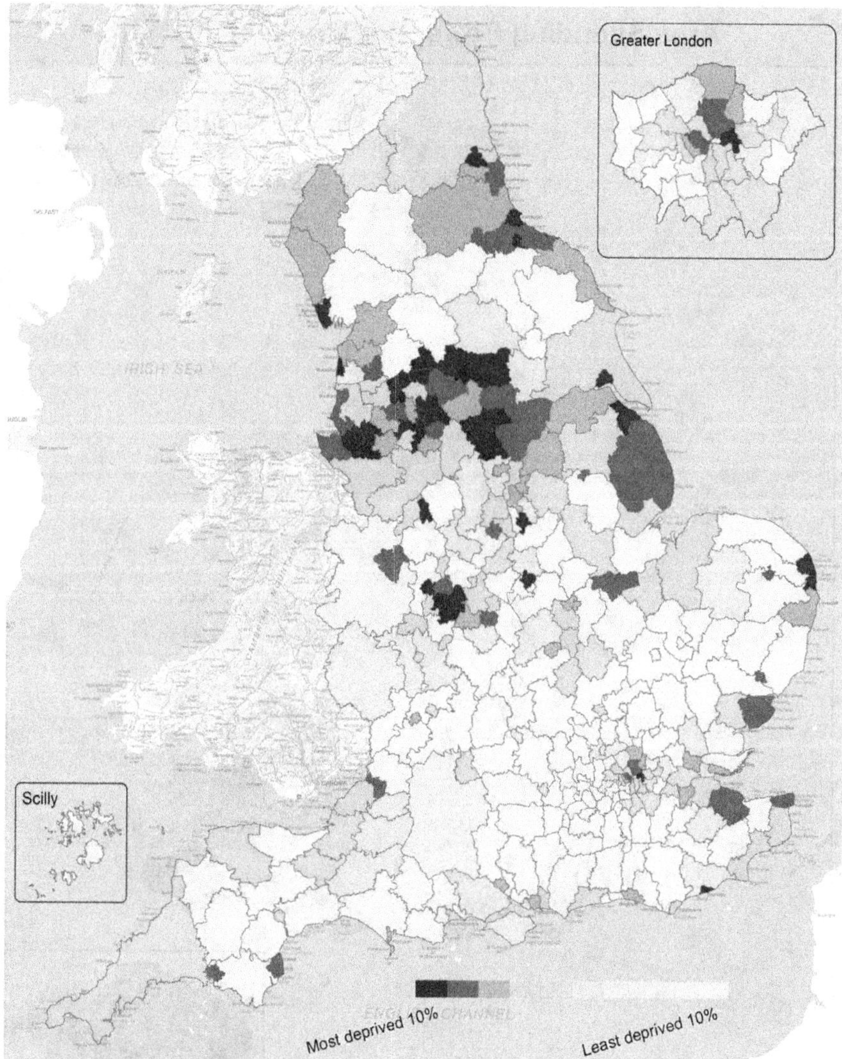

FIGURE 14.1 Index of multiple deprivation

Note: There are 127 districts with no neighbourhoods in the most deprived decile nationally. These are shown in the least deprived decile.

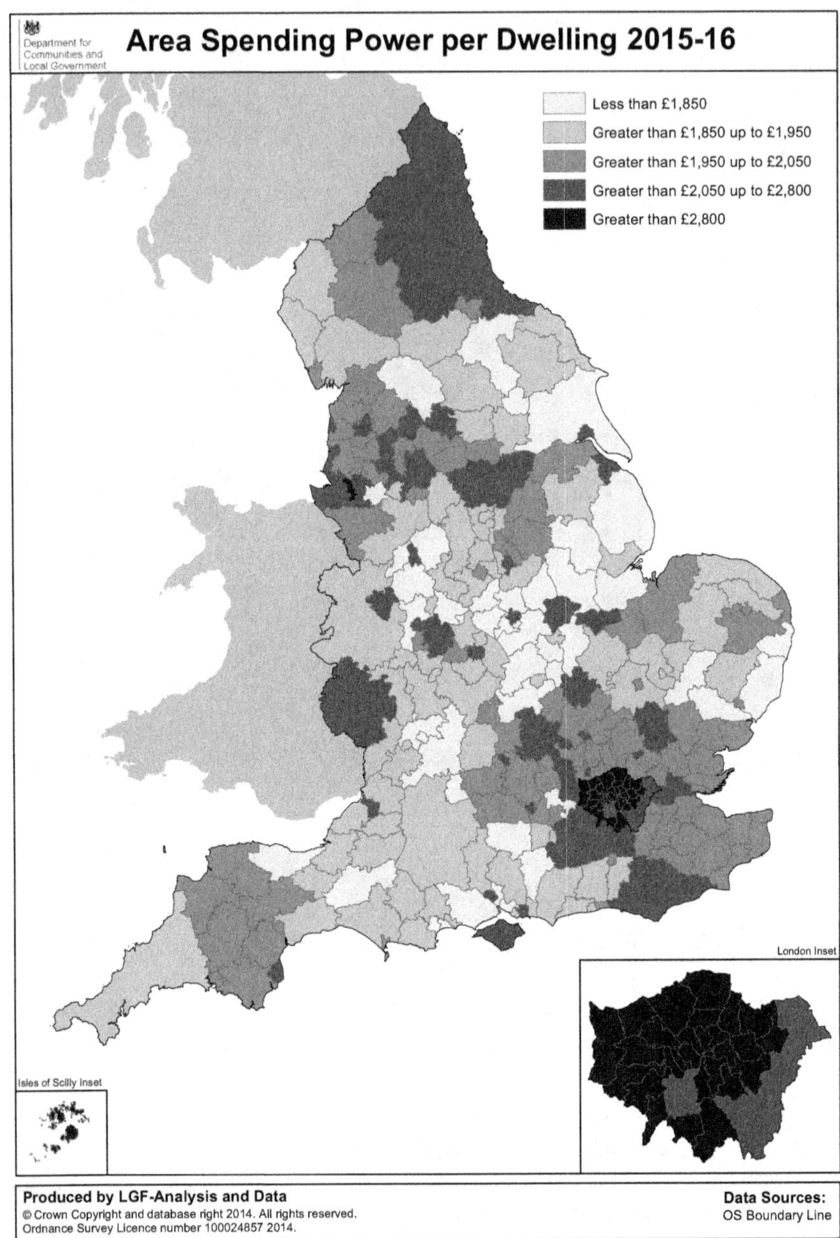

FIGURE 14.2 Spending power of local authorities per dwelling

The IMD works well in urban settings but other disadvantaged groups can also be identified, such as people with disabilities, disadvantaged racial groups and isolated rural people, who will not necessarily be living in areas scoring high levels of multiple deprivation as shown by IMD scores.

Currently, Scotland and Wales use different forms of the Index of Multiple Deprivation (IMD) to measure inequality while Northern Ireland uses the "Noble" indicator, which includes social capital.

Community development and public services

The goal of improving community development and well-being for the UK was recognised in 2010 by UK Prime Minister David Cameron who launched the National Wellbeing Programme to "start measuring our progress as a country, not just by how our economy is growing, but by how our lives are improving; not just by our standard of living, but by our quality of life".

In November 2010, the "Measuring National Well-being Programme" was introduced by the Office of National Statistics (ONS 2018) to monitor and sreport UK progress using indicators of well-being included in the Annual Population Survey of over 300,000 respondents. Well-being is assessed using what are known as the ONS 4 questions which ask respondents how they feel in terms of life satisfaction, feeling that things you do are worthwhile, happiness and anxiety. The combined score (out of ten) in response to these questions is considered to provide a Personal Wellbeing Measure. While this is rather a crude measure, these well-being scores are highest in Northern Ireland and Scotland.

Between 2010 and 2015 a number of initiatives were introduced across different public services in England to try to support the improvement of community development and well-being. The importance of social capital and community development as aspects of well-being was recognised in 2018 by changing the name of the English government department to the Department of Housing, Communities and Local Government. None of these steps appears to have been particularly successful, perhaps because they were top-down gestures, measurements and guidance rather than truly community initiated and led local initiatives.

The Scottish Government introduced the National Performance Framework (NPF) in 2007; this was updated in 2018 to include goals and targets for the economy, the environment and communities, with 11 outcome targets and 81 indicators, with links to the UN Sustainable Development Goals (Scottish Government 2018). At a personal level the NPF includes measures of social capital in four domains: social networks, community cohesion, community empowerment and social participation.

The NPF is intended to bring together national and local governments, businesses, voluntary organisations and all people living in Scotland, to work together towards common targets for well-being. Community Planning Partnerships were established to co-produce and implement local improvement plans, funded by the Scottish Government and local partners. The outcomes of these programmes are tracked at national level by indicators including measures of well-being and equity. Later in 2021 the Scottish "Fourth National Planning Framework" will set out plans to show how these aims can be achieved while transitioning to a net zero economy by 2045.

The Welsh Government has also established national goals for well-being, formalised in the Wellbeing of Future Generations Act 2015 (Welsh Government 2015). The seven national goals are:

- A prosperous Wales
- A resilient Wales
- A healthier Wales
- A more equal Wales
- A Wales of cohesive communities
- A Wales of vibrant culture and thriving Welsh language
- A globally responsible Wales

At a personal level, Welsh well-being indicators include measures of being safe, having somewhere suitable to live, being involved in decisions that impact your life, having friends, being part of good, strong communities, having every chance to do well in education, feeling good about your life, for adults being able to work and for children being able to grow up happily and successfully, and being well-looked after.

The Social Service and Well-being (Wales) Act 2014 also provides a legislative imperative for actions to achieve the well-being goals of individuals. It focuses on a number of themes including prevention, co-production, voice and control, and multi-agency working to give people access to services. In particular, people be given greater "voice and control" over the services they receive which should work with them and their family, friends and carers to co-produce support designed around what matters most to them. This should be supported by advocacy to help vulnerable people access information and services and express their needs and wishes. Public services such as health, social care and housing are required to work with the community and voluntary sector to ensure that seamless multi-agency services can be delivered to local communities. The draft Welsh Government, National Development Framework 2020–2040 (Welsh Government 2019) builds upon proposals set out in the Act, and puts forward measures to support employment, well-being, equity and Welsh culture in distinctive urban and rural areas while achieving net zero carbon emissions.

For Northern Ireland the devolved administration Department for Communities was established in 2016. This has focused on developing social capital and community cohesion, to address the history of social division in the province.

The NI Continuous Household Survey measures these trends and examines a variety of topics, such as internet access, the environment, tourism, libraries, health, sport and education.

It is apparent that community development initiatives in the devolved parts of the UK have generally been more successful than those in England, perhaps because they are seen as more relevant to local communities than those in England. This provides a model for English regional government to follow.

Community development approaches can be effective or ineffective dependent on how they are applied. Quite often lip service is paid to community development by service professionals who should not be surprised when their approaches prove ineffective. Particular issues which will contribute towards the effectiveness of community development are as follows (Prowle 2010):

- **Meaningful consultation** – where change to the pattern of service provision in a community is being proposed, it is important that the community is consulted about such changes. However, it is also simportant that the consultation involved is seen, by the community, as being meaningful and not pseudo-consultation taking place after decisions have already been made.
- **Information** – community groups need to be provided with accurate and comprehensive information about various aspects of health and social care in their area. This would include information about needs and demand for services, technical aspects of service delivery, resource availability etc.
- **Skills** – much of the information about public services has a degree of technical complexity. Hence, community groups need to be provided with the skills to correctly interpret and apply this information in a meaningful way.
- **Involvement** – community groups need to be actively and meaningfully involved and supported in the issues surrounding health, social care and well-being. Such involvement needs to be facilitated and respected by statutory and voluntary organisations.
- **Feedback** – community groups need to be provided with adequate feedback from statutory and voluntary organisations. This would include feedback from consultations and on the actual provision of services.
- **Empowerment** – community groups need to be empowered to undertake the roles described above. This implies the provision of suitable training, mentoring and advocacy for the groups themselves.
- **Honesty and trust** – for community development to be effective it is important that a strong degree of honesty and trust is fostered between the groups and statutory and voluntary sector organisations operating within the community. This implies a strong degree of transparency in the decision-making procedures of statutory and voluntary organisations.

There are many examples, from many areas, of the ways in which community development is an essential pre-requisite for and product of well-functioning public services. Examples are given below:

Health

Health services are dependent upon community development because:

1 Healthy behaviour, which is the main determinant of non-communicable diseases, depends upon the norms of behaviour amongst community groups; these will be far more influential than any doctor's warning: For example: is it considered normal to smoke or drink excessive alcohol? Is daily exercise expected at all ages? Are eating habits healthy and moderate?
2 Infectious diseases such as Covid-19 require communities to accept vaccines and behave in a responsible way by wearing masks and maintaining social distance. These behaviours depend on community norms of behaviour.
3 Most care is provided by family and friends, with the support of patient groups, religious and social groups and volunteers from the community.

Social care

Social care professionals play a leading role in supporting the process of community development. They also recognise that well-developed community relations are essential to the social care and well-being of children and adults; see the following examples:

1 Community social workers help communities function. Some work directly with individuals, conducting needs assessments and making referrals to resources in the community. Others assess and support community organisations.
2 NICE guidance for looked-after children and young people stresses the need for support for the child or young person to participate in the wider network of peer groups, school and community activities to help build resilience and a sense of belonging.
3 NICE guidelines for the care of older people with multiple conditions recommend that social workers ensure there is community-based multidisciplinary support. The health and social care practitioners involved in the team might include, for example, a community pharmacist, physiotherapist or occupational therapist, a mental health social worker or psychiatrist, and a community-based services liaison worker drawing on community resources.

Schools and further education

These depend upon family and community support and can help build stronger communities; see the following examples:

1 The values instilled in schools of personal and community responsibility are keys to community development, for health, care, probity and hard work.
2 The educational attainment of different ethnic groups reflects the family and social culture of the pupils' home and community. This has been identified as key to the exceptional performance of children from ethnic Chinese families (Francis et al.).
3 The value placed on education also reflects community norms in respect of adult education participation, as for example in the University of the Third Age and Workers Education Association courses.

Policing

Without minimising the responsibilities of offenders for their behaviour, it is apparent that a great deal of offending reflects instances of the failure of health, social care and education services and the level of community development that shaped their lives (Lister 2014).

1 On entering prison more 70% of prisoners had drug abuse problems and infection rates of HIV and hepatitis C are between 15 and 20 times those of the general population. But 80% of them had never had contact with drug treatment services. Nearly 75% of prisoners in custody suffer from two or more mental disorders.
2 Of the offenders over 18 released from prisons: about a quarter were formerly in some form of social care. Prior to conviction, two thirds were unemployed, and one third homeless.
3 Many have low levels of literacy and numeracy and a variety of learning difficulties and disabilities including dyslexia, 50% have reading skills at or below that of an 11-year-old and 7% have an IQ less than 70. Nearly half of all males and one third of females in custody were excluded from school and 50% of male and 70% of female offenders achieved no qualifications at school or college.

Housing services

These also depend upon community development amongst residents. The Housing Association Community Trust (HACT 2021) uses the outcome of the Annual Population Survey to derive measures of social value of the outcome of interventions to improve housing, community development and social activity. This is assessed by comparing the increase in life satisfaction score associated with a specific condition (other things being equal) with the increase in household income associated with a similar increase in life satisfaction; see the following examples:

1 The average social value of moving from rough sleeping to secure housing is assessed by this measure as some £24,467.
2 The average value attributed to feeling belonging to the neighbourhood (community engagement) is assessed as £3,753; the social value of being active in a tenant's group is assessed at an average value of £8.116.
3 The average value attributed to regular volunteering is assessed as £3,249.

These examples of the links between public services and community development show that public services both build community development and are dependent upon it. As each instance in which community development is supported by public services and vice versa is unique, it may be helpful to illustrate this relationship and the development of co-production by a specific example (Lister et al. 2016):

> A project to develop community social capital and support the integration of new immigrant women, in a coastal city funded by the EU Integration Fund, was led by an English City Council. As time was tight proposals for the project were only specified in outline. This turned out to be helpful as it allowed the women who joined the project to define their own goals.
>
> The council staff who initiated the project held discussions with many community leaders at the outset. They were helpful, but it soon became apparent that these men, were not going to lead the project. The women who joined, first in groups from different immigrant communities, soon recognised that they had many shared experiences and needs and so became a cohesive multi-racial group and developed their own leaders.
>
> They defined their own goals, for example, to learn English and supporting information to help them discuss their children's education, their own health needs, employment opportunities and how to deal with the bureaucracy they faced as migrants. They developed their own agenda including developing as Community Advisers, setting up a web site for immigrant women and supporting advocacy on issues such as Female Genital Mutilation.
>
> The council staff learnt many lessons from the experience of co-production, most importantly they learnt not to assume they would know what the participants would want. They learned to listen to, trust and respect the women who joined the project. And they learnt to work together across departmental and organisational boundaries.
>
> Evaluation of the project in terms of the Social Return on Investment achieved showed a positive return for the immigrant households, for

employers and for the City Council. This project was recognised by the EU Integration Fund and UK Home Office as a model of successful co-production for community integration and was asked to host an international meeting so that the women and the council staff could share their experience.

Co-production with community organisations is an essential starting point for a whole society approach to community development, whatever the starting point or objective of public services.

The role of the third sector in community development

The third sector is an umbrella term which includes voluntary organisations and groups, local and national charities, not-for-profit social enterprises and other non-government organisations. The sector can also be described as civil society. These organisations and groups play a vital role in supporting vulnerable and disadvantaged people in our society working with local authority and NHS services. They may provide services from their own resources, at their own discretion, or they may deliver services on contract from a local authority or another commissioning agency. They also play a key role in community development.

According to the National Council for Voluntary Organisations' (NCVO) UK Civil Society Almanac 2020, there are some 167,000 third sector organisations, with a total annual income of over £54 billion, with almost 1 million employees and over 20 million people who volunteer at least once a year, more than half of whom volunteer at least once a month (NCVO 2020). People in the age range 65–74 are most likely to volunteer, more than a quarter volunteer at least once a month. It has been noted that while the greatest challenge we face is the care of older people in poor health and needing social care, the greatest resource available is the increasing number of older people in good health.

Third sector organisations work in all areas of public service including social care, culture and recreation, health, education, offender support, climate change, employment, training and housing. The workforce of employees and volunteers is larger than the NHS. But civil society is not simply a source of volunteer support for public services, they also lead the way in developing innovative solutions to social problems, advocating for national and international causes and giving voice to local opinions.

In Chapter 5, on public finance futures, it was suggested the dire public finance situation, in the UK and overseas, coupled with limited economic growth might mean that the post-war model of delivering public services through, mainly, public service professionals might no longer be sustainable. There is almost an expectation that the third sector will be able to "fill the gap". For example, some NHS health organisations in developing strategies for dealing with mental health problems (which will be severe post-Covid) are incorporating the involvement of third sector organisations into the delivery of services to low intensity patients. Whether the sector can deliver on this remains to be seen.

It is suggested (Prowle 2010) that the third sector can contribute in a number of unique ways:

- **Infrastructure** – community groups often have or can help develop an appropriate infrastructure within their communities. The term "infrastructure" is not meant to imply physical facilities but also repositories of information, guidance about key issues and human resources in terms of volunteers. Community groups will have an in-depth and virtually exclusive knowledge of the community in which they reside. This will facilitate the implementation of more achievable strategies for improved health status.
- **Ownership** – the involvement of community groups in the process of formulating a health strategy can induce a high degree of ownership of that strategy. Community groups can often provide leadership in the community area and thereby inform, influence and empower individuals living within the community in a way that "outsiders" (be they from the statutory or voluntary sectors) cannot. Community groups can also provide credibility and trust amongst the individuals within the community in a way that outsiders cannot. They can also engender a feeling of empowerment with individuals feeling able to influence service provision rather than having services foisted on them. Finally, community development provides a means for achieving greater inclusivity from groups and individuals in the community than might otherwise be the case.
- **Innovation** – community groups can be a source of inspiration and ideas about how best to approach and resolve particular problems. The "grass roots" perspective of community groups can aid in identifying solutions which will not necessarily have been identified by health professionals.
- **Monitoring and feedback** – community groups can be the medium whereby information about changes within the community is monitored by the groups and fed back and explained to the individuals and other groups within the community in a manner which will be regarded as unbiased and robust.
- **Relevance** – there are examples of where services delivered to clients by third sector organisations are seen as more relevant by the clients themselves than services delivered by statutory public agencies.
- **Accessing hard to reach groups** – the difficulties of communicating with "hard to reach groups" are a particular challenge with regard to health and social care. Some examples of such hard to reach groups might include teenage parents, long-term unemployed, gypsies and travellers. Community groups will have an almost unique perspective on how to reach such groups which is not available to "outsiders".
- **Provision of support** – community groups are uniquely placed to organise and deliver appropriate support to vulnerable members of their

> community including carers. In some circumstances this support could prevent inappropriate admissions to hospital for social reasons or facilitate early discharge. Another aspect of this concerns community support in civil emergencies.

However, for this to work, it is important that relationships between local authorities and the third sector are good. This is not always the case. In some cases, local authorities (fairly or unfairly) see third sector organisations as amateurish and not capable of delivering the services needed. In other cases, third sector organisations see local authorities as protectionist in nature and unwilling to involve "outsiders" in service delivery. Both of these perceptions are probably true in some cases but the key point is for them to be improved. The local authority-third sector link is a vital one for local public service delivery and a key role for regional governments must be to try and improve this relationship rather than get involved, directly, themselves.

The roles of statutory agencies in community development

To some extent the roles of statutory agencies in community development might be seen as taking actions to promote improved community development and to avoid taking other actions which might inhibit it.

In considering this issue, we can think of statutory agencies as being at three levels:

- National UK government
- Regional governments including Wales, Scotland and Northern Ireland
- Local government – local authorities and other local public service agencies such as NHS organisations, police authorities, and fire and rescue authorities

National UK government

Over the years, UK governments have tried to undertake a variety of initiatives in this area. The "Big Society Agenda" was launched in 2010 by David Cameron to support civil society, described as "the biggest, most dramatic redistribution of power from elites in Whitehall to the man and woman on the street". The agenda was led by a Government Minister and Department supported by a £200 million fund from private and public sources for non-governmental community organisations and youth organisations and a training programme for 5,000 community organisers. It promised a substantial increase in public funding for civil society from the 18% noted in a survey undertaken at the time. Unfortunately, this was introduced during a period of substantial cuts in local authority funding. Public funding reported by the NCVO is now just over 15% of civil society income. Hence, it is now generally regarded as yet another Whitehall policy failure.

In June 2019 Lord Heseltine (2019) produced the "Empowering English Cities Report" which reviewed progress since the 2015–2016 "Cities and Local Government Devolution Bill". The report commends the introduction of metro-mayors but notes that "no government with a parliamentary majority will accept the right of elected politicians at a subordinate level to frustrate its manifesto pledges". This illustrated the dilemma posed by the delegation of authority within a parliamentary system. Authors such as Gavin Esler (2021) and Ed Straw (2014), and indeed the authors of this book, suggest this must be resolved by a written constitution that sets out the roles and powers of national, regional and local governments and guarantees freedom to act without interference within these delegated authority levels.

More recently, the Johnson Government has emphasised an agenda of "levelling up" the regions of the UK, in the Conservative Party Manifesto of 2019 and the Queens's Speech of May 2021. This is to be supported by a range of funding sources including the "Levelling Up Fund", the "UK Community Renewal Fund", the "UK Community Ownership Fund", the "UK Shared Prosperity Fund", the "UK Infrastructure Bank" and the "Towns Fund". In addition to funding promised for regional and local initiatives, action is promised to support jobs and economic development in areas considered to have been "left behind". A further White paper on devolution is promised later in 2021.

The "UK2070 Commission" independent inquiry into city and regional inequalities in the UK led by Lord Kerslake (2021) published its report "Make No Little Plans – Acting at Scale for A Fairer and Stronger Future". The commission noted growing inequality in wealth, child poverty, health, housing, education, social mobility, access to basic services and the internet and environmental standards. The Commission found that the UK is one of the most spatially unequal economies in the developed world. The report notes that too much public spending is dealing with the consequences of failing to tackle spatial imbalances rather than creating the conditions for success. It calls for a large-scale, comprehensive, long-term and devolved plan of action to deliver change. Actions proposed to deliver change, while moving to a net zero emission economy, include a comprehensive framework for inclusive devolution. The range of powers devolved to Scotland should be similarly devolved to the regional level and beyond within England. In a postscript to the report published in October 2020 it is noted that the Covid-19 pandemic and issues arising from Brexit have made these steps even more urgent.

However, under a system of regional government, it does seem that the national UK government will have a very small role to play in relation to community development. This is because all of the public services where community development is an important factor would fall under the remit of regional governments. However, the various initiatives described above (particularly the Kerslake report) suggest some important lessons for regional governments. Change is required, not just in *what* is done by governments but *how* it is done.

Regional governments

Regional governments should aim to develop services reflecting local needs and priorities by engaging local populations, councils and mayors in decisions and action. The creation of regional governments for the nine English regions should bring decision making closer to people across the UK and encourage innovation in policy making for community development and well-being. However, even regional governments should recognise that they are too distant from their local communities to fully understand local needs and the key public agency is the local authority.

Public engagement with local decision making "giving voice to local opinions" is made more difficult in England by the complexity of current public service accountability structures. The public must attempt to engage with public services through a myriad of structures including various forms of local authority and mayoralties, health commissioners and different types of NHS trust, police commissioners, transport user groups, housing associations, local education authorities and academy school boards, school forums and local enterprise partnerships. These bodies each have their own catchment area and responsibilities and different levels of accountability to the public.

A regional government in England could provide a single focus for public engagement with regional economic development and public services, just as the devolved administrations already do. This would ensure that measures to "level up" the regions of England would be founded on local needs and opportunities and could bring together all public services, community organisations and groups as well as business partners in the region in a whole society approach.

To achieve this, it will be essential to engage the public, not only through elected regional governments but also through local authorities that people recognise and feel they own. It is therefore essential to review the catchment of all public services so that they provide clear coterminous areas that match how people view their locality, so they can participate in community actions and decisions and be seen as accountable.

Local government

Local government is perhaps the key statutory agency in relation to community development. Currently, it might be argued that people identify more with localities: villages, towns, districts or counties such as Cornwall or Yorkshire, rather than English regions. It will therefore be important to stress the role of regional governments in supporting both local community initiatives and region-wide programmes. It will also be necessary to gain public support for the transfer of powers to local administrations and regional governments.

Public engagement with services at a personal level is further complicated by a lack of understanding and trust of public officials. This is most evident for disadvantaged groups which are sometimes described as "hard to reach" or "seldom heard". These include ethnic minorities, as illustrated by the low level of vaccine take-up amongst these groups. To address this issue community engagement at a regional level must extend not only to localities but to communities of ethnicity, faith and interest. Regional media outlets, such as ITV and BBC regions, could play an important role in engaging communities and developing awareness of regional issues and interests, if they were aligned with regional government catchment areas.

Conclusions

The topics of this chapter, namely community development and the role of the third sector, have always been important in relation to public services delivery. However, they will become of increasing importance in the years ahead as the public sector grapples with the challenges outlined in Chapter 2. The role and importance of community development in the effective delivery of public services is discussed earlier in this chapter but this theme is also picked up by the authors of the individual policy chapters in Part C of the book. Unfortunately, there are many difficulties and barriers getting this message across. Many public service managers sometimes have a negative view (sometimes justified) about the role and capabilities of the third sector in delivering effective public services but often this view is based on past experiences as opposed to the current situation which has probably improved considerably. Also, belief the creation of regional government will make it easier to promote these themes compared to the difficulties with monolithic central government departments. The experiences of the devolved governments lend weight to this view. Hence, it is vital that policy makers and managers in regional governments gain a good understanding of the issues of community development and the roles of the third sector.

References

Arnstein, S. (1969) "A Ladder of Citizen Participation", *Journal of the American Institute of Planners*, 35(4), 216–224. https://doi.org/10.1080/01944366908977225

DCLG (2015a) "Deprivation by English Local Authority areas and Regions in 2015", Department for Communities and Local Government, Infographics London.

DCLG (2015b) "Spending Power per Dwelling 2014–2015", Department for Communities and Local Government, Infographics London.

Esler, G. (2021) "How Britain Ends: English Nationalism and the Rebirth of the Four Nations", Head of Zeus, London.

Francis, B., A Mau, and L. Archer "The Construction of British Chinese Educational Success: Exploring the Shifting Discourses in Educational Debate, and Their Effects", available at https://discovery.ucl.ac.uk/id/eprint/1549042/1/Francis_Template%20Copy%20Francis%20Mau%20Archer%2031102016.pdf

Frontier Economics (2010) "Estimating the Costs of Inequalities: A Report Prepared for the Marmot Review", Frontier Economics Europe, London.

HACT (2021) "Ideas and Innovation in Housing", available at https://hact.org.uk/

Heseltine, M. (2019) "Empowering English Cities", available at https://englishcitiesmichaelheseltine.premediastudio.com/MichaelHeseltine

HM Government (2007) "Putting People First a Shared Vision and Commitment to the Transformation of Adult Social Care", HM Government, London.

Kerslake, R.W. (2021) "Report of the 2070 Commission Report: Make No Little Plans – Acting at Scale for a Fairer And Stronger Future", Turner and Townsend, Leeds.

Lau Wai Kei Rosamond, Community Development, De Montfort University, available at http://wiki.our.dmu.ac.uk/w/index.php/Community_Development

Layard, R. (2011) *Happiness: Lessons from a New Science.* London: Penguin Books.

Lister, G. (2014) "Assessing the Value for Money of Health Trainer Services", report for Department of Health available at https://www.building-leadership-for-health.org.uk/evaluating-behaviour-change/health-trainers-health-economics-behavioural-economics-new-media/

Lister, G., A. Strang, M. Ali, J. Leech, U. Schmidtblaicher, M. Chowdhury, and S. Cheverton. (2016) "Co-Producing Integration with a Community of Migrant Women and Measuring the Social Return on Investment Achieved", available at https://www.building-leadership-for-health.org.uk/co-producing-community-integration/

NCVO (2020) "UK Civil Society Almanac 2020", National Council for Voluntary Organisations, available at https://data.ncvo.org.uk/?tag=skills

ONS (2016) "Social Capital across the UK: 2011 to 2012", Office for National Statistics.

ONS (2018) "Measuring National Well-being: Quality of Life in the UK", Office for National Statistics.

Prowle, M. (2010) *Managing and Reforming Modern Public Services: The Financial Management Dimension.* Pearson UK.

Scottish Government (2018) "Launch of National Performance Framework 2018" and "National Performance Framework", available at https://nationalperformance.gov.scot/

Stiglirz, J.E., A. Sen and J.P. Fitoussi (2009) Report by the Commission on the Measurement of Economic Performance and Social Progress, available at http://www.stiglitz-sen-fitoussi.fr/documents/rapport_anglais.pdf

Straw, E. (2014) "Stand and Deliver: A Design for Successful Government", Treaty for Government, York.

Vanhoutte, B. (2015) Hedonic and Eudemonic Wellbeing. *In: ESS ERIC (2015) Measuring and Reporting on Europeans' Well-Being: Findings from the European Social Survey.* European Social Survey (ESS ERIC).

Welsh Government (2015) "Well-being of Future Generations (Wales) Act"

Welsh Government (2019) "National Development Framework 2020–2040 Consultation Draft"

INDEX

Printed in the United States
by Baker & Taylor Publisher Services